D1605846

The Case

DATE DUE			

THE CASE
OF HOTEL POLSKI

An account of one of the most enigmatic
episodes of World War II

by Abraham Shulman

HOLOCAUST LIBRARY
NEW YORK

Cover Design by Michael Meyerowitz
Printed in the United States of America

Contents

INTRODUCTION

Before the Second World War, the Hotel Polski was a small, insignificant building on Dluga Street in Warsaw, an obscure hotel with a restaurant on the ground floor. The hotel stood in a section of the Polish capital which belonged neither to the elegant center inhabited by the rich nor to the rundown areas of the poor.

One end of Dluga Street was bordering on the beginning of Nalewki Street, the Jewish quarter and heart of Jewish life in Warsaw — the largest Jewish community not only in Poland but of all Europe. The other end of Dluga Street ran into Freta Street, the beginning of Warsaw's Old City, the center of which was its picturesque square surrounded by ancient buildings and 'a maze of winding little streets, remainders of the capital's Middle Ages.

The Hotel Polski stood on 29 Dluga Street. The adjoining building, a similarly-built four-story house, was a Jewish high school, or *gymnasium*, named "Spójnia" (Unity), geared to the children of assimilated Jews. All the subjects were taught in Polish, and the orientation of the school masters was to educate their students in the spirit of Polish culture, to make of them Poles "of the Mosaic persuasion." But not all the students of that school were so inclined; there were some exceptions who had chosen this *gymnasium* not for its assimilationist attitude but for the superior level of its instruction. This writer, a child of Yiddish-speaking parents, was one of those few exceptions.

I attended the Spojnia *gymnasium* for several years, from the fifth to the eighth and last class, which provided the student with a *matura*, the equivalent of the French baccalaureate, which opened the way to higher studies.

My parents lived at the other end of Warsaw, in a suburb named Wola. I usually travelled each morning to school by electric tramway, but I very often chose instead to walk, a real excursion which took over an hour. This taste for walking offered me the opportunity of gaining a familiarity with all the streets and squares between the distant suburb and Dluga Street, and to know intimately all the buildings surrounding the school. I knew every house and store, the display windows and the gates, the quadrangular blocks of the sidewalks and the pavement cobblestones. A few steps away from the school stood such attractions as the *Kinematrograf* — the Municipal Cinema, and the spacious Krasinski Square with the imposing iron railing fence surrounding the Krasinski Park, one of the few gardens in Warsaw, in which sat Jews dressed in traditional black fashion clothes, reading Yiddish newspapers and engaging in loud political debates. Farther down was Tlomackie Street with its magnificent synagogue, the most imposing in all of Poland. And, on the other end, there was the greatest attraction of them all: a twenty-minute walk through the Old City and onto an elevated Viaduct which led to the Kerbedz Bridge over the majestic Vistula River.

But the Hotel Polski, which I passed twice daily, was no attraction at all. It had neither the glamour nor the mysteries I associated with a hotel. The ground-floor restaurant, announced by a black-lettered sign over one of the windows, promised no culinary delights. But it was the will of fate that this colorless and obscure, unnoticed hotel should survive to this day — not in its physical form, for it was eventually razed to dust and ruins together with the rest of the city — but in its spirit. It became, for a brief span of its existence, the stage for one of the most puzzling, bizarre and still enigmatic episodes of the war. The hitherto unknown hotel became an Affair.

But in order to do this, it had to first undergo all the stages of the Nazi occupation.

On September 1, 1939, the Germans began what they called a *blitzkrieg* or *Feldzug in Polen*. Two weeks later Poland's army was crushed and the entire country, save the capital, was occupied by the two partners, the Nazis and the Soviets. The only city to resist, pathetically and hopelessly, had been Warsaw. On September 27, Warsaw, reduced to ruins, with its gardens, squares, streets and courtyards full of civilian graves, surrendered.

Now the Germans' interest switched to the Jews. On October

8

4, the leader of Warsaw's Jewish Community Council, Adam Czerniakow, was ordered to set up a Judenrat within 24 hours. In November, a census was taken of the Jews in Warsaw, which showed their number to be 359,827. The Germans now began a *blitzkrieg* not against armies or fortifications, but against these 359,827 people.

On January 26, 1940, congregational worship was forbidden, and, out of compassion for animals, ritual slaughter was banned. In September, 1940, the Germans outlined what they called a "quarantine area," later to become the ghetto, and which at that time contained 240,000 Jews and 80,000 Poles.

On October 16, the Germans ordered these 80,000 Poles to move out of the quarantine area within four weeks, to be replaced by all those Jews of Warsaw who lived outside that area. Meanwhile, Jewish and Polish workers were ordered to erect a six-foot-high wall around the area, and, on November 15, 1940, the ghetto was sealed. The Jewish Council census in January, 1941, showed the number of people imprisoned in that largest human trap in the history of mankind to be 378,979.

From that time on, until July 22, 1942, the ghetto became the stage for an extraordinary range of statistics. Mortality in the ghetto rose. Each week, many hundreds, and later, thousands, died of starvation, and yet the total number of Jews kept growing. But this increase in numbers had nothing to do with the commandment to "increase and multiply." The Germans replaced and multiplied the number of Jews who had died with others whom they chased out of surrounding small towns and villages and dumped into that infernal trap.

In May, 1941, the census showed 430,000 Jews to be in the ghetto. In September, Governor Frank, head of the General Government, announced a reduction in the ghetto's food rations. On October 5, a death edict was issued against anyone leaving the ghetto without permission. On April 12, 1942, the first rumors reached the ghetto inhabitants about the arrival of an "extermination brigade." This was the only time that the organized criminals called themselves in such explicit terms. From then on, they would use euphemisms — mass murder would be termed "resettlement" or "colonization of the Eastern territories."

In April and May of 1942, news reached the ghetto of the

massacres in Lublin, Biala Podlaska, and Pabianice. On July 22, the rising fears gripping Warsaw's Jews, the expected nightmare, was realized. From that day on, cattle trains began setting out from the Umschlagplatz, "resettling" eight, ten, and even twelve thousand Jews daily to the East. Officially sent to work, they were in actuality slain in Treblinka.

On January 18, 1943, the second resettlement operation began, and then, in April, following a heroic, desperate and hopeless resistance, the Germans liquidated the ghetto. The entire area, within the walled boundary, was utterly razed.

All that remained was the wall — so as to trap those few living corpses who might have survived among the cinders — and the Pawiak prison. For the first time in seven hundred years, Warsaw was *Judenrein*. The Nazi dream was fulfilled.

The Hotel Polski continued to exist. Its location shielded it from German barbarity. It had the good fortune to be located outside the ghetto walls, on the "Aryan" side of the city. The Poles, according to German scientists, belonged to a lower form of the "Aryan" race, as opposed to the Jews, who were subhumans. After the destruction of the ghetto, the name "Aryan" side" became superfluous, for the non-"Aryan" side was destroyed. But the name persisted.

During the years of 1940, 1941, and the first five months of 1942, the Hotel Polski continued to serve as a second-rate establishment, housing visitors from provincial towns. The little restaurant continued to serve meals to its few guests and to an occasional passer-by. But in May, 1943, it became the center of an unusual event.

Warsaw was only officially *Judenrein*. In fact, Jews still lived in the city illegally. Some had never entered the ghetto, but had disguised themselves as Gentile. Others had smuggled themselves out before and during the deportations, or even after the uprising, and now either lived in hiding with Polish families, or walked around openly, pretending to be "Aryan" Poles. The number of Jews thus clandestinely hidden isn't certain — there may have been ten, twenty, or even thirty thousand.

But that number kept diminishing. Both types of "underground Jews" — those who possessed "good looks" and dared to come out, and those who hid in basements and attics, behind false walls, locked in wardrobes, or even in mausoleums in the

Jewish cemetery — lived in incessant terror. Every day, a few of them were caught by Polish blackmailers, stripped of their possessions, and handed over to the Germans.

But suddenly a rumor reached the "illegal" Jews that they could be saved. All they had to do was to discard their disguises, come out from their hiding places, and present themselves at the Hotel Polski. There they would be able to procure for both themselves and for their families — if anyone of their families was still alive — documents of foreign countries. And then, equipped with this proof that they were *Ausländer*, they would be sent abroad in regular passenger trains and exchanged for German citizens in the foreign countries.

The immediate result of that rumor was that a great number of hidden Jews actually came out of concealment and rushed to the hotel, first in trickles and then in the hundreds and finally a few thousand. Soon the Hotel Polski went through the greatest prosperity it had ever enjoyed. Instead of the usual few dozen guests who had quietly occupied the rooms on the four floors and took their repast in the little restaurant, the building literally swarmed with people. All the corridors, lobbies, stairs and the courtyard were packed with men, women and children. It was almost impossible to get a room, and the people had to be content with a place to sleep in a corridor or on the stairs.

Almost all of those who had so suddenly invaded the hotel were Jews who had emerged from darkness to this unexpected above-ground haven. There were also some Poles who had accompanied their friends on the dangerous journey to the hotel, for every step outside was still forbidden territory to the Jews, and anyone recognized as such, though he be just one step from the hotel, could be stopped, robbed and slain.

The hotel attracted another sort as well: Poles, or Jews disguised as Poles, who came to the hotel to do business. Many of the Jews who had run to the hotel with the anxious hope of becoming foreigners had brought along with them their entire fortunes in the form of gold, diamonds, or foreign currency. They needed local currency to pay for the hotel, for the restaurant, and above all for the foreign documents which were either in the form of passports or "promises" — promises of visas from South and Central American countries.

The hotel contained yet another category of people — those

11

who ran the show. These were a few Jews who collaborated with the Germans, and who, with the help of the Gestapo, organized the entire operation which came to be known as the "Hotel Polski Affair."

The gate to the hotel was only half closed, entrance being granted to all. The necessary password, the "Open Sesame" was "I'm Jewish" and the door swung open. The word Jew, which, only a few steps away signified terror and death, here meant life. And so, the Hotel Polski bordering on the razed ghetto's still glowing cinders on one side, and on the living hostile "Aryan" city to the other, became an island of life to those who managed to arrive safely.

How was this possible? Was it a trap set by the Gestapo? Was it a new trick to entice the hidden Jews — who would eventually be caught anyway — to emerge from their hiding places? Was this pleasant-seeming oasis in reality a trap in which the Nazis planned the destruction of the remaining Jews?

As mentioned above, the German murder operations were clothed in euphemisms. Deportation to the death camps was termed "resettlement" or "replacement"; murder was called "special treatment." The trains arriving in Auschwitz stopped before a gate engraved with the message, "Arbeit Macht Frei." The railway station in Treblinka was built by a stage designer to resemble a genuine station with a buffet and signs announcing arrivals and departure times. Jews in line to enter gas chambers were handed out towels and soap and told that they were going to have a shower. Before the final deportation from Warsaw a high Gestapo official took part in the opening ceremony of an orphanage in the ghetto and spoke of the importance of children for the future of a nation.

The Jewish survivors knew all this — and yet, when the rumors about the Hotel Polski reached them, so many of them went. Why?

There were some positive signs — there are always signs for those who are in desperate need of them — that this time it would perhaps be different. The leaders of the Hotel Polski and organizers of the affair — the several Jewish Gestapo men who demanded fantastic sums of money in payment for the so-called "foreign documents" — shared the loot with their German bosses. This therefore meant that the Germans were this time

12

interested not in Jewish lives but in their fortunes. Another sign: some well-known Jewish personalities, including the director of the American Joint, had procured such documents for their own families. And the third and strongest sign: the Jewish Gestapo men had registered as foreigners not only their families, but themselves as well.

This book is based on memoirs and diaries written by those who themselves went through that bizarre, often grotesque and dramatic episode, and on interviews conducted with such living witnesses of the affair as well as abundant documentation. One would think that the greater the number of documents, the closer we would approach the truth, but this book would seem to prove the opposite. The greater the details of evidence, the more confused the conclusion seems to be.

Why did the Jews on the "Aryan" side give up their disguises or abandon their hideouts and present themselves at the hotel, proclaiming openly that they were Jews? In order to answer that, one must attempt to form in his mind an image of the conditions under which the Jews on the "Aryan" side lived.

On the "Aryan" Side

There are hundreds of personal narratives written or told by Jews, and sometimes by Poles, which relate their experiences in Nazi-occupied Warsaw. But the most authentic, most encompassing and most shattering is the account given by a young Jewish historian, Emmanuel Ringelblum.

In September, 1939, Ringelblum was 39 years old, married, the father of a seven-year-old boy, and the author of four books and a large number of monographs.

Two months after the Germans had overrun Poland, he set himself the task of recording for posterity the history of that Jewish tragedy.

As a trained and professional historian, Ringelblum knew that such a task could not be performed by one individual, however zealous and well-informed — it had to be a coordinated effort. The informants had to be carefully selected according to the criteria of representative occupations, social status, and geographic distribution. He succeeded in persuading people to collaborate with him, and turned the individual notes into a collective archives.

Emmanuel Ringelblum lived and carried out his work in the ghetto until he was smuggled out on the "Aryan" side. Living on the "Aryan" side, he never ceased his work, collecting and writing down the reports which were delivered to him in his various hideouts by underground couriers.

His last hiding place was a cellar under a greenhouse on Grojecka Street, in the suburb of Ochota, where he lived with his wife, son, and 35 others. On March 5, 1944, the Gestapo, tipped off by informers, surrounded the hideout and took all the people in it to the Pawiak prison. On March 7, Emmanuel Ringelblum was executed among the ruins of the ghetto together with his wife and son.

But most of his work survived. It was buried in milk containers in various locations in the ghetto and on the "Aryan" side, and dug out and published after the war. The following quotations from his work, *Polish-Jewish Relations*, are therefore the most authentic and also the most harrowing documentation we possess of that era, for they were written by a man who was both a competent historian, and, above all, a Jew who wrote about life in the underground on the "Aryan" side when he himself lived in hiding.

> When a Jew finds himself on the "Aryan" side, he has two alternatives — either to remain "visible" or to "go underground." In the first case, the Jew is transformed into an "Aryan" — he provides himself with "Aryan" papers and lives legally, registered in an appropriate registry office. In the second case, a Jew with a Semitic appearance hides either in a hideout or in a camouflaged room, where he remains illegally, unregistered. Jews on the "Aryan" side generally use Roman Catholic papers.
>
> Life "on the surface" is not at all easy. A Jew who has taken this option lives in constant fear, under harrowing tension. Danger lurks at every step. In the blocks of flats, the landlords smell a Jew in every new subtenant, even if he produces a guarantee of "Aryanism" from a trustworthy source. The gas and electricity employees, the janitor, porter, a neighbor — all constitute a danger for him because any of them might identify him as a Jew.
>
> Another prerequisite for survival on the "Aryan" side is an occupation. A Jew must be employed somewhere, otherwise he

will give himself away, sooner or later. A Jew "on the surface" has to possess "Aryan" papers, for it is only on the basis of these that he can get work. Baptismal certificates, fabricated in Warsaw, usually give as the birthplace parishes that had been burnt down mostly in the eastern borderland. On the basis of such a certificate, the counterfoil of the register, one can receive a genuine *Kennkarte* (identity card). Other documents such as work papers, diplomas of institutes of higher education, etc., can be acquired from competent printing firms. If a Jew does not work, he must at least keep up every appearance of working. He must leave his flat in the morning in order not to give rise to suspicions. Many inspections take place in parks and public places, so Jews spend long hours riding in tramways in order to pass the time somehow until lunch time or the evening.

Individuals who are getting ready to cross to the "Aryan" side try to adapt themselves to their future environment while they are still in the Ghetto by growing a moustache; so the joke went round the Ghetto that a Jew on the "Aryan" side could be spotted by a moustache, knee boots and a *Kennkarte*.

Only individuals with a so-called "good" — that is, "Aryan" — appearance can survive "on the surface." ... In the Ghetto, "studies" were carried out in order to establish what features characterize a Jew or Jewess. The results of these "studies," these incessant discussions in the Ghetto, were as follows: a Jew can be recognized by his nose, hair and eyes. As for the Jewish nose ... some people had surgical operations performed. However, conditions in the Ghetto were not suitable for this, and besides it was very expensive. It was difficult to change a Jewish nose — it stayed on, and in the Ghetto as a result of insufficient nourishment it became even longer and even more Jewish than before! People had their characteristically Jewish dark hair bleached, but this did not help much either, because the agents checked the roots. In practice it turned out that platinum blondes gave rise to more suspicion than brunettes. Jewish eyes, the experts claim, can be recognized by their melancholy and pensiveness. The whole suffering of the Ghetto, the many years of torment, the loss of the family — all this was concentrated in them. ... Women disguise themselves by wearing mourning, bleaching their hair, combing it out smooth, etc. There are some people who have a first class "Aryan" appearance but know little Polish or pronounce Polish badly, people who cannot even pronounce their "Aryan" surname correctly. This difficulty can also be circumvented — one pretends to be a deaf-mute and wears an armband saying *taubstumm*.

Jews on the "Aryan" side have to act like real conspirators. No one knows their addresses. One brother does not know the address of the other, children do not know the addresses of their parents — they use the addresses of go-betweens. Visits are undesirable as they can lead to exposure. Jews usually meet at tramway

15

stops, in cafés, etc. It is forbidden to write down the addresses — they must either be memorized or put down in some code form.

Jews on the "Aryan" side are least unwilling to go out after dark, since then it would be difficult for a *shmaltzovnik* to distinguish between Jew and non-Jew. Crossing to the Aryan side takes place after nightfall or at dawn. . . .

The majority of Jews on the "Aryan" side remain "under the surface." They live either in a hideout, or simply in a back room. I have heard from someone who has lived for six months in a back room in a flat. Extreme cunning is needed to prevent neighbors and acquaintances from knowing that a Jew is staying there. If someone is paying a visit, one has to resort to stratagems and move from the room to the kitchen or to other rooms in such a way as to enable the visitor to see the whole flat and not allow him to realize that a Jewish family is hidden there. I heard about a Jewish family that lived for five months in a two room flat without there ever being a single collision, despite frequent visits from friends and relatives of the owners. But these Jews had to leave that flat, as the owners' mother could no longer stand the nervous tension connected with the Jews' stay there, and moreover this street was frequently cordoned off by gendarmes searching for arms and there was no place to hide in the flat. . . .

Among the most popular kinds of hideouts were parts of rooms that had been cut off, disguised rooms, recesses, cutoff parts of attics, cellars, etc. In ground floor flats, the cellars were converted into hideouts, which were connected with the flats by trap doors. In other parts of the city, building hideouts presented great difficulties. Bricks had to be carried in briefcases to avoid suspicion by the neighbors. One bricklayer, an expert in building hideouts, carried the bricks on a pushcart, on which there was an iron stove that served to simulate the need for using the bricks. Building a hideout required a lot of money, tens of thousands of zlotys and sometimes even more. . . .

The stay of a Jew on the "Aryan" side means the torment of constant fear, day and night. Every murmur at the entrance of the block of flats after curfew, the sound of an automobile horn, a ring at the door, every sound and every noise in general cause the heart to beat faster for fear of an informer, blackmailer or gendarme. For Jews on the "Aryan" side to be "nabbed" or denounced is an everyday affair. The Polish agents of the criminal police, Gestapo agents and Polish police are all under orders from the German authorities to pursue Jews. When the police — both plainclothes and uniformed policemen — were deprived of their ample takings in the Jewish district, where the scope of their activity was dwindling, they passed over to the "Jewish region" on the "Aryan" side. It was not so much a matter of giving Jews to the Germans as of making profits, and ample ones at that, for themselves. Jews of limited means who were not able to buy themselves out of the hands of their tormentors, were handed over to the Gestapo.

The position of a Jew on the Aryan side becomes particularly difficult if he is taken ill. There have been cases of betrayal by "Aryan" doctors to whom Jews were forced to turn for help. In one particular case, a Jew hiding on the "Aryan" side, a former high official of the Ministry of Agriculture, had a serious heart attack. An "Aryan" doctor was called and stayed the entire night with the patient. In the morning, the doctor discussed the patient's further treatment with his wife. He advised her to have the patient hospitalized, to which the wife, half unconscious after her sleepless night, replied that that was impossible due to certain reasons. Half an hour later, the Gestapo arrived and sent the couple to the *Umschlagplatz* as part of the "resettlement" action in progress. The husband went to Treblinka while his wife managed to escape.

It is still worse if a Jew dies on the "Aryan" side. In a certain hideout a little girl died, and she was buried in the adjacent garden. When the ghetto was still in existence, Christian undertaking establishment would smuggle in the bodies of deceased Jews to the Jewish cemetery. After the liquidation of the ghetto, the situation became more difficult. However, for a few thousand zlotys the deceased "on the surface" will find eternal rest "under the surface."

Jews often unmask themselves by their unsuitable mode of life. Wealthy Jewesses often show off their rare and valuable furs, put diamond rings on their fingers, squander their money, drive around in rickshaws and carriages. The results of such behavior are surveillance, searches and finally arrests. Jews are often "nabbed" as a result of their own imprudence, for example by meeting in large numbers in restaurants and cafés. Some move about the streets of the capital too frequently until an "Aryan" acquaintance gives someone away to the authorities. . . .

Plainclothes and uniformed police have made great progress in spotting Jews. As far as men are concerned, it is not a difficult matter: the trousers are pulled down and there is the evidence, and the trousers are pulled down at every turn without ceremony. "Aryans" suspected of being of Jewish origin are often checked this way. A remedy was sought for this too. Some people are of the opinion that it is possible to make a Jew's male sex organ look like an uncircumcised one by means of an operation. The attempt has been abandoned for the most part, because of sexual disorders connected with this very costly operation. In some cases the authorities required medical examination of suspected Jews. If the doctor happens to be a decent man, he will certify that so-called *phimosis* was performed, that is, the removal of the foreskin, as the result of venereal disease. A medical certificate like this has saved the life of many a Jew. More than one Jewish

17

"Aryan" walks around with this certificate of *phimosis*.

The agents have much more trouble in spotting Jewish women, though rumor has it that they recognize Jewish women by a protruding bone in the neck or by the ears, a notion with a striking resemblance to the eighteenth-century folk belief that Jewesses give birth after their death. But the agents find ways here too. A Jewish woman of even the "best" appearance can rarely give references about her family. The agents also know of another weak point of Jewish women, namely, their purely superficial knowledge of Catholic ritual rites. To the question, "What does a priest do after the confession?" very rarely can a Jewish woman answer that he taps the confessional. Sometimes a Jewess is trapped and ruined by so simple a question as, "When is your nameday?" The newly Christian Maria or Stefa has not yet had the time to look at a calendar in order to check when her nameday is.

Next to the police agents, the blackmailers and the *shmaltzovniks* are the endless nightmare to the Jews on the "Aryan" side. There is literally not a Jew "on the surface" or "in hiding" who has not had something to do with them on one occasion or another, who has not had to buy himself off for a sum of money. There is hardly a single family or individual who has not been subjected to these human jackals. It is not unusual for these cases to end with death by suicide or by the liquidation of the victims by the Germans into whose hands they are delivered by the blackmailers. In *shmaltzovniks* terminology, a Jew is a "cat" slinking through the city streets. The blackmailers keep their eyes glued on the Jews so that at the right moment, when he takes off his armband and goes into the entrance of a block of flats, they will be able to catch him red-handed and demand a suitable ransom. A more cunning *shmaltzovnik* will make a note of the number of the flat and will join forces with a policeman to raid the Jew and the Christians who are his hosts. The *shmaltzovniks* operate in every place where Jews have some contact with the "Aryan" side — at all the posts near the walls, at the exit gates, along the routes to the work posts, at the work posts, etc., in short, wherever Jews try to "break loose," to detach themselves from the work post and go to a flat on the "Aryan" side.

The *shmaltzovniks* walk around in the streets stopping anyone who looks Semitic in appearance. They frequent public squares, especially the square near the Central [Railway] Station, cafés and restaurants, and the hotels where Jews who were foreign citizens used to be interned. The *shmaltzovniks* operate in organized bands. Bribing one of them does not mean that a second will not appear in a little while, then a third and so on, a whole chain of *shmaltzovniks* who pass the victim on until he has lost his last penny. The *shmaltzovniks* collaborate with plainclothes police agents, the uniformed police and in general with anyone who is

18

looking for Jews. They are a real plague of locusts, descending in the hundreds and maybe even thousands on the Jews on the Aryan side and stripping them of their money and valuables and often clothing as well. A *shmaltzovnik*, like a real street thief, will sometimes take not only his victim's money away from him but his belongings as well. . . . Fortunately a *shmaltzovnik* is usually satisfied with moderate booty or, to be more precise, whatever [money] the victim has. . . .

An even more dangerous plague for Jews on the Aryan side is constituted by bands of blackmailers. The difference between the *shmaltzovniks* and the blackmailers is that the former's area of activity is the street and the latter's is the flat. Through surveillance in the streets, in the cafés, by collaborating with the *shmaltzovniks*, the blackmailers find their victims; they call on them in their flats together with agents and uniformed police. If the *shmaltzovniks* are wasps that sting their victims, the blackmailers are vultures that devour them. The demands of the informers-police-blackmailers partnerships are set very high and come to at least thousands of zlotys and more often to tens of thousands. An instance is known where sixteen Jews caught in a suburban villa paid half a million zlotys. Only the very rich can afford to buy themselves out of the blackmailers' hands. Usually, there is only one thing left to do — to escape, leaving all one's belongings to the landlord, who is usually collaborating with the blackmailers.

While the Ghetto still existed, one could observe the return of great numbers of blackmail victims to the Jewish district, broken in spirit, stripped of belongings and money, cursing the Aryan side which had deprived them of their last haven. The returning Jews kissed the earth of the Ghetto, blessed every day spent there and claimed that there they could rest without continually watching out for the police and the "Black Maria" with the Gendarmerie. Some people returned to the Ghetto even without having been blackmailed, just for fear of this nightmare which prevented Jews on the Aryan side from sleeping at nights and imbued them with deadly fear. Some people returned to the Ghetto for a holiday: their shattered nerves could no longer stand the constant tension.

Blackmailers, *shmaltzovniks*, agents, uniformed police and all sorts of other scoundrels held and still hold their revels with impunity in the streets of the capital. The murder of thousands of Jews, sentenced to death by the Gestapo after being caught, is their handiwork. Yet no harm befalls them. They know that where Jews are concerned, there is no law and no punishment, nobody will stand up for them. Jewish political and social organizations constantly demand that extortion and blackmail be fought. The Polish Underground, however, has as yet done nothing to save the handful of Polish Jews on the Aryan side. The Home Plenipotentiary of the Polish Government [-in-Exile] has indeed issued a very belated warning that blackmailing Jews is a crime, which the Government will punish now and after the war. Words, however, have not been followed by deeds. Though energetic action was taken to liquidate denunciators and informers, very little has been done in the sphere of fighting blackmailing of Jews. This complete impunity for the blackmailers and the *shmaltzovniks* has wounded and still wounds the handful of Jews, who see in this a clear sign that nobody is anxious to save Polish Jews.

The united anti-Jewish front of agents, uniformed police, blackmailers and *shmaltzovniks* gets considerable help from the anti-Semitic propaganda which has built up the ideological basis for the infamous deeds of these unified scoundrels. Anti-Semitic propaganda . . . provides this gang with material which in the eyes of the Polish population mitigates the criminal nature of handing over Jews to the Germans. . . .

Legends are spread to the effect that Jews who are caught by the Germans ruin their "Aryan" landlords by affirming that the latter knew that their subtenants were of Jewish origin. These rumors and others like them are spread on purpose, constantly and secretly. As a result, the position of Jews "on the surface" and "under the surface" gets worse every day. The number of Jewish victims shot down pitilessly becomes larger and larger. Woe to the Jew whose apartment is getting "hot." Even for big money it is difficult to find an "Aryan" willing to hide a Jew in his apartment. A Jew who has lost his room will not find shelter anywhere, even for a day or two. He has to hide in the ruins of bombed buildings or in the open fields, with his life in danger until he finds a place which costs more every day. The noose is constantly tightened round the neck of Warsaw's remaining Jews and there is no prospect of help from anywhere.

The Polish police, commonly called the Blue or uniformed police in order to avoid using the term "Polish," has played a most lamentable role in the extermination of the Jews of Poland. The uniformed police has been an enthusiastic executor of all the German directives regarding the Jews. The powers of the uniformed police in the sphere of collaborating with the Germans concerning the Jews were as follows: (1) guarding the exit gates of the Ghettos or the Jewish districts; (2) participating in "resettlement actions" in the capacity of catchers, escorts, etc.; (3) participating in tracking down Jews who were in hiding after the "resettlement actions"; (4) shooting Jews sentenced to death by the Germans.

. . . The uniformed police has had a deplorable role in the "resettlement actions." The blood of hundreds of thousands of Polish Jews caught and driven to the "death wagons" will be on their heads.

Emmanuel Ringelblum devotes a large part of his report on Jewish-Polish relations to the question: Why did so few Poles aid their Jewish fellow-countrymen? Why did so few of them offer hiding places to Jews?

He begins by pointing out the dangers that threatened any Pole who would shelter a Jew. As soon as the ghetto was formed, the Germans issued decrees on the Aryan side threatening heavy prison terms for any Pole caught hiding Jews, facilitating their escape, or offering them any aid. In mid-1942, the Nazi authorities posted notices announcing the introduction of the death penalty for anyone discovered aiding Jews. At the same time, the Gestapo spread rumors that the inhabitants of a building in which a Jew was found would suffer under the rubric of collective responsibility. Prodded by rumors such as these, anti-Semitic tenants would on their own initiative conduct searches of neighbors' apartments to look for Jews.

"The anti-Semitic note," says Ringelblum, "expresses itself most clearly in the general satisfaction that Warsaw had become *Judenrein*, that the old dream of the Polish anti-Semites had come true. Some loudly and others discreetly expressed their contentment that the Germans had done the dirty job of exterminating the Jews."

There is always a danger in generalizations: All Jews, all Poles, all French . . . Were all the Poles hostile to the Jews? Did they all enjoy the Jewish catastrophe? Of course not. Poland had its heroes, those who proved their humanitarianism with their own lives. A forest dedicated to the "Righteous among the Nations" has been laid out near Yad Vashem, full of trees planted in honor of Poles who risked their lives to save the lives of Jews. There are hundreds, perhaps thousands, of such Polish men and women whose courageous humanity and self-sacrifice deserve to be remembered as lighthouses for a humanity sunk in the darkest depths. But their number is so pitifully small.

Equally shocking was the behavior of the Polish government-in exile in London, which was made up of all the political groups of prewar Poland. For a very long time, until the end of 1942, the Polish government kept silent about the anti-Jewish atrocities, about the German "Final Solution" which had already been made known to the entire free world. Only on November 27, 1942, did the Polish National Council in London pass a

21

resolution condemning the German crimes. This resolution had been drafted not by a Pole but by the representative of the Jews in Poland, Ignacy Schwarcbart, and was made public only after protracted and obstinate endeavors on his part in the face of constant and systematic obstructions.

As for the Polish underground, while it conducted an energetic fight against the Polish traitors who collaborated with Nazis, it displayed far less determination to deal with the plague of blackmailers who attacked, robbed and handed Jews over to their killers. Only in April, 1943, did the Polish "Committee for Civilian Struggle" (Komitet Walki Cywilnej) issue a warning to these blackmailers. Consequently about ten death sentences were carried out against those who had murdered or persecuted Jews in hiding. These steps, although of a positive nature, were unfortunately minuscule efforts as compared to the magnitude of the number of crimes committed against the remnants of the Jewish population. In fact, the Jews on the Aryan side could expect no help except from a handful of individuals. They were a hunted pack, living twenty-four hours of the day and every second of the hour in torment and terror. Their chances of survival were negligible, and the prospect of death ominous and all-pervading.

And suddenly a ray of light indicating a chance for life emerged from an unexpected corner — the Affair of the Hotel Polski.

Was this why so many heeded the rumor, why they discarded their disguises or emerged from their hiding places and went to the Hotel? Perhaps — if the Jews on the "Aryan" side were still governed by such a trait as reason; if in an irrational universe they still clung to logic. But the Jews must have been spurred by other motives besides a desire to escape their nightmarish and untenable existence. They must have sensed some probability of truth in the story of an exchange of foreign citizens.

Faith in the Hotel Polski

The fever that had taken hold of the Jews on the "Aryan" side prompted over five thousand of them to flock to the Hotel Polski between May and July of 1943. There must have been some smidgen of hope based on at least a molecule of reality. And such a hope — or at least the mirage — indeed existed.

In fantastically remote places such as Berlin, Washington, London and Geneva, talks were being held on the subject of exchanging foreign citizens. But these places were beyond the reach of the Jews in the ghetto. Jews were cut off, in fact, not only from the free world, but from any place which lay beyond the ghetto walls.

And yet, during all the days of the ghetto, the minds of the Warsaw Jews were filled and swarming with fantasies, yearning for miracles, one of which was the dream of going abroad.

Dr. Hillel Seidman, who was archives director in Warsaw's Jewish Council, and who later wrote *The Diary of the Warsaw Ghetto*, often describes in his book the extraordinary ideas which the Jews entertained. Here are a few excerpts from the diary:

> . . . A new spirit has descended today on the ghetto. There has been good news. From where? From whom? No one knows. But everyone knows the following:
>
> 1. America has recognized all the Jews remaining in Poland as American citizens.
> 2. Great Britain has recognized all Jews in Poland as citizens of the land of Israel.
> 3. President Roosevelt has warned Germany against the destruction of the Polish Jews. The Germans who live in the USA will be held responsible for the fate of the Jews in Poland.
>
> The news travelled from street to street, from house to house. A number of Jewish personalities who came today to the archives offices of the Jewish Council spoke of the news, above all of the granting of Palestine citizenship to Polish Jews.
>
> One of those present recalled that a similar proposal had been discussed and even adopted in the British Parliament, but had never been enacted.
>
> The Jewish historian, Dr. Itzchok Schipper, an eternal optimist, analyzed the news from the legal viewpoint and came to the conclusion that judicially it seemed probable. He mentioned a number of historical precedents and said that the news was borne out by them. He also pointed out that the whole matter seemed

possible because Jewish leaders all over the world had most certainly shaken the conscience of the world — the news which now arrived was the result of the world's reaction.

Dr. Edmund Stein, the rector of the Judaistic Institute in Warsaw, agreed with him: "Our calls for help have not gone unanswered. This proves that the world hasn't lost its conscience. . . ."

And another entry from Hillel Seidman's diary:

> Everyone asked the same question: "Does the world know? And if they know, what are they doing for us?" Rumors spread that all surviving Jews would receive foreign citizenship; that England had issued a guarantee of protection for all Jews; that all Polish Jews had been recognized on the basis of the Balfour Declaration as citizens of the land of Israel.
>
> There were further rumors that the Americans, in retaliation for German atrocities against Jews, had begun applying similar measures against the Germans in the USA; that Morgenthau, Bernard Baruch, and Samuel Rosenman had intervened with Roosevelt, and Hore Belisha with the Archbishop of Canterbury; that Churchill was threatening the Nazis.
>
> And another "news item": Roosevelt and Churchill, through the intermediary of Switzerland, which safeguards both American and British interests, have demanded that Germany give all Polish Jews the rights of foreigners, including those set out in the Geneva Convention.
>
> The news was being discussed. Orthodox Jews argued that it was true and found proofs in prophecies and mysterious hints in holy books and in pronouncements of great *Tzaddikim*. Some proved the news true by kabbalistically interpreting Biblical passages.
>
> Even those who were less optimistic and didn't believe in the authenticity of the news maintained that, however, news items such as these were a positive factor in the ghetto, for they strengthened the will to survive.

But that mood among the Warsaw Jews and their hope for miracles was based not only on metaphysics and a belief in miracles. There also existed some real and tangible signs that showed the hope in foreign papers to be more than merely the product of feverish minds.

On May 13, 1942, more than two months before the "great deportations," Adam Czerniakow, chairman of the Warsaw Judenrat, wrote in his diary,

> I went this morning to Brand and Mende. Mende took me to Nikolaus, who declared that he was proposing to the Council an

24

emigration exchange of Jews for Germans in the USA and South America, excepting Chile and Argentina. Palestine too was included. Women who had husbands in Palestine would be allowed to leave for that country.

The inhabitants of the ghetto knew at that time little or nothing about that private conversation between their Judenrat chairman and the chief of the German *Auslandstelle*. But soon after, the news was made known to the whole ghetto population in an official and public manner. And the reaction was not joy but, rather, fear and despair.

Dr. Hillel Seidman noted the events and the state of the people's mood in his diary:[1]

> Wednesday, July 15, 1942. A *Verordnung* from the *Auslandstelle* of the Gestapo has been issued that all Jews who are foreign citizens are to go to the Commandant Building of the Jewish Police, from where they will be transported. Where to? To be exchanged to their native countries, explains the Gestapo.
>
> Friday, July 17. This morning at seven o'clock a group of foreign Jews gathered before the house of the Jewish Police on 17 Krochmalna Street. They were arranged in rows and marched to the prison building of the Pawiak. The scenes of farewell with relatives were very moving. There were many who said, "Who knows if our good-bye is not forever . . .?"[1]
>
> In the afternoon, when we returned from saying good-bye to relatives and friends, we began to think: Why had they been interned?
>
> Some said, "They will be sent to America through Portugal." Others: "They'll be kept there until the end of the war."
>
> There are, however, pessimists, who explain that sudden affair with the foreigners as the Germans' desire to protect them from an imminent deportation of Warsaw's Jews.

These fears proved to be realized. Five days after the foreign Jews were isolated, the Germans began the mass deportation. Between July 22 and October 1 of 1942, over 300,000 Jews had been sent to die in the death camp of Treblinka. Hillel Seidman was one of the 40,000 survivors whom the Germans had left before they finally razed the ghetto to the ground. He noted on many occasions an event which later became an important factor in the affair of the Hotel Polski. The Jewish ghetto post office began receiving letters from abroad, some which contained foreign papers, documents, visas and even passports. But most of those to whom these documents had been sent had been deported. The post office officials began feverishly to seek those who may still belong to the world of the living. On December 4, 1942, Hillel Seidman wrote in his diary,

A great sensation: Certificates have arrived from Palestine. Everyone thought with a spark of hope: Perhaps for me? It appeared that 54 certificates had arrived, almost all for women whose husbands are in Palestine. The head of the Jewish post office, H. Jaszunski, came to my archives, bringing with him all the letters and documents and asked for advice: How could he find the addresses? All the addresses are no longer valid. The streets have long since been "Aryanized." I took the letters into my hands. The certificates had been sent from the Palestine Agency in Constantinople. Most of them bore photos of the wives and children. Each envelope contained also a letter written by Dr. Gildin, in which he wrote that after they obtained the exit visa from the German authorities, the wives would receive transit visas through Turkey as well as travelling expenses to the land of Israel.

I found among the names many acquaintances and friends: the wife and child of Pinchas Lewin (Mindel and Sarah); the wife of the editor of the Warsaw *Togblatt*, Samuel Rotstein; the family Kaminer of 9 Ceglana Street, and others.

Since it was impossible to reach some of the people at their former addresses, we decided to look for them in the "shops" [factories]. We typed out their names and began distributing them in the "shops." We also posted them on the walls of the Council building.

As I knew personally some of those who had received letters, I gave their addresses to Mr. Jaszunski. But before these people received their certificates they already knew about them — news in the ghetto travelled very fast. It finally appeared that of the 54 certificates, only about 20 of their owners were still in the ghetto. The rest had already been deported.

The vice president of the Jewish Council, Engineer A. Stolzman, went to the Gestapo to inquire about the received certificates and returned with more news: the *Auslandstelle* of the Gestapo had an additional list of 21 people who should be living in the ghetto. When Stolzman remarked to the Gestapo men that they may have already been deported, he received the reply, "You can send replacements." And indeed, who would be able to check who is who?

And so there was another very tiny ray of hope.

Meanwhile, the "foreigners" who had been interned in the Pawiak on July 17, 1942, suffered from hunger and sent letters out to their friends and relatives in the ghetto asking for food parcels. Only a small percentage of the internees were genuine foreign citizens. Most had procured their foreign documents during the war. Most of these passports or other papers were from countries in Central or South America.[2] It appeared from the very beginning that the Germans divided the internees into groups of citizens of countries hostile or friendly to Germany. All those who possessed documents of countries friendly to Nazi Germany, such as Argentina or Chile, were sent from the Pawiak to the death camp in Treblinka. Among these were the Joint director, Neustat, and his wife; the well-known Yiddish actress, Klara Segalowicz; and the famous lawyer, Alexander Margolis. They had all had Argentine passports. All calculations and strategies were misleading. Only citizens of hostile countries such as Paraguay, Peru, and so on, who had declared war on Germany, remained to be exchanged for Germans, while those of neutral or friendly countries were murdered.

Among the "foreigners" in the Pawiak were Tamara Schorr, wife of Prof. Moses Schorr; her daughter, Felicja Cohn, and her four grandchildren; the two children of Mrs. Cohn; two children of Mrs. Artur Miller; and the well-known writer and pedagogue, Guta Eisenzweig, who played a prominent part in the cultural life of the ghetto.

Towards the end of 1942, the Germans brought Jewish foreigners from other towns to the Pawiak, such as Rabbi Shabse Rapaport, the rebbe of Pinchev and author of many religious books, together with his family; the pedagogue and social activist, Alte Rapaport Bergluz; the family Weingort from Bielsko; and Mrs. Szajn, the daughter of the Mizrachi leader in Cracow, Dr. Bulva.

Hillel Seidman had managed to survive until the winter of 1943, thanks to his post on the Jewish Council. (Despite that, he had been twice dragged to the *Umschlagplatz*, from where he had miraculously escaped.) Now he found himself with the rest of the remaining Jews in a hopeless situation, threatened from within the ghetto by deportations and outside its walls by blackmailers and informers.

He received at that time, through the Jewish underground, which he was using to send food parcels to the internees in prison, an offer from the parents of a Warsaw University classmate of his, Eisenzweig, to register as a member of their family, for they had South American papers. Seidman agreed to their proposal, changed his name to Eisenzweig, "procured" with bribes and payoffs Paraguay documents and notified the Jewish Council and the *Auslandstelle* of the Gestapo that a South American citizen named Szyja Eisenzweig lived in the ghetto. He was arrested and sent to the Pawiak. There the internees lived in the administrative section of the prison, men separated from the women and children.

A large transport, including Seidman, was sent from the Pawiak a few weeks later. The group was taken in German police cars to the Central Railway Station, put in first-class compartments and travelled under the auspices of the Red Cross across the breadth of Germany to a luxurious French resort area, Vittel.

Hillel Seidman was one of the many "fabricated" foreigners who became part of a family by changing his name. Many of the Pawiak internees were in the same category. Others had received their authentic papers from relatives abroad after the war had broken out. But there were also a number of real foreigners, who had come to Poland on a visit and got stuck because of the outbreak of the war and the occupation.

One of these people was an American Jewish woman, Sylvia Berg, with her daughter, Mary. At the outbreak of the war, the girl was fifteen years old. Mary Berg later wrote a book, *Warsaw Ghetto*, which was translated into several languages. It is the first and most detailed eyewitness account of what it meant to be a foreigner in the Warsaw ghetto, written with great accuracy and the talent of an acute observer. The chapter of the "Jewish foreigners in the Pawiak prison" can be regarded as the Prologue to the later story of the Hotel Polski Affair.

A Foreigner in Warsaw

Mary Berg mentions the possibility of going abroad in her entry of June 9, 1942:

> Today we learned that the Swiss Commission which takes care of American citizens in German-occupied countries has permitted

an American woman to take her child and husband to an internment camp. She recently left the ghetto for Berlin under German escort. My mother is in despair, because she failed to register in April when women began to be interned. She wrote to the Commission some time ago, but we are still awaiting their answer. My mother also wrote to the representative of the American colony on the "Aryan" side, Mrs. Lawrence, asking her for information about the exchange of prisoners. Mrs. Lawrence answered that the list of prisoners to be exchanged was closed, but advised my mother to report as soon as possible to Nikolaus, Commissioner for Foreign Affairs in the Gouvernement General. However, it is not easy to get to see this dignitary.

After many attempts, her mother quite accidentally found a way to Nikolaus's office, through a Jew who was working for Nikolaus's deputy. She knew this man, whom Berg calls Z, from Lodz. He told Mrs. Berg how he had fallen into the clutches of the Gestapo. He had been arrested while trying to cross the German border with a false passport, and, after long tortures, had been compelled to work for the Gestapo. He was now employed as an interpreter on Szuch Avenue. It was with his help that Mrs. Berg and three other families in the ghetto in the same situation — that is, three foreign women whose husbands and children were native Poles — were registered in the *Auslandstelle*.

From that day on, writes the young girl,

> there is a real pilgrimage to our house now; an endless line of persons keeps coming to my mother to give her the addresses of their relatives and friends in America so that she can ask them for help. The exchange is supposed to take place on July 6. Everyone wants the same thing: they must send us affidavits, they must help us get out . . . and don't forget to tell them what we are going through here . . . and please let this be the first thing you do when you get to America, don't delay one minute, so that we may live to see the moment of our liberation. . . .

But Mrs. Berg had her own difficulties. She was terribly upset, because Nikolaus

> registered only her and my sister Ann. He says that only children under sixteen are allowed to stay with their mothers, and Ann is fifteen. So it looks as if father and I will have to remain here. But although we have little hope, our friends say that all this will be smoothed out and that the whole family will go. I wish I could believe them.

29

The great day came on July 15, 1942.

> Today while returning from school I met the janitor's wife from Number 16. She rushed up to me in great excitement and told me in one breath that a policeman had just come from headquarters and brought an order from the Gestapo that all foreign citizens should report to the Pawiak prison on July 17, early in the morning. I rushed home, and my mother, who was just eating dinner, dropped her spoon upon hearing the news, and I thought she would faint. But she soon rose from the table and went to see Z. to learn the meaning of this sudden order. . . . It seems that everything will be decided tomorrow. Later, captain Hertz came with the same news. "Now," he said, "you'll see that I was right. We are all doomed. The foreign citizens are being removed because the Germans do not want them to witness what they are preparing for us.

Next day Mrs. Berg went together with Z. to the Gestapo to Assistant Commissioner Orf's office. He declared that she was entitled to take all her family with her. She was told that she would stay with her family in the Pawiak only three days and would then be sent for exchange to America. All their relatives, friends and neighbors came to bid them good-bye.

> It is now close to midnight. Mother is packing. There is a terrible disorder in our apartment. It was crowded with people until ten o'clock; all of them came here for the same purpose: to give us the addresses of American relatives and ask for help. There were many wives with children, whose husbands and fathers had gone to the World's Fair in 1939 and had remained in the United States. They brought us dozens of photographs. It was a horrible farewell. All over the house people were sobbing and there was no end to the heartfelt wishes and tearful embraces.

At seven in the morning, two Jewish policemen came to escort them to the Pawiak. It was a sunny Friday. They were led to the yard of the police station on Ogrodowa Street, where they met about seven hundred "citizens of various European and American countries." A police commissioner checked everyone's papers. Then a group of policemen lined people up in two rows, formed a closed circle around them and ordered them to walk. They came out into the street, hundreds of people stood waiting on both sides of the pavement. Everyone

> wanted to have a look at the lucky seven hundred foreign citizens. At the corner of Zelazna and Leszno Streets the police were

compelled to make use of their sticks to disperse the crowds that barred the passage. From all sides came remarks: "It's a bad sign if they're being taken away," said one. . . . "Now they'll finish us off."

Literally all the able-bodied inhabitants of the ghetto were up that morning. Beginning at the corner of Smocza Street, that is to say, in the most crowded part of the ghetto, access to the street was completely closed. At last our procession reached Dzielna Street and stopped in front of the Pawiak gate. The German officers who were waiting for us there ordered the Jewish policemen to leave. . . .

The Germans called out the names in alphabetical order and ordered each internee to pick up his own suitcase. All of us said good-bye to our friends among the Jewish policemen and to our close relatives, who were the only persons allowed to accompany us to the Pawiak. Finally, the prison gates opened and we found ourselves behind the bars. The Germans kept counting us. . . . We were led through various winding corridors until we reached the large prison yard. . . .

A table and chairs were set up in the courtyard, and the German officers sat down and spread out their lists. Then Assistant Commissioner Orf ordered the American and British citizens to form one group and the neutrals another. Now the real registration began. Each name was read several times, and the person named had to appear before the table and answer questions. When my turn came I was seized by the fear that my father and I would not be recognized as entitled to be exchanged. I approached the table with shaking knees. The Germans asked us why only my mother's and sister's names had been reported. My mother explained that at first Commissioner Nikolaus had refused to register my father and me, but that later the order had been changed. Without saying a word, the German officer put our names down in the files.

The internees were led through intricate corridors. Finally, the Americans and British were brought to a one-story building which had formerly been inhabited by prison employees. They were placed in several rooms, ten people per room, women and men separately. The other foreign citizens of neutral, occupied and South American countries were locked up in prison cells, the women going to the women's wing, called "Serbia."

The next day, they were summoned for a new registration which took place in the little prison yard. Berg saw that most of the Jews were citizens of varous South American republics. There were only twenty-one United States citizens. The others were citizens of Paraguay, Costa Rica, Nicaragua, Ecuador,

Haiti, Bolivia and Mexico. The sixteen-year-old girl remarks on this:

> Thus it is clear that many Jews could be saved from the ghetto with the help of South American passports. The Germans recognize the validity of such passports, although their possessors can speak neither Spanish nor Portuguese. It seems that the Germans need human material for exchange against the Germans interned in the American republics. How can the world be informed that human lives can be saved with these little slips of paper?

Four days later, on July 22, 1942, began the great "resettlement" of the ghetto Jews to Treblinka. On July 21, sixty hostages were brought to the prison, among them prominent members of the Judenrat. The ghetto was in a panic. From their windows in the prison, the internees could see what was going on outside. At daybreak on the twenty-second they could see the first crowds of terrified Jewish men, women and children surrounded by armed gangs of German, Ukrainian, Lithuanian and also Jewish policemen being led to the *Umschlagplatz*.

The internees in the Pawiak experienced all the terror which was felt in the ghetto. In August, in the midst of the deportations, a group of "neutrals" was taken out of the Pawiak to the *Umschlagplatz* for deportation. Mary Berg remarks, "So our turn may come soon, too. I hope it will be very soon. This waiting is worse than death."

Meanwhile, the shootings and cries from the streets didn't cease. One night forty Jews were shot under the windows of the prison. There were also continuous executions inside the Pawiak. Besides having to bear that constant nightmare, the internees suffered also from lack of food, although some received parcels which their families or friends brought to the prison gates, despite everything.

> My mother lies on her mattress all day long; she is so starved that she cannot move. Ann is like a shadow, and my father is terribly thin, just skin and bones. I seem to bear the hunger better than the others. I just grit my teeth when the gnawing feeling in my stomach begins. At night I begin to wait for the next morning, when we are given our four ounces of bread and the bitter water that is called coffee. Then I wait for lunch at noon, when we are brought our first soup, a dish of hot water with a few grains of kasha. Then again I wait impatiently for the evening, when we get our second dish of hot water with a potato or a beet.

One of the internees, Felicja Kohn, the daughter of the grand-rabbi's wife, Madame Schorr,

told us that should we be sent to the *Umschlagplatz* we would do better to take poison. She assured us that she would get us special pills for that purpose. I shuddered when I heard these words, and, strangely enough, at that moment my will to live was stronger than ever.

By October 12, all other American women who had until then lived on the "Aryan" side had been taken to the Pawiak — a sign that the exchange would soon take place.

Some of these women are Jewish, and they told us that an unpleasant anti-Semitic mood prevails even among the internees. The Jewish women are constantly made to feel that they are outsiders. Only the nuns who are in this group protect them and condemn the anti-Semitic remarks of certain women. The nuns take care of the children without discriminating between the Jews and the Gentiles. They display true sisterly love and Christian charity; everyone respects them.

On October 20, 1942, Commissioner Nikolaus visited the internees and told them that next Friday

exactly at ten in the morning: all the American citizens would be sent away. The citizens of South American countries are in despair, they think that they will probably be sent to Treblinka.

But three days later only the "American" men were sent away, among them Mary's father.

We are glad that father has gone. He has no American papers; he is really a Polish citizen, and here he was in constant danger of being deported to Treblinka. In the camp he will at least be under the supervision of the Swiss Exchange Commission. . . . My father must be in the train by now. Shall we ever see him again?

A week later the internees were examined by a physician and all those who were ill received permission to live on the Aryan side. A date was fixed for the departure — December 16 — but because of the constant flow of unfulfilled promises, nobody believed in this one. And indeed, they were notified on December 17 that the departure had been again postponed, this time until next year.

On that same day, new internees were brought in from the provinces, among them

several members of the W. family, and Rabbi R. of Pinczow with his family. All of them have South American passports. These people were at the last moment removed from a transport going to Treblinka. When the Pawiak commissioner led them through the yard they looked terrible, their clothes were ragged and dirty, and the shadow of death lay on their faces. The Rabbi came first, followed by his wife, his two unmarried daughters, another daughter with her husband, and his son, whose wife held their six-month-old child in her arms.

It was a dreadful procession, and I felt as though they were following a funeral. The newly arrived women were put in our room.

Suddenly, on January 17, 1943, the hoped-for day arrived.

We are about to leave. Our suitcases are packed. We are sitting in our coats, waiting.

Early this morning *Obersturmführer* Fleck came to take us to Gestapo headquarters at Szuch Avenue to say farewell to our friends on the "Aryan" side. Permission to say good-bye to our Gentile friends was obtained by our representative, Mr. S., who had to negotiate with Commissioner Nikolaus for a long time before he would agree.

At ten in the morning we left the Pawiak in trucks. The streets of the ghetto were empty and dead. In many houses the windows were wide open despite the cold, and the curtains fluttered in the wind. Inside one could see the overturned furniture, broken cupboard doors, clothes, and linen lying on the floor. The looters and murderers had left their mark.

At the ghetto exit on Nalewki Street I saw a Jewish policeman adding coal to a little stove. A German guard was warming his hands at it.

On the "Aryan" side few people could be seen. Here and there a passer-by hurried along a deserted thoroughfare. When such passers-by saw our truck filled with people under a Nazi escort, they sadly shook their heads. They surely thought that we had been rounded up to be sent to labor camps in Germany.

At Szuch Avenue we found Mrs. Zofia K., our Gentile friend who had been so helpful to us. She brought us a package of bread, cookies, and candy, and wept as she bade us farewell. The Nazis did not allow us to stay long, and an hour later we were taken back to the Pawiak. We were told to be ready to leave at a moment's notice. But we waited endlessly. . . .

While we are waiting here we can see transports of people being sent out of the Pawiak to the Oswiecim camp. Is that where the Nazis intend to send us, too?

34

But the entry in her diary of January 18, 1943, reads,

> At two A.M. Commissioner Nikolaus and his assistant Fleck arrived at the Pawiak in an elegant limousine, which was followed by a dozen closed police cars. We were ordered to go to the yard, where we have taken our walks during the last six months. A thick layer of snow covered the ground. The Ukrainian soldier who stood on guard in a long fur coat with his rifle on his shoulder, said to us "*Do svidania!*" (Good-bye) The women attendants also came out to say good-bye. From the sad expressions on their faces we felt that they thought we were being sent to our death. Not one of them believed that we were really being sent to an internment camp.
>
> Commissioner Nikolaus read the names of the internees in alphabetical order. Armed soldiers led the persons named to the police cars. By three o'clock we had left the gates of the Pawiak behind and, for the last time, traversed the streets of the ghetto.
>
> It was dark everywhere, except for the little fires of the stoves near the sentry posts. I felt choked by tears when we drove down Leszno Street. How much Jewish blood has been shed here . . . We were silent, and our Gentile companions sympathized with us.
>
> My own feelings were mixed. Of course, I was glad to be rescued from this valley of death, but I could not help reproaching myself and wondering whether I really had the right to run away like this, leaving my friends and relatives to their fate.
>
> Our train was not at the station but on a siding some distance from the city. When we finally got on board day had begun to break. We sank exhausted on the hard seats. . . . Our train is moving in the direction of Poznan, not of Auschwitz. . . .

In Summation

These were the two reasons which caused so many Jews hiding on the "Aryan" side to voluntarily enter what they themselves called the Hotel Polski trap. The first was the nightmare of their daily existence, and the other was a belief that the exchange plan contained a grain of probability. In their condition of shattered nerves and a fevered and self-deluding imagination, any trifle pointing to hope would gain in credibility and whet anticipation.

There was a detail in the rumors which emanated from the Hotel Polski which lent the affair an air of realism: the news that those who came to the Hotel had to pay enormous sums of money, often in gold and diamonds, to be entered onto a foreign document.

It was known from the beginning of the German occupation that the killers were also thieves, that each one of them was open to bribery and corruption. To each one of them, from the top to the bottom, from Reichsmarschall Göring, who plundered all the treasures in occupied Europe; to Goebbels, Streicher, Funk and the rest of the Nazi heads who wallowed in luxury in requisitioned palaces with stolen furniture and looted cutlery; to the lowest Gestapo man, SS man or member of the *Einsatzgruppe*, the motto and rule to follow was: Kill and inherit.

Millions of German civilians in the *Heimat*, the Homeland, wore the clothing taken from murdered Jews. Millions of German children received from their papas underwear, dresses, shirts and toys of slaughtered Jewish children. German *Hausfrauen* slept on mattresses stuffed with the hair of Jewish girls and women. One of the Jewish survivors of Bergen-Belsen, quoted in this book, relates that, when the prisoners freed after the liberation were put up in a house formerly occupied by high SS officers, they found spoons, forks and knives with the Hebrew inscription, Kosher for Passover. All Nazi Germany lived on slavery and on plunder.

The news from the Hotel Polski that the Jewish Nazi agents, who were certainly sharing everything with their German bosses, charged colossal sums for forged documents lent probability to the authenticity of the Affair: the Germans, concluded Jewish optimists, had found a new way to enrich themselves; there is perhaps a chance.

And so they flocked to the Hotel.

And what happened? It turned out that all their anticipations, the logical and the irrational, those impelled by despair and based on faith, were built on a foundation of sand. The terror which had dwelt in the heart of every Jew on the "Aryan" side accompanied him to the Hotel and, from there, to the camp to which he was sent, allegedly for exchange. And the most sinister premonitions which had lived with each Jew every second of the day finally materialized: for the Jews were taken from the camp, put once more on trains and taken on the second part of the trip to their final destination: Auschwitz. In the end, with the exception of those few who, unable to afford an expensive American document, had to content themselves with a place on the disdained Palestine list, most of those who went to the Hotel Polski and bought themselves foreign documents, perished. And in that short span between hope and death lay an ocean of human suffering. The tragic journey of these people is the subject of this book. We shall trace here their Golgotha which began in the Hotel and took them over three torturous roads, to Vittel in France, Bergen-Belsen in Germany and to the Pawiak prison a few blocks away from the Hotel, all of which led to the same destiny.

We shall tell the story of these Jews from their own accounts, their own diaries and testimonies, as well as interviews given the author of this book and available documents. This is the only way the drama can be recreated. No outside story-teller, not even the most competent historian, can equal the truth which lives in the memories of these people.

Chapter One:

HOTEL POLSKI,
THE IRRESISTIBLE TEMPTATION

The Hotel Polski represented the third stage in the drama of Jewish foreigners in Warsaw.[3] It started with the announcement of the Gestapo that foreign Jews should come to the headquarters of the Jewish police on Krochmalna Street and from there they were taken to the Pawiak prison. Those who presented documents of neutral or friendly countries (friendly to the Fascist Axis)[4] were immediately separated and taken in trucks to the *Umschlagplatz*, and from there to the death camp Treblinka. The others remained — some of them for over six months — until they were transported to the international camp of Vittel in southern France.

But this did not hold for all of them. After the uprising and ultimate liquidation of the ghetto, a number of Jews were allowed to leave the Pawiak prison and go to one of the more elegant hotels in the center of Warsaw — the Hotel Royal on Chmielna St. next to the Central Railway Station. This was the second stage preceding that of the Hotel Polski.

The Hotel Royal had a clientele of prosperous Poles as well as Germans who came on various missions to Warsaw. Now, with the arrival of Jews, the sight was unbelievable . . . Jews, Poles and Germans were living in the same building, sharing the same lobby, eating in the same restaurant, and all this at a time when being a Jew was synonymous with death only a few steps away.

The news about the existence of the Hotel Royal spread quickly, and Jews began coming directly from their hiding places on the "Aryan" side. One of the "attractions" of the hotel, which gave the Jews some excuse for hope, was the presence of the Joint director, David Guzik, who sat in the hotel legalizing doc-

39

uments with the German *Auslandstelle* or adding the names of those without papers to those of others to form artificially fabricated families. The Jewish man who was in charge of all of these operations was a certain Wladyslaw Garbinski, who stayed at the hotel together with his wife.

The entrance to the Hotel Royal was open. There were no guards nor German sentry. Everyone could freely enter or leave. Inside, at first, neither the Poles nor the Germans seemed to bother about their Jewish neighbors. The German *Auslandstelle* promised the assembled Jews that they would be taken to a transfer camp for foreign internees in Vittel. And indeed, on May 21, 1943, it was announced that the train would leave that same day. One car only was designated for the Jews, with eight compartments and eight seats in each compartment, meaning that no more than sixty-four Jews would be able to leave. The Jews in the hotel were overcome with panic — an equal number was to remain and wait for another chance.

David Guzik and Garbinski went to the *Auslandstelle* and begged them either to add one more car or to allow the Jews to travel in less comfort — why exactly eight to a compartment? The Jews were ready for less luxury . . . to sit on the floor and in the corridors. But the Germans were adamant — eight times eight is sixty four — no more no less.

The departure scene was unbelievable. A group of sixty-four men, women, and children, dressed in the most fashionable clothes and loaded with elegant suitcases arrived in special cars to the railway station, where they boarded a normal looking passenger train. To an outsider it looked as if everything were happening in the 1930's, in prewar, peaceful Warsaw, where there were no Germans, no ghettos, deportations or death camps. The only Germans who accompanied the sixty-four Jews were the almost normal Ausland police. Inside, everyone, even the smallest children, had a separate seat and a comfortable place for luggage.

The news about the circumstances under which the train had departed caused more and more Jews to come to the Hotel. Only a few possessed any foreign documents. Some arrived in normal dress, some were elegantly attired, while others came in tatters. Guzik let them all in, and the number of Jewish guests soon exceeded one hundred.

And then, the inevitable happened. Some of the Hotel's Polish guests, and, above all, the Germans, who had come here expecting to find the entire city "Judenrein," could no longer stand the presence of Jews under the same roof as they. The result was that the Jews were ordered to move. The question was — where to?

After a feverish search, somebody discovered the little known Hotel Polski on Dluga Street. Like most of the hotels, this one too had a few dozen rooms, a restaurant, and a great spacious courtyard. And this is where the Jews were moved. Soon, more and more Jews began to arrive, and the stage was set for the last part of the drama — Hotel Polski.

In this chapter, we shall first give accounts of testimonies of the affair given by authors who at the time of the events lived on the "Aryan" side and were active in underground Jewish movements, and who were thus in a position to observe the Hotel from the outside. Their accounts will be followed by those of the real dramatis personae (which characteristically for those "times of absurdity" contain some discrepancies and errors) — those who personally went through the hotel, either as inmates — owners of foreign documents who had survived to tell their story, or by those who frequented the hotel for other purposes.

The final entry in this chapter will be a short story written by the renowned Polish author, Adolf Rudnicki, a Jew who lived on the "Aryan" side, and who, after the liberation, wrote a number of important fictionalized accounts of the Jewish drama under the Nazis.

Excerpts from Published Books

BERNARD GOLDSTEIN

Bernard Goldstein was one of the few Bundist personalities who remained in Warsaw after the outbreak of the war. He later was one of the active leaders of the Bundist underground.

The ghetto was still burning. The Jews in hiding on the "Aryan" side lived in constant fear of falling to the Nazis' hands. Then suddenly, a ray of hope shone forth.

41

During the month of May, there were many rumors that the Gestapo had obtained a large number of visas from foreign consulates of several neutral countries. According to these rumors, most of the people for whom the visas had been intended were no longer alive. Now the Gestapo was prepared to sell these visas to other persons for large amounts of money and to allow them to assume the names of the dead people.

Jewish Gestapo agents, such as Kenigel, Adam, and others, were the official representatives of the Gestapo in these transactions. Those possessing these visas were to be sent to temporary camps for foreign citizens near Vittel and Hanover, and from there would be sent abroad.

An office was set up in the Hotel Imperial* and on Chmielna Street for the registration of foreign citizens. The rush of people was so great that there wasn't enough room for all the applicants. The office was therefore transferred to the Hotel Polski on 29 Dluga Street. Registrants were transferred from the hotel to the Pawiak prison, where they were held in the women's section awaiting transport to Vittel or to Hanover.

The Jewish foreign citizens were allowed to take luggage and valuables with them. Many who were afraid to carry large sums of cash exchanged their money for gold or jewels.

It was a good business for the Gestapo. Entire families put their faith on this doubtful salvation. They readily paid tens of thousands of zlotys for a single passport. I know of a family that paid 750,000 zlotys.

Letters arrived from Vittel and Hanover and other places, describing the excellent conditions under which the people lived, protected by the Red Cross. These letters reinforced the faith in this road to safety, and the eagerness to buy passports increased.

The Joint Distribution Committee contributed financially to obtain passports for a number of organizational leaders. The Joint Director, David Guzik,[5] sat in the Hotel Polski helping people in their search for foreign papers. Guzik himself believed so strongly in the whole plan that he obtained passports for his own wife, children, and a brother.

Then the Polish underground issued a warning. According to

*Should be: Royal.

42

information it had received, the entire affair was a trap, which meant that the Gestapo planned to get their hands on the remaining Jews in Warsaw and kill them.

Our own underground had also had serious doubts about the scheme from the very start. But our warnings were in vain, especially after it became known that many of the Jewish Gestapo collaborators were providing their own families with these passports. Adam, for instance, had sent his entire family on the first days of registration, and he himself went to the camp in Vittel. Ganzweich, the Nazi collaborator and leader of the infamous "Thirteen," sent his own wife. The popular dancer and Gestapo collaborator, Madame Machno, went to the Hotel Polski as did many other important and minor officials of the Jewish police.

One night, the Gestapo surrounded the Hotel Polski. Scores of those who hadn't yet registered were arrested, and, the following day, shot. Still, the desperate refused to heed any warnings, but stormed the Hotel Polski, offering anything for a visa. The holder of such a visa considered himself to be lucky beyond belief. Inside the Hotel was a continuous round of joyous parties to celebrate the acquisition of visas.

The Hotel Polski affair lasted until November, 1943. In February, 1944, we received the tragic news that our warnings and fears had been well founded. Most of those who had gone through Vittel, Hanover, and other camps as foreigners, had perished.

TUVIA BORZYKOWSKI

Tuvia Borzykowski was born in Radomsk. In 1940, he was summoned to Warsaw to help conduct the work of the Hehalutz, an organization preparing young Jewish men and women for emigration to what was then Palestine, in a communal framework. In the summer of 1942, Borzykowski joined the Jewish Fighting Organization, participated in the revolt, and was one of the last handful of fighters to leave the ghetto, by way of the sewers.

In 1949, he left Poland for Israel where he joined the Kibbutz of Ghetto Fighters, and died ten years later, following a prolonged illness. His book, Between Tumbling Walls, *from which the following passages are excerpted, originally appeared in Yiddish, in Poland, in 1949.*

A new rumor was spread among Jews living in "Aryan" Warsaw and caused an upsurge of hope. People are whispering that one can buy for money a passport issued by a neutral country and thus be able to travel abroad as a foreign citizen. Those who still have some dollars make efforts to establish contact with the source of the life-giving documents. They pay money to all sorts of characters who claim to have the right connections. Those who have barely enough money to pay their landlords, if that, bewail their ill luck.

The source of the rumors is, of course, the Gestapo. It is they who spread the news that they have received from consulates of neutral countries a number of visas for citizens of those countries, and since most of those people are no longer alive, they are ready, they say, to pass them on to others — for a price.

Jewish Gestapo men, Adam, Kenigl, and others, register Jews and collect five-figure sums. Then they are all housed in the Hotel Polski from which they are to be sent to the special camp for foreigners in Vittel, and from there abroad. The hotel is already packed. From time to time groups of Jews are transferred to the camp, and the vacated rooms are taken over by new arrivals. All are allowed to take along baggage without any limitations. Thus Hotel Polski has become the only island where Jews live legally under the eyes of the Gestapo. Among the Jews there are also individuals who have no foreign documents, but lost their hiding places, have not yet found others, and meantime find shelter in the hotel. The Gestapo has already found out about it, and one night they raided the place. Those without documents were taken to the Pawiak prison and shot.

The "foreigners" are not quite sure of their luck; it does seem strange to them that the Gestapo who hunt every Jewish man, woman, and child have suddenly become willing to save some Jews. Germans enter and leave the hotel without bothering them. Is it not a trap?

Those things happened before. During the "actions" in the ghetto the Germans gave some of the Jews the illusion of being safe, then sent them to death. Even the fact that letters were received from Jews in the Vittel camp with the information that they arrived there safely and remain under the protection of the International Red Cross does not alleviate the fears. There had been letters from the Treblinka death camp too, bringing news that the Jews there were living peaceful lives. Despite all these fears, more and more Jews register at the Hotel Polski. They are tired to death of hiding, of being afraid of every noise, of every whisper from outside; they figure that the war will last a long time, sooner or later the Germans will get them, so there is nothing to lose. Perhaps this time the Germans will not betray them? Perhaps they want to save a handful of Jews in order to show to the world that they are not *such* heartless murderers?

Even such a serious person as the head of the Warsaw office of the Joint Distribution Committee, David Guzik, believes that he may in this way help save some Jews, and he spends J.D.C. money for this purpose.

JACOB CELEMENSKI

Jacob Celemenski is an active member of the Jewish socialist Bund. Thanks to his "good looks," he was able to live as a Pole since the early days of the Nazi occupation, while acting as an underground courier, bringing financial aid and distributing illegal literature to Jews who lived in hiding. These included Jews who lived in Warsaw as well as those who lived in towns and camps across Poland. He is the author of a book of memoirs entitled, With My Slain People *(Yid.)*

. . . One day, when I came to one of our hideouts on Grzybowska Street, our comrade, Leybl Szpichler, said to me, "We need your help." And he proceeded to tell me something that I had known before, but this was the first time that I was being confronted with it directly. There were rumors circulating in Warsaw that Jews in possession of foreign passports could save themselves. The Germans had assembled a number of Jews holding foreign documents in the Pawiak prison as early as the eve of the great deportations from the Warsaw ghetto, with promises to send them abroad. Now, they had begun bringing together Jews in the Hotel Polski on Dluga Street, where they were to be exchanged for Germans. How true this was I didn't know. Neither did I know who the organizers of this affair were. I suspected that this was simply another new German trick to kill Jews.

I now learned from comrade Szpichler that he was in touch

with a Hotel committee which was trying to get citizenship papers from South American countries, and that, together with his wife and child, he would soon be sent to a special camp for foreign Jews in Vittel, located in the French Vosges mountains. I didn't like the whole thing. I knew from experience that one shouldn't trust the Nazis, and that all their schemes inevitably ended with the deaths of more Jews.

Two days later, when Leyb Szpichler was already in the Hotel with his wife and child, I went there to see what was going on. At the gate stood a guard wearing a policeman's cap. He allowed only those with foreign papers to enter. Neither Polish policemen nor even Germans were allowed inside, except those who came on special missions from the German authorities. This was a sealed island, surrounded by an ocean where being a Jew meant certain death. I myself entered through a side door. To my great surprise, I met not only my friends the Szpichler family here, but also the wife of a friend, Yoshke Lipszyc, as well as comrade Zyman and his wife. Esther Lipszyc told me how she had come. She had lived in a room on the "Aryan" side which she had attained with the help of an activist of the Polish Socialist party, whom she had known well before the war. He was the administrator of the house, and had told her to stay there. He had carried out all the necessary formalities and provided her with official papers. Nevertheless, she didn't "look well." To remain in her room constantly was very difficult, but she was afraid to go into the street. On hearing of the Hotel Polski, she immediately went there to buy foreign papers and wait for a transport. I told her that considering her good connections with the administrator of the house, she should remain there. A good hideout on the "Aryan" side was much more certain than this Hotel, which looked very suspicious to me. It seemed very improbable that the Nazis intended to save Jewish lives.

Other people in the Hotel informed me that the Committee was in touch with the Center of the Orthodox Jews in Switzerland; that the *Va'ad Hatzala* was sending passports from Switzerland — mainly Palestinian papers and also South American citizenship. Most of the Jews in whose names the documents were sent were no longer alive, and so other Jews were now being "adopted" by these documents. The same thing was going on not only in Warsaw, but also in a number of other towns, and in other occupied countries. Two transports had already left the Hotel and arrived in Vittel. Among the people in these transports were several rabbis, Itzhak Katzenelson the poet, the writer Hillel Seidman, Dr. Nathan Eck, and others. I immediately went to Dr. Leon Feiner, the leader of the underground Bund, and told him about the visit to the Hotel, and all that I had learned. He didn't think long before categorically replying, "The Bund will have nothing to do with it."

The news that one could buy a foreign passport and go abroad spread like wildfire among the rest of the "Aryan" Jews. The very thought that one could enter the Hotel and discard the mask of "Polishness" made everybody restless. The Jews began to leave their hiding places and went to the Hotel. The rich had themselves added on to existing passports for exorbitant prices, and those without money were helped by the Committee, which forced the rich to pay for the poor.

Sometime later, I received a letter from the Szpichler family announcing that they were leaving with the next transport. They asked me to come and bid them farewell. I received a special pass card from the Joint director, Guzik, which I showed to the guard at the gate, who let me enter. This time, I had the impression that I was in the middle of a ghetto. The stairs were crammed with families and their luggage. Hysterical scenes took place before the Committee door. Poor Jews were crying and asking to be put on the list of the lucky ones. Most had given up their apartments on the "Aryan" side and had nowhere to go, except to throw themselves into the river. Everyone looked feverishly at the door, where life or death was decided.

The great courtyard was packed with people. I saw Jews in heavy expensive furs and rings on their fingers, while others were frightened, nervous and starving. Everyone talked and bargained. As in the ghetto, there were beggars who went around asking for charity. Most of these people didn't realize that the entire affair was a hoax. Instead, they clung desperately to this last hope.

With a heavy heart, I entered room 12 where I met the Szpichler family, Esther Lipszyc, the teacher Zyman with his child, and comrade Solnik. Before the war, he had been a member of the Bundist militia. Everyone was in a gloomy mood when we said our good-byes.

The next day, they were sent not to Vittel, but to a camp called Bergen-Belsen where they were all murdered.

The inmates of labor camps also learned about the Hotel and tried to get out to some well known political and social activists from Poniatowa and Trawniki. One day, I was approached by a member of the Polish Socialist Party in Cracow, who had been active in Warsaw, named D. Steinberg. She asked me in the name of the Polish Socialist leader, Zygmunt Zaremba, if it was possible to save three Jewish party members from the Poniatowa camp. I replied that according to a resolution of the Bund, I wasn't allowed to have any dealings with the Hotel Polski, and couldn't intervene in any way. I had a similar case with our comrade Solnik, who gave me a desperate heart-rending letter he had received from several of our comrades in the Poniatowa camp, to save them from certain death. It was signed by Shmuel Kruk, Israel Hofman and others. Alas, we could do nothing for them.

During my last visit to the Hotel, a Polish worker arrived on a mission to procure a foreign passport for comrade Helena Szefner, wife of Boruch Szefner, the famous Bundist writer. The Polish worker brought a photo of Helena, who told him, however, that he should consult with me before making any arrangements. I advised her to return to her apartment in Pruszkow, and to give up this idea completely. She should not trust her life to the Germans if she had an alternative. She took my advice and stayed there until the end of the war. She later joined her husband in the USA.

Very few people who went through the Hotel Polski survived.

DAVID KLIN

David Klin was a member of the Jewish Socialist Party, the Bund, and was active in Jewish and Polish underground fighting groups in Warsaw. After the liberation he wrote a book, Arm in Arm with Death. *One of the chapters is devoted to the affair of the Hotel Polski:*

A rumor suddenly spread about an exchange between foreign citizens in occupied Poland and German internees in America. This exchange was to take place in neutral countries. Since many of the Jewish foreign citizens in Poland were no longer alive, or their whereabouts were unknown, their places could be filled by others who would use their names. The Germans wouldn't be very particular.

How this news reached the hidden Jews is a great mystery. The chief people in charge were, of course, the few Jewish-German collaborators. They had the names of the passports or documents which were to be distributed. For the Jews who lived on the "Aryan" side, constantly in the shadow of death, the news presented the illusion of rescue. It was seen as a good omen especially because a few of those who were promoting the affair were well-known Jewish personalities who themselves believed in this chance of saving some of the hidden Jews. The Jewish collaborators demanded enormous amounts of money in return for bestowing on people the privilege of setting their names on foreign documents. But in order to demonstrate their "Jewish heart," the collaborators arranged that the rich pay for the poor.

The point of assembly was the Hotel Royal on Chmielna Street. The first transport went from there to Vittel, a French resort, where the exchange was to take place. All those who came to the Hotel to get themselves registered were well-treated. No Germans appeared in the hotel. The first transport left with great pomp. It seemed that those on it had avoided death. Letters came from Vittel with detailed descriptions of how smoothly the trip had gone, and of how they now lived in hotels and were well fed.

The second transport was arranged from the Hotel Polski on Dluga Street. Among those who this time came to the Hotel were many well-known political and community leaders along with their families, such as the wife and daughter of the Joint director, Guzik; the family of another Joint director, Czerski; the lawyer, Orzech, who was the brother of the Bund leader, Maurycy; the Yiddish writer, Yoshua Perle; and the Zionist leader Kirszenbaum with his wife and daughter.

The Jewish Nazi collaborators too had sent their families and this strengthened the general belief that this was indeed a way to escape the hell of Warsaw. Everyone stood before a choice: either remain in the cellars, bunkers and hideouts and live like hunted animals, or take a chance. This had confused the greatest pessimists and the over-cautious. Even Jewish underground groups on the "Aryan" side took no unqualified stand on the affair.

The second transport was sent out not to Vittel, but to Hanover. The Germans explained that Vittel was overcrowded. From the second transport also came news, but this time only postcards from Poznan and Berlin describing the trip.

My brother-in-law, Lipszyc, and Gala Leszezynska, were ready to go to the Hotel, but I convinced them that they shouldn't trust the Germans. They promised not to go there.

I personally went to the Hotel Polski one day where I met Jacob Celemenski, the Jewish socialist and underground courier, and we both expressed our doubts and reservations. But it was difficult to convince others, in view of the letters which we had received. Almost everyone answered us in the same vein: Here we are all the time exposed to death. Perhaps over there we'll have a chance.

When I returned home, I saw, to my regret, that Gala Leszezynska had left. She had gone to a friend of hers, the wife of the Zionist activist, Lazar, and both had decided to join the next transport. I ran back to the Hotel to convince her to return, but it was too late. The transport had already left. Four days later I received a postcard from her mailed from Berlin, which contained only a few words: "Best regards, Berlin-Friedrich Bahnhof." My brother-in-law rebuked me for not having let him go. Now, he said, he would definitely present himself for the third transport. We had a long and violent argument and he finally gave in. From Gala we received no more news.

Later we learned that before the departure of the second transport, the Germans took the Zionist leader, Kirszenbaum, out of the train together with his wife and daughter. Someone had informed on him that he had taken part in preparing the ghetto uprising. The family was shot in the Pawiak.

The second transport went from the Hotel Polski directly to the extermination camp of Bergen-Belsen.

In the meantime, a third transport had assembled in the Hotel Polski. This time the Germans made no more ceremonies. They surrounded the Hotel and took all the four hundred assembled Jews to the Pawiak. This was the last road those Jews travelled.

The Jews from Vittel as well were later sent to extermination camps. Only two of them managed to escape from the railway station in Paris. One of them — Gitler — leader of the children's organization, Centos, now lives in Poland. Some of those who didn't escape managed to survive, among them Miriam Novitch who lives today in Kibbutz of Ghetto Fighters in Israel.

Earlier in his book, David Klin explains how the Hotel Polski affair began:

A group of four or five Jewish collaborators who were active on the "Aryan" side formed a group, Himmelblau. They lived close to the Gestapo Headquarters on Szuch Avenue, Swieta Teresa Street 2. Among them were Lolek Skosowski, Kenigel, Lubraniecki and others. Lolek Skosowski had recovered from the bullet wound he had received from the attempt of the Jewish Fighters' Organization (ZOB) to execute him in the ghetto brush factory. He now continued his criminal activities.

The Himmelblau group began, under order of the Gestapo, to spread news that a number of foreign documents for Jews in Warsaw had arrived from abroad. The documents were in the hands of the Gestapo. There was a chance for those in whose names the documents were sent to use them by being exchanged for Germans interned in Allied countries.

VLADKA MEED

Wladka Peltel Miendzyrzecka, known as Vladka, was a member of the Jewish socialist youth movement, the Tsukunft, and was active as a courier in the underground on the "Aryan" side. This is her account, that of an observer, of the Hotel Polski Affair in her book, On Both Sides of the Wall:

While I was still in the country, a number of visas became available for Jews hiding in Warsaw. The visas came by way of Switzerland, Palestine and South American countries. The Jews for whom those visas originally had been issued were no longer alive, but the Gestapo authorities agreed, in exchange for cash, to give them to other Jews, who then would assume the names written on the documents. Jews acquiring such visas were immediately classified as aliens and transported to a special detention camp in France, where aliens and prisoners of war were

51

kept until they could be exchanged for Germans held in Allied countries.

The glad tidings about the visas spread among the Jews in the city like wildfire. At a time when the Germans had devastated the Warsaw ghetto, when special SS troops were assigned to the task of ferreting out and killing Jews, when any Gentile harboring a Jew was doomed, when Polish homes were set on fire and hideouts were reported to the police — at such a time of terror against Jews, the Gestapo suddenly instituted a center for the new Jewish emigration.

Wherever one. went, and whomever one encountered, Gentile or Jew, this new emigration was the topic of conversation. Just imagine — Jews, whom the Nazis had been exterminating until now, were suddenly granted the right to live! The Gestapo was according the status of alien to Jews!

On the other hand, it might really mean freedom. Some Jews were skeptical. Perhaps this was just another German trap. On the "Aryan side" death lurked everywhere for the Jew; sooner or later he was bound to be trapped there. But in this instance, the Germans had to deal with foreign consulates and with the free outside world. Abroad, the Germans would have to account for the visas.

True, the Germans were not to be trusted; but how could one neglect such an opportunity? Indeed, the visa transformed an outlawed Jew into a citizen who was respected and protected.

Thus the Jews rationalized, throwing their lot in with this risky venture.

The new hope seemed to be confirmed by letters which arrived from the first of the evacuees. This group of Jews had arrived in Vittel, a city in France, just as the Germans had promised. Conditions at the camp were good, and Jews were treated with the courtesy the Germans accorded the other citizens.

The fact that David Guzik, who had been an executive with the Polish branch of the American Jewish Joint Distribution Committee before the war, had taken part in the feverish emigration "undertaking," served more than anything else to raise the hopes of the Jews.

Wealthy Jews began to abandon their best hideouts and children were being retrieved from churches and orphanages so as to be ready to leave for France at a moment's notice. Anyone who could get his named placed on to the emigration register considered himself as good as saved. Jews sold their last trinkets — rings, gold chains, diamonds.— to raise the money needed for the coveted passports.

The offices at which these visas were issued were located in the Hotel Royal, on Chmielna Street, later in the Hotel Polski, 29 Dluga Street. Crowds were waiting there for this transfer to France. Some thirty Jews had been sent from the Poniatowa camp near Lublin. I, too, was anxious to appraise the situation for myself.

Unauthorized persons were not supposed to enter the hotel, but the Gestapo was not too strict and admitted everybody. Immediately upon entering the office one was struck by the 'voyage departure' atmosphere. The courtyard was teeming with chattering Jews. Frenzied men and women kept dashing inside to see whether the office was already open for business. Others hurried up the stairs or hauled bundles and luggage to their living quarters in the hotel building. Still others called their friends aside and conversed in whispers.

"Did you talk to them?"

"Well, how much do they want?"

"What kind of passport will you get?"

One day Palestine immigration certificates were available at a reasonable price, while the price of South American visas was high; the next day, the values were reversed. The prices fluctuated with the demand. The restlessness seemed haunted by fear. Amidst the feverish preparations for departure, faces reflected inner misgivings: were they being duped?

Before the evacuees left for the detention camp in France, the Germans addressed them, explaining courteously that once they reached their destination they would have to be patient for a while until exchanges for German prisoners of war could be arranged. The Germans apologized for the hardships and inconveniences of the journey.

"There's a war on, you see," they said. "You have to make allowances for us; we Germans can't get everything we want, either."

These speeches caused some perplexity; never before had the Jews heard Germans apologize or even explain. Some Jews were not only perplexed but dubious; some sought out Guzik for his counsel. Guzik commanded the respect and trust of the Jewish community. His word was the decisive factor. After all, he had sent his own family abroad! If he had such confidence in this process it had to be reliable. Why, he was even able to maintain direct contact with friends overseas! How else could one account for his retaining a position of prominence?

The Gestapo, moreover, did everything it could to emphasize the privileged status of the Jews at the Hotel Polski. There were known cases of arrested Jews being released upon their showing that they were registered there.

Two incidents caused a great stir at that time. Jews were forbidden to leave the hotel, but some occasionally ventured out despite the prohibition. One woman who had obtained a visa was picked up by police while she was out for a walk — a normal occurrence in itself. The woman's friends promptly lodged a complaint with the Gestapo officers in the Hotel Polski. Using as their "intermediaries" Skosowski, whom the Jewish Fighting Organization had at one time beaten up in the ghetto as a Gestapo agent, and Zurawin, another Gestapo collaborator, these friends protested against the "illegal" treatment accorded to the woman, who was now officially an "alien." The woman was set free within hours.

The other incident involved a Jew registered at the Hotel Polski who sought to retrieve some belongings from a Gentile friend to whom he had entrusted them. The Gentile now refused to return the articles. This was an occurrence so commonplace that to challenge it was almost absurd. But, in this case, the Jew insisted to the Hotel Polski "intermediaries" that, as an alien, he was privileged to take his belongings with him. Two Germans were dispatched to help him reclaim his property.

While such instances helped to enhance the credibility of the new passports, doubts increased during the month of June. By that time, passports could be obtained for a pittance, or even for the mere asking. All applications were approved almost routinely. Uncertainty began to gnaw at us. Somehow, it all went too smoothly. Could not the entire operation be some kind of trap, after all?

I heard such questions from friends and acquaintances to whom I gave modest aid from our relief funds before they left.

54

Zyman had misgivings. My friend of long standing, he had a very good hiding place at Grzybowska 29, and had placed his five-year-old daughter with a Gentile woman. He was at the Hotel Polski, waiting for his turn to emigrate, having already attended to the formalities. He voiced his doubts;

"I have settled all the details, but I'm not sure whether I'm doing the right thing. You're actually putting your life in their hands!"

Indeed, a number of our leaders had begun to feel the same way. Yet they could not be absolutely certain. They cautioned against trusting the Germans, and sent out inquiries through underground channels. But they could not definitely denounce the operation. Isolated as we were from the world outside Warsaw, we had no means of proving that the passports were really a German ruse to coax Jews out of hiding. How could we assume the responsibility of urging fellow Jews to stay where they were likely to be liquidated, instead of taking the chance offered them to escape?

Eliezer Geller reasoned along similar lines. I met him at the hotel, his scorched hands still bandaged from the fire at the cellophane factory. "All I want is to get out of Poland; afterwards, I'll be on my own," he told me earnestly. Eliezer was waiting his turn together with Israel Kanal, another group leader in the ghetto uprising, and survivor who had recently returned after staying with a partisan unit in the Wyszkow woods. Even before the uprising he had gained fame by shooting Szerynski, the notorious chief of ghetto police.

After all the wavering and questioning, the majority decided to go, despite the risks.

Only when the last transport of Jews was ready to leave did the duplicity of the Germans become fully apparent. As usual when Jews were being assembled for the journey, the hotel was surrounded by German armed guards, and all exits closed. Several military vehicles were in readiness. Amid growing uneasiness, someone whispered that he had overheard Gestapo officials say something about being "rounded up." And, when the order was indeed given for all Jews present in the Hotel Polski to board the vehicles, there was an eruption of clamor and tumult. *All* Jews were to go? Heretofore, only those registered had been selected! Among those present were many whose documents had not yet been processed or who were waiting for their families to join them.

Running to the office for an explanation, the horrified Jews found it swarming with police. Some Jews refused to get into the vehicles, contending that they would join the next group. But protests proved futile. The Germans searched thoroughly. They left no one behind — not even Guzik.

Among the very few who escaped was my future husband, Benjamin Miedzyrzecki. He hid in an attic and was not detected. Some four hundred Jews were deported to the Pawiak prison.

Within a few hours it became known in Warsaw that half of the Jews with passports had been shot by the Germans in the prison courtyard; the others were deported to the Bergen-Belsen death-camp. Only a few escaped through bribery, among them, David Guzik.

Those of us remaining on the "Aryan" side were both heartbroken and enraged. The Germans had played craftily on the Jews' last hope for survival. Jews who had miraculously escaped death in the ghetto had now been duped into surrendering themselves to their torturers and executioners under the lure of a legalistic procedure promising final release from the inferno.

Of the more than 3,000 victims taken out of the city as emigrants, it turned out that only 40 or so held genuine foreign passports, which were honored. Only they escaped this final roundup.

After the war, I learned more about this tragic episode. The Germans at first respected foreign passports and treated the Jews who possessed them in a fairly decent manner. Jewish organizations abroad made every effort to obtain fictitious passports from Latin American countries for Jews living in the Nazi-occupied countries. And there were even negotiations, carried out with Nazi officials for the release of a certain number of Jews against a corresponding number of German prisoners of war held by the Allied powers. But, tragically, only a handful of Jews were saved by all these efforts. The rest found themselves saddled with forged papers which the Germans refused to honor, and ultimately met the same end as so many of their brethren who had elected not to take the chance.

Diaries, Reports, Testimonies and Interviews

SIMCHA KORNGOLD

The Yad Vashem archives in Jerusalem contain a manuscript written by Simcha Korngold, a native of Warsaw, who survived the war and came to Palestine on September 8, 1945, together with his three children. He now lives in Haifa.

Korngold and his family went through all the stages of the destruction of the Warsaw Ghetto. His wife perished during the great deportations. He himself took part in the ghetto uprising, and then together with his children, aged 5, 6 and 7, crawled through the sewers to the Aryan side, where he lived in various hideouts with Polish families, while the three children were hidden in three different places, in villages around the capital. On hearing of the Hotel Polski he went there and managed to get their names inscribed on the Palestine list. He then brought his children over to the hotel and together with them, was sent with a transport of about 3,500 Jews, the majority of whom held South and Central American papers, to the camp of Bergen-Belsen. During all this time, starting from the beginning of the war, he wrote his memoirs in which he described his experiences and thoughts. Several of his notebooks were lost while he was still in Warsaw; after the war, one of them was found by a Pole who brought it to the Jewish Historical Commission.

His last hideout in Warsaw before he decided to enter the Hotel Polski was in an underground bunker in the apartment of a Polish friend, Jasio, who lived next to the Jewish cemetery in the suburb of Bródno. One night the bunker collapsed and Korngold, together with a Jewish woman who was hiding with him, was forced to spend several days and nights with no food or water in a mausoleum in the cemetery. It was then that his Polish friend brought him the news about the Hotel Polski.

. . . Jasio told me: Hundreds of Jews are inside the Hotel Polski. They wear no armbands and are free to come and go.

The rumor was that the United States had declared all Polish Jews as American citizens. They had gathered in the hotel from which they expected to be sent to Switzerland for an exchange with German nationals. All this sounded reasonable and I decided to go there the next day, July the eleventh. Maybe this was our last-minute salvation.

Early in the morning I went with Jasio to the hotel to see what it was all about. I had nothing to risk, for I was already in a desperate situation. I had no more money, and I couldn't afford to provide for the eight persons who depended on me and for whom my friend Puharski was presently paying the expenses. He kept consoling me: The Russians will soon come. And so I went to the Hotel Polski. The gate of the hotel was not guarded from the outside. On the other side stood a Jewish man. I knocked and he refused to open. I said to him, "I'm Jewish. I want to get in." Then he opened and Jasio and I entered.

The courtyard was crowded with a great number of Jews, among them many acquaintances. I met neighbors who had lived together with me on 12, Muranowska Street — Shim Friedman with his wife and children, Haim Friedman with his wife and child (he had had a store on 20, Gensia Street), Basia Friedman, and others. I started to make inquiries — what was it all about? They told me. There were a number of foreign citizens from Argentina, Honduras, and other countries who lived in Poland, and who, according to the law, should be interned. But they had perished, and since they no longer existed, we were going to take their places, assuming their names. The Germans were doing this to show the world that their murderous country obeyed international laws, because the outside world was full of rumors that all foreigners had been killed. The Germans wanted to demonstrate that these rumors were false. This is why they began this action in cooperation with the International Red Cross, which would be free to come and check the truth. At the same time, other countries which held German citizens would send them to Switzerland for an exchange. This is why they had created this Hotel Polski affair. All of this was clear to me and made sense.

I looked around. Everyone was free as befit foreign citizens. That entire section of Dluga St. had been transformed into a neutral area. I likewise began to breathe the foreign atmosphere. This sudden feeling of freedom was like an epidemic, a foreign disease. And that was the way the criminal Germans cheated hundreds of Jews who had lived on the Aryan side.

The leading part in the affair was played by Jewish col-

58

laborators who had long Gestapo records, and whose names I want to mention here — Kenigel, Skosowski, Adam and others. At the end of June 1943, the Germans, with the help of these Jewish traitors, organized a search for Jews to replace those who had been murdered.

For the privilege of registering one's name on such a foreign passport, one had to pay tens of thousands of zlotys. Those who could afford to pay were added to an artificial family consisting sometimes of forty members. The demand was large. Those who paid were added as sons, sons-in-law, daughters-in-law, children, grandchildren. Everyone was warned to remember his new name, to what family he belonged. People went around memorizing their new names. But not everybody could belong to these privileged ones — only those who had money. Not only were these people tricked into their death, but they had to pay a high price for it. Among these privileged ones were, ironically, dozens of Jewish Gestapo collaborators. On July seventh, the first transport was sent to Switzerland. The same German criminals who had carried out the mass deportations in the Warsaw ghetto now treated these foreign Jews with great courtesy — "Bitte schön, danke schön." Trucks arrived before the hotel and the Germans told everyone with indescribable politeness to get into them. Each truck was accompanied to the Gdansk railway station by two SS men.

Knowing all this I immediately began to look for foreign documents for myself, my three children, and the three women who were under my care on the "Aryan" side: Eta Bernstein, Danka Rubinstein and Roza Lampart. I couldn't leave these three women unprotected — I had to take them along with my own family. I was introduced to Adam, the veritable ruler of the hotel. He was running around the hotel with a gun, screaming and from time to time shooting into the air. But no one was afraid of him. Everyone was running after him; he couldn't shake off the people who wanted to become foreigners.

After some bargaining, I agreed to pay thirty thousand zlotys for my people, and I told Jasio to get in touch with Puharski about the money. Jasio ran in haste to Puharski. After some time Puharski arrived at the hotel. We talked about the whole affair. He advised me not to go. He didn't trust the Germans. I convinced him and he gave me the 30,000 zlotys, wishing me that it should all turn out well. He promised to come to the Hotel the next day.

I asked him to send out messengers to bring my people and the children to the hotel. He offered the help of Michal Lange who was very clever and who would bring all my people to the hotel by the thirteenth of July, for this was the day that the last transport was supposed to leave.

I didn't return to Jasio's apartment but told him to bring the woman, Mrs. Bernstein. In the meantime, I paid 15,000 zlotys and promised to bring the remainder the next day. They said it was all right. I had to rely on their word, for I had nowhere to go.

I looked around the hotel, talked with people and got acquainted with the procedures. I saw how everyone was repeating his newly-acquired name to himself. I had a premonition that something was wrong, that this would all end in a catastrophe, for the children couldn't memorize their names. They kept making mistakes; if there were an identity check, the whole affair would be uncovered. I was hot and cold with worry. I had already paid 15,000, and they were supposed to bring the children and the other people. I kept thinking, What should I do?

I slept through the night. It was the morning of July 12. I suddenly heard of a list of 223 persons who were being searched for by the government of Palestine. I had a quick thought, that Palestine is better than America — first of all, because the number of people on the list was small. I entered one of the rooms where a man sat with a so-called Palestine list before him. I won't divulge his name for he came together with me to Israel on September 8, 1945, together with a wife and child, and I'm not sure what part he played. A Gestapo man was collecting the money. (I don't recall his name — Reisman or Reisberg). I saw from the list that they were looking for two women and three children. Of these five people, only one was alive, a woman who was being searched for by her husband, and she was none other than Eta Bernstein.

I was electrified by that fact. I was also worried by the thought that I should let the sum of 15,000 zlotys, which I had paid for the American papers, get lost. First of all, here were no individual papers but a collective list, and the Germans couldn't prove that I wasn't the right person mentioned in the list. Above all, I had with me the authentic Mrs. Bernstein about whom I knew all the data. And so I made my decision. There was place only for five people on the list, so what was I going to do about myself and the other two women? Everything had to be decided that very day. I offered 15,000 zlotys for all eight persons. At first they refused to accept it. They wanted more. I told them that these papers were real, not false, and also that this was all the money I had. I didn't tell them about the other papers. I didn't even remember what name I had been given on the American documents. So everything was settled.

Mrs. Bernstein arrived at the hotel without any luggage. She had nothing, nor had I. We had only the clothes which we were wearing. I watched how other people brought enormous and elegant suitcases, as befit people going abroad. All I possessed were the eight people — this was my entire "luggage." But I was satisfied. My only wish was that we would arrive in peace to Palestine, and then I would be happy.

I told Mrs. Bernstein about the Palestine list, asked her all the personal details I need to know, and the names of her two children. She told me that two of her brothers in Palestine had left wives behind in Poland, Eta and Brakha. Brakha was the mother of one child, and Eta had two children. The children had perished, and she now remained all alone. (I had saved her while we were both working at the Schultz Shop in the ghetto.)

We therefore decided that Eta Bernstein would receive two of my children as her own, and that my sister, Pearl Korngold, would from now on be Brakha Bernstein, the wife of the second brother, Bernstein, and that my third child would be hers. In this way both Palestine brothers became the husbands — on paper — of the two women, and the fathers of my three children. I received the name of a brother of the Bernsteins, who was killed by the Germans, and who was called Shlomo Bernstein. So from now on I was Shlomo Bernstein. And the third woman, Royza Lampart, became my wife.

There still remained the young woman, Danka Rubenstein, who became transformed into Szayndla Korngold, the daughter of my uncle. (My father's brother, who also lived in Palestine, had left a daughter, Szayndla.) In this way we constructed an entire artificial family.

But that wasn't all. Now it was necessary to fabricate Palestine documents (Ausweise) together with photos of the new family members. There was a Jewish man in the hotel who manufactured such Ausweise papers to which we attached our photos, signed by every one with the newly-adopted names. I dictated the exact names and addresses, and after I finished, I felt that a heavy weight had been removed. I was glad that I had gotten away from the American visas, and was safely on the Palestine list.

The hotel was very crowded. People sat on their suitcases and bundles; nobody slept — there was no room. The courtyard was packed. Everyone tried to believe in happy endings. We were all looking forward to the lucky day when we would arrive in Switzerland.

The next day was July 13, 1943. Lange brought my oldest son, nine-year-old Leib Aryeh Korngold. Mrs. Bernstein immediately took care of him. At 10 o'clock Leon brought my little sister, Pearl. Mosciuk came with Danka Rubenstein, along with my youngest son, seven-year-old Emanuel. I gave everyone the Ausweise which they signed with their new names. I told them to memorize all the details. I was beginning to grow terribly nervous, for my little girl and also the woman, Royza Lampart, were still not here. While everybody was beginning preparations for the transport, they arrived, almost at the last moment. Now I had everyone, including my girl, Sonya Korngold, who, in January of that year, had stood at the ghetto wall on Zelazna Street, about to be shot by a German guard, and who had been miraculously saved.

We were all here. Everyone held on to his children, and I stood together with my "new" fabricated wife, while Danka Rubenstein, whose name was now Korngold, stood alone. All our papers were in order. My Polish friend, Puharsky, was here, as was Jasio with his wife, and a number of my other Christian acquaintances. They had all come to wish us luck.

I noticed a Jewish comrade with whom we had crawled through the sewers outside the hotel. He stood on the other side. He had decided not to go, but to remain in Warsaw. Suddenly the whole area was surrounded by SS men. The hotel was sealed — no one could enter or leave. At 12 o'clock sharp Brandt arrived with Mende and a number of other Nazi criminals. Every possible entrance — the courtyard, the street, the stairs —

was now guarded by the Nazi murderers. We were ordered to come down to the courtyard with our luggage. Everyone was to stand together with his family and wait until his name was called out.

I watched this whole game — how the bloodiest Warsaw murderers with their SS assistant-executioners stood in the courtyard of the hotel, with every exit guarded. It looked like a blockade. We stood with pounding hearts — was this the last moment of our lives? Were we on the threshold of death?

The gate opened and the first German truck rolled in. Brandt held a pack of papers in his hand. Those whose names were called out began getting into the trucks. One of the Germans politely brought a chair from inside the hotel so that the people could more easily mount the trucks. The SS murderers were very courteous and helpful. They advised us not to jam together, so that we would be more comfortable. I hardly recognized them, the bloody killers, with their new behavior. The mood of the people was good, even cheerful. We were treated like real foreigners.

One truck left full of people and luggage, and another moved in, then a third, a fourth, until finally, everyone left. All the trucks were now arranged in a row, each guarded by two SS men. They then began slowly to move in the direction of the Gdansk railway station. They moved along the ghetto walls. We looked over the walls and saw the ruins. The eyes of many were filled with tears. Our Warsaw had been destroyed by these same criminals who were now helping us to go abroad.

We arrived at the Gdansk railway station. The truck stopped. The Germans helped us descend. We saw a train with elegant passenger cars, surrounded by representatives of the Red Cross, as well as representatives of Switzerland. We were photographed, our names were called out, and everyone received a food parcel from the Red Cross. There were also Swiss journalists who wrote down everything — including what sort of gentlemen the Germans were.

We went to the train. Everyone had his own upholstered seat. The people's mood was cheerful. Now the Germans collected signatures from the Jews testifying to the Germans' fine behavior. The train began to move.

MIECZYSLAWA TOMKIEWICZ

Mieczyslawa Tomkiewicz was a lawyer and the wife of a lawyer and Zionist activist who was shot while jumping from the train to Maidanek. In 1945, she was liberated from Bergen-Belsen by the American army. Her story appeared in the Polish-language publication in New York "Nasza Trybuna," 1946.

In May, 1943, I lost everything. On the third of that month the Germans deported my parents, my younger brother and my husband from the burning ghetto. They all jumped from the train which was taking them to a concentration camp in Lublin. Only Stasio, my brother, survived.

One evening in May, Stasio returned. I cannot recall the date — after the third deportation in the ghetto every hour seemed an eternity. Stasio was trembling with fear, wild, half-frenzied with the awareness that he was still alive. He told me in detail how they had fought, how they had been caught, what had happened on the *Umschlagplatz* and then in the train. Then he told me how they had jumped.

I was faint from pain as he clung to the soft blanket, crying that life is beautiful.

An apartment and false papers had been prepared for mother, father, Piotr, Witek and Helenka on the "Aryan" side. Now they were dead. Piotr, my husband, had been with me two days before the uprising in the ghetto and had then returned to that apartment, to be with my parents for Passover. So he had told me. But that was not the only reason for his return. I haven't even mentioned that the remnants of my extended family also perished in that deportation: my mother-in-law, my brother-in-law, and my aunts. But at that time this was so unimportant to me. I remained on the "Aryan" side with my child, four-year-old Bobush, and with Stasio, whose Jewish appearance and adolescent clumsiness would create additional troubles.

Compounding the problem was the fact that I had no money, which made my situation appear hopeless. Death seemed, then, in relation to life, as easy as a dream. However, since only those who desperately cling to life die — because this is the caprice of fate — I naturally didn't die, and I had to think seriously about

64

how to save the last few members of the family: Bobush and Stasio, with myself as protector and guardian.

I was the pampered only daughter of wealthy Jewish parents. I was a 27-year-old woman who had never earned a penny in her life — a non-practicing lawyer, an amateur journalist, an intelligent wife who was one of those whom the ex-husband has to "carry on his hands." And on top of this I was over-sensitive, high-strung, overintellectual, and now, very unhappy. Against my will I was pushed into an arena of heavy fighting. Against my will I had a boxer's clumsy gloves put on my hands, to enter a fight for life. The stakes were high: Bobush, Stasio, and myself.

Once again, it appeared that a human being has in himself inconsummable forces, and that human vitality is proportional to the difficulties of life. I began somehow to survive. My first disappointments undermined my naive trust in man. The struggle transformed the trusting into the untruthful, the oversincere into the secretive. My character began to change completely. I spent two hard months paying people with the last money I had to seek close ones, although I had no doubts about their fate. I took part in some negotiations and did some business. I earned some money but my new experiences taught me that this wouldn't be so easy, that it was necessary to look for other ways.

And then I heard about the Hotel Polski. Lusia came with a detailed report of this place which sounded as strange as the tale of a thousand and one nights. Over there one could get American "promesses," one could sign onto a "Palestine list" on the basis of a "general certificate" — and in these ways one could be exchanged for German nationals in Turkey and Switzerland. But all this, according to Lusia, was a gigantic hoax. Who would go and voluntarily give himself into the hands of the Germans? Nonsense. In Radom the Germans had shot all those on the Palestine list. The hotel was being run by Gestapo collaborators, who were making lots of money. How could we trust an arrangement set up by them? Lusia, as well as a great number of acquaintances with whom I was in contact on the "Aryan" side, were all of one mind: the security offered by the hotel was a dangerous illusion — this was really but another road leading to death.

Stasio, who lived in difficult conditions, sleeping on the floor in the little cell of our hideout, wanted to go to the Hotel Polski. He knew how hard I was struggling to earn money to pay the exorbitant rent; and because of his "bad" — meaning, non-"Aryan" — features, it was a painful problem every time he wanted to go to the toilet and each time he wanted to speak aloud, thus risking discovery. On top of this, he was forced to stay in the company of a woman broken by pain who cried her eyes out day and night — all this didn't belong to the pleasures of a sixteen-year-old boy. He wanted to get away, whatever the price.

At first I didn't want to let him go, deciding that what I didn't consider fit for my child was not good for him either. For several days we considered the good and bad factors concerning the hotel. During that time, the first group of the so-called Auslanders, the foreign nationals, left the Hotel Polski, travelling out of Warsaw in Pullman cars, with flowers, luggage, packages and an excess of politeness from the Germans. I was impressed. I began to wonder if I were right not to let him go, if I weren't depriving him of a chance which might not soon reappear. I admit that I didn't think much of my own fate — I was indifferent to what would happen to me, apathetic and depressed. Nevertheless, I had had enough of the atmosphere of the "Aryan" side. I wanted some radical change, to escape from my thoughts and memories, and from those barren reproaches of "if" and "whether"; that I hadn't done enough, that I had no intention to act, that I was wasting time. These thoughts tormented, and I could find no rest.

Finally, one evening I decided that it seemed that our going to the hotel was Piotr's last will, for he had spoken so enthusiastically about Vittel, the "promesses," letters and so on. I grew certain that had Piotr been with me, we would certainly have gone with that Auslander transport. The next day I went to the hotel.

I walked through sun-flooded and movement-filled Warsaw, wearing my landlady's used raincoat as I went among elegantly-dressed women. My eyes were swollen and my hair dyed a peroxide-blond, in which the black roots were already beginning to show. I stopped at Miodowa Street for an ice cream at a pastry store which I had often visited when I had gone to the courthouse. In spite of everything, the ice cream tasted good. I remember that I was strangely affected when I saw the enormous cherries in display windows. It seemed to me that I had never seen such big cherries and strawberries before the war, or, in any case, that I had never eaten them. These strawberries and cherries were full of life, and so gay — they seemed to laugh loudly with their many colors at the world and at people.

* * *

The hotel created a strange impression on me — it was indeed an anomaly. In the very heart of Jew-hating, German and *shmaltzovnik*-controlled Warsaw which, according to all official declarations was to be "Judenrein," existed a building full of Jews. They walked about a courtyard, greeted each other, and drank vodka and beer in the hotel's restaurant. The women, wearing elegant and chic dresses, walked up and down the stairs as in the good old days, smiling and flirting with gentlemen who sported close-cropped and little "Aryan" moustaches. "Hello, Janina!" "How are you, Zbyszek?" And no one dared approach these Jews to demand, "Your money or else" — and no one shouted after them, "Judek! Judek!"

All the efforts of the local *shmaltzovniks* were in vain — Adam and Lolek would defend us. Adam and Lolek were two almost mythological figures, the leaders of this entire affair. The talk about Adam was that he wasn't a Jew and that he was good. As for Lolek, he was an old Gestapo collaborator, an important figure in this enterprise, a go-between linking Jews and Germans. They took enormous sums of money from those who wished to escape by obtaining "promesas" from Chile, Venezuela, Paraguay, Peru and Honduras. They took 100,000, 200,000, 500,000 zlotys, or diamonds, dollars, gold. This was divided among Adam, Lolek and their entourage of Gestapo-collaborators, kapos, half-kapos and swindlers, who knew how to catch fish in muddy waters. Not a small part of the money fell into German hands, in the form of expensive dinners, drinks, gifts and the like for officers and important members of the SS and the Gestapo.

Everyone expected the war to be over soon: "The war will end in three or four months." "Yes sir, at the most four." In order to save their reputations for this future, our benefactors accepted some people for no fee at all. As a rule, such a case also required cash to lubricate mediators and any influential people, but it wasn't a very large sum. Some people who knew how to cry incessantly, stubbornly and without respite, into the ears of our dignitaries, Adam and Lolek, could be helped absolutely free. These were the people who had nothing more to lose. Their hideouts had been discovered, the *shmaltzovniks* had robbed them of everything. They were without means or acquaintances and were threatened at every moment by death, either from starvation or from the Germans. They had nowhere to lay their heads — they wandered about the railway station, on streets, constantly exposed, being stopped and denounced. There were also those who had escaped from the burning ghetto and came here directly, or those who had jumped from trains and who now sat in the Hotel Polski, their last refuge.

It was said that these people who had no resources remaining got special treatment from Adam and Lolek. These "leaders" of the Hotel reserved greatest preference for the swollen-bodied people from the bunkers who could faint in a very convincing way in the over-crowded corridors, or in Adam's and Lolek's rooms.

It is commendable to be noble for such people. Adam and Lolek had even established a sort of social assistance fund: they distributed clothing, food and money. In this way, sensing how they might be judged in the future, they paid off their sins.

Wandering about the hotel, I met some acquaintances who gave me information and news. What could I do to be permitted to join the next transport? In order to talk to Adam and Lolek, one had to stand for a long time on line, or else catch one of them when he passed by and hold him firmly by a jacket button so that he couldn't get away. Then one had to present his case at an accelerated tempo and with a proper amount of histrionics. This trick of grabbing one of them by the button, I was advised, was the more radical method. But I couldn't bring myself to do it, so I decided to wait in line. This meant that I would have to remain there throughout the night, for our benefactors began their office hours at ten to eleven P.M.

While standing on line, we could hear many interesting stories — how people had sat for weeks in damp, dark bunkers with hardly any food or water, bitten by lice and rats; how others had escaped from burning houses under a hail of German bullets; how one had jumped through the barred narrow window of a cattle train bound for Treblinka; how another had lost his hiding place; how *shmaltzovniks* had robbed Jews, leaving the terrorized victims half naked and without means, and so on ad infinitum.

That line for foreign documents was a rosary of Jewish misfortunes. A husband killed, a child murdered, a wife burned, a mother dead of starvation, a husband who had jumped from a fifth floor — relatives deported, murdered, gassed, beaten to death with sticks. All this was related quietly, without a display of emotion. Such is fate. Yesterday, him . . . today, me.

Those who stood in line were the unhappiest people, and, on top of everything else, penniless. If a person had money or diamonds, our benefactors received him during the day. The others stood here for hours and hours until late into the night, waiting for an audience which might save them. Those people who had money calculated, hesitated, were afraid. But those on line had no scruples or hesitations — they risked nothing, and no longer feared anything.

And so I too stood on that line. A feeble light bulb illumined the yellowish faces of these people made up to look "Aryan": peroxide-bleached hair and moustaches, names like Zbyszek, Joanna, Bogumil. We waited nervously and without strength, jammed together.

Eleven, twelve, one o'clock — the pilgrimage to the small hotel room to be received by Adam and Lolek continued. The happy ones who managed to enter related their adventures and troubles — and the more bloodily one could present one's story, the greater was his chance to travel.

I was advised to cry a little before Adam and, perhaps, to faint. But I knew that I wouldn't do it. I would be cool, sober and to the point. And if it wouldn't work — so be it!

The atmosphere was becoming unbearable. I was one of the last on line, by what miracle I didn't know, because I had been standing since the beginning, when the line had formed. I was sleepy, I was suffocating, I was feeling bad. My husband's colleagues were wandering about, so sure of themselves, so calm, so alive. He had fought, jumped, perished. Perished. My head was spinning, my throat choking. Your last will, Piotr, your last will.

Someone announced the end of receptions. People still pushed, and someone shoved me into the sanctuary of Adam and Lolek, but I didn't say anything. I couldn't. It was three in the morning, I was completely exhausted and irritated. If Piotr were here . . . I sat on the floor in the corridor. I clenched my teeth so as not to howl. All around me on the floor, on top of packages, on the stairs, were dozens of sleeping people bent in the most bizarre positions. I couldn't weep aloud, for no one there cared how I felt and suffered. I was all alone. I felt terrible, and had achieved nothing. Early in the morning, with great effort, I got up from the horribly filthy floor. I wandered around some more, listening to more promises, but I knew already that all these would come to nothing. I already knew the value of people's talk.

I returned to my little cell on the "Aryan" side.

Since I was beginning to believe in that whole affair, I came to the conclusion that Stasio should attempt that route. And he would surely succeed better than I. He was young, he had jumped from the train — he had nothing to live on, they should help him. I packed some of Piotr's shirts and a few other small things for him. He added the Iliad, with which he had jumped from the train to the parcel, and off he went.

"Good-bye, Stasio."

"Good-bye, Sis."

We didn't hold by sentimental farewells in those times, when every hour's parting might mean a last and fatal departure.

He left on Sunday morning. The next morning I received a telephone call. Stasio was speaking. He mumbled something about a Palestine list, about a man with whom he had jumped together — and that I too could come, together with my child. I didn't believe what I heard, and told him to repeat his news again. Finally I decided to check the news out on the spot.

I called Grandma Sendzina, with whom I was hiding my Bobush, and asked her to bring the child from the village. About ten o'clock the next morning, I went to the Hotel, looking at all the display windows on the way, gaping at this and at that. I did this with complete clarity, expecting to be stopped at any minute by a Polish policeman, who comprised the worst of the *shmaltzovniks*.

At the hotel, I learned that the chief of the Palestine list had jumped from the same train as Stasio, and that when, on the famous line to Adam and Lolek, he had met Stasio, the partner of such tragic moments, he immediately made arrangements for Stasio, myself and the child. This meant that our names had been added to the list of those confirmed by the *Auslandstelle*, on what basis I didn't know. Departing into the unknown was fixed for early the next day, a Tuesday.

I returned home, buying such small items as soap, a brush, and powder on the way. In our housekeeper's apartment, I found Bobush in a pink flannel gown and sandals. This is the way Grandma Sendzina had brought him from the country, having no idea of our situation. I began feverishly to look for proper children's clothing. I had none of my own, having lost them when I had been forced to leave my last hiding place in a great rush.

When Grandma Sendzina learned that I was going to take Bobush on such a dangerous adventure, she began to cry and implored me to leave the child, that she and her family would save him, that I shouldn't take such a splendid boy to certain death. I was unbending — I had no presentiment of death. Toward evening, my landlord left in a droshky to the hotel together with Bobush and my wedding pillow in a blue satin pillow case, the only remnant of my six-room apartment in our own house. As a precaution, I left separately and went by rickshaw through Marshalkowska Street and Saski Park. My school at the corner of Marshalkowska and Królewska was in ruins. In the droshky rode Bobush in his sandals with the enormous pillow. And I rode in the rickshaw wearing my landlady's raincoat. We were leaving Warsaw. Good-bye, then, perhaps forever!

There was a great commotion in the hotel. People were bringing in trunks and suitcases, bidding each other farewell, and milling around in all directions. Bobush was frightened, very polite and calm. He was cold in his little pink gown, and had lost his attachment to his unfamiliar mother whom he hadn't seen for more than a year and a half, having in that time acquired a whole range of mamas, grandmas and uncles. I put my jacket on him, and he looked ridiculous. I hoped that Grandma Sendzina would have enough time to bring his things.

I bade my landlord a warm farewell, having arranged that he would come the next morning with the rest of the things brought by Grandma Sendzina, and I began a new chapter. I gave Bobush for the night to some acquaintances in the hotel, who had — oh luxury! — their own mattress, and I spent the night squatting on some sacks. At six in the morning I used the telephone and began alarming Grandma Sendzina and my landlord about the things. Everything was in order — everything was there.

On the stairs I encountered a German gendarme in a helmet with a pointed top. It appeared that the hotel was surrounded — no one could enter or leave.

I thought to myself, "What bad luck, my things are lost." Other people thought that this was the end — death, the gas chamber — and were frantic with terror. Some of them, who had paid thousands, didn't want to go. They hid themselves in corners and in the garrets. They wanted to wait for the next transport. They didn't like this — they were afraid, they had unfavorable premonitions.

I had no bad premonitions. In the meantime, half of my belongings — a few handbags and a briefcase with food — got lost, and I was very busy looking all over for them.

Finally, we were leaving. At the last minute I stopped to think: perhaps I should select the next transport and wait for my things? The child was almost naked and barefoot — I too had nothing to wear. But I tried to console myself: "Ah, it will somehow work itself out. The Red Cross, Palestine, there will be enough things for my child."

Finally, names were called out. A lot of Germans stood around, including Brandt and Hantke, who, two months ago, had carried out the deportations from the ghetto and its final end. Now they politely helped us to board the trucks. They courteously asked some questions which I, as a matter of principle, didn't answer, pretending not to understand.

BER BASKIND

Ber Baskind was a merchant in Warsaw before the outbreak of World War II. He had a wife and two sons, one of whom had returned from his studies in Holland shortly before the war began.

After the Germans invaded Poland, Ber's sons attempted to escape to Hungary, but were both caught and perished. Ber's wife was taken to a camp in Lublin, and from there to Majdanek. He was taken with others after the uprising to Poniatowa, a labor camp which held 14,000 deportees from Toebbens. There he found two brothers-in-law.

Prisoners in the camp received a daily food ration of seventy grams of bread and a meager ration of soup. The conditions were cruel and, in effect, amounted to slow murder. For the slightest offense, such as stealing a potato, the penalty was death. Ber had one aim: to escape. His condition was somewhat eased by a Polish worker who often went to Warsaw and brought him food, soap, a coat and a hat.

Ber wrote to friends in his attempts to prepare an escape. Once he paid 25,000 zlotys in advance to a man who had promised to come in a car to free him for a total of 800,000 zlotys, but the man never arrived.

One day, Ber met two Polish mailmen. They agreed to take him out of the camp together with a man named Abraham Rosental, of Lodz, who had a wife, sisters and brothers in Warsaw.

On May 31 [1943], the two men were smuggled out wearing mailmen's uniforms, and went by train through Demblin and Otwock to Warsaw. They stayed at 84 Leszno Street in the four-room apartment of a tailor, Koflewicz. Another man and his daughter were also hiding there. Conditions were very poor. They all had to be extremely careful to prevent detection – they couldn't move around, and had no running water. It was as if they were in a cage. After some time, Rosental's sister was allowed to come and bring food and newspapers.

On June 17, bad news arrived. Rosental's wife and sisters had been arrested. Rosental left the apartment and was also arrested. He admitted being Jewish, but because he was a tailor, he wasn't killed. Instead, he was taken to Pawiak. The apartment hideout was now unsafe. The postman promised to find another room. But in the meantime, what were they to do?

. . . It was my sister-in-law who found a solution. She told us of a Hotel Polski at 29 Dluga Street, which was being used as an internment camp for Jews registered as citizens of an American republic or as Palestinians. The principle was that the Germans would exchange them for German nationals in American countries or in the Middle-East. Perhaps this would be our salvation.

Without hesitation I sent a messenger to the Hotel Polski. He found a few of my friends there. They gave him all the necessary information. They said that if I had enough money I could arrange to enter the hotel under a false name, as a member of one of the families already interned in the hotel. It would be best for me to come as soon as possible.

I followed my friends' advice, and for $1,000 obtained a promesa and other identity documents certifying my name to be Bretsztein.

I was no longer an unfortunate Polish Jew exposed defenselessly to the caprices of the German executioners. With the acquisition of this false document, I became, at least in principle, a free man. I was no longer just a Jew, but a citizen of Paraguay.

No longer did I have to fear when I heard steps on the stairs; no longer did my heart pound madly when I heard someone knock at my door. No longer did I have to live in a hideout, now that I had the good fortune to be interned in the Hotel Polski. I still couldn't go into the street, but I could at least walk in the courtyard.

And an important detail: Jews interned in the Hotel Polski were allowed to receive visitors, and we could thus communicate with the outside world. After a few attempts, I succeeded in sending some messages to Lublin and for the first time received indirect news about my wife. I was assured that she was interned in one of the concentration camps in Lublin. But, alas, I could neither hear her nor talk to her.

A week after I entered the Hotel Polski, I received a letter brought by my sister-in-law from Rosental. He wrote that he was in Pawiak prison and asked me to try to get him out.

The Germans had arrested him and taken him to the Gestapo headquarters with his hands manacled, as though he were a dangerous criminal. There he admitted being a Jew and that he had escaped from Poniatowa. He was allowed to live because he was young — thirty years old — and because he was a tailor. People like him were as a matter of course sent to Pawiak, where they were used as workers. However, because of the bad conditions there, they usually didn't live more than a few months.

At the moment there were 2,000 internees in the Hotel Polski, most of them registered with the Bureau of Foreigners as Americans or Palestinians. But there were also those possessing no papers at all. With no other place to go to, they somehow drifted here. Some were forced to flee from hiding places discovered by the Germans. Others had wandered about the ruins of the ghetto and at last managed to escape through the sewers after everything around them had been turned to ashes. Still others had exhausted all their resources and turned to the hotel as the only place where they could exist. But the fate of all of them depended on their passing the first official check, and they therefore made desperate attempts to be officially registered as foreign nationals.

This enterprise of obtaining and registering false documents was a large affair, managed by two young men of about thirty — our "protectors," they might be called.

These two men were entrepreneurs who had good relations with the Gestapo and who possessed exceptional rights. We didn't know very much about their activities or why they were granted such remarkable favors. We were simply left with vague surmises about which it was best not to insist. Whatever their position and activities were, one must admit that in the Hotel Polski their behavior was far from criminal. On the contrary, they deserved much praise, for they carried out great services for people.

Papers arrived in Poland almost constantly from Switzerland, Honduras and Paraguay. These papers, sent as a result of requests made by the internees' relatives living in those countries, were the "promesas." They stated that the person or family named in them was under the jurisdiction of Honduras, Paraguay or Palestine, and that therefore, their legal status was that of a foreign national. But the Germans, using methods characteristic of them, would keep these documents as long as possible, and after they expired, would send the persons named in them to camps. Then they could produce the documents, saying that they had arrived too late.

A principal job, then, of these two "patrons," was to get as many "promesas" as they could from the Gestapo. They also had good connections in the Department of Foreign Citizens. Using these "promesas," they could register entire families and augment their size to twenty people by claiming other refugees to be family members.

Obviously, in order to perform such a job they demanded exorbitant amounts of money from those in a position to pay. But it must also be said that in some cases, they registered poor people and took no payment at all — sometimes they even provided them with material assistance.

75

Since Rosental was still alive and kept asking me to help him, I asked one of these "patrons" if — for sufficient payment — he could get someone out of Pawiak prison. He replied without hesitation that this didn't fall within his purview and advised me to see an engineer* who came to the hotel every day.

I therefore began asking about that engineer, and when someone pointed him out to me, I saw, to my surprise, that he was one of my old customers. I approached him and told him of my friend Rosental's predicament. He wrote down all the details and arranged that we should meet again in two or three days.

Meanwhile, a former partner of Rosental's by the name of Pinchanek arrived at the hotel. He had succeeded in registering together with his mother. When I told him of Rosental's plight, he immediately offered to help financially.

A few days later, at the meeting with the engineer which we had arranged, he told Pinchanek and me that Rosental was still in Pawiak prison, and that there was a possibility of getting him out. It would cost a thousand dollars and we would have to pay in advance. Rosental would be freed eight days after we paid the money.

With our friend's problem now apparently solved, I presented my wife's case to the engineer, telling him that I was prepared to sacrifice all I owned in order to save her. He promised to do all he could to get her out of the camp. It was clear that, as always, money was not only the last but also the only resort. We knew from numerous experiences that the Germans were bribable. A hope still existed to achieve results with the help of money, but we had to act very quickly.

Meanwhile, we were told that those who were to be exchanged for German nationals in American countries must leave the hotel in two days for another camp.

Pinchanek, for his part, had used up all his resources to save Rosental and to register his family — his mother, father and three sisters. As for me, I promised the engineer an advance of $1,000 to save my wife and Rosental. I also added the condition that he see to it that I not be included with the first group to leave the hotel, for I wanted to wait to see the results of his efforts regarding Rosental and my wife.

*This "engineer" was the Gestapo collaborator Kenigel.

Two days later, on July 5, the first group, numbering about 1,300 people, left the hotel. But the hotel wasn't any less crowded, due to the constant influx of unfortunates who came to save themselves, or simply to hide.

On July 13 another group of 300 left. I wasn't one of them because our cases hadn't yet been finalized.

But suddenly — an unexpected event transpired. At two o'clock, just after the group of three hundred had left the courtyard on their way to the train, all the hotel exits were blocked off by police vans. All of us who remained in the hotel were ordered to prepare to quickly leave the hotel with only some of our luggage.

We were all well enough acquainted with the enmity that the Germans were capable of to be terrified by this new measure. What lay hidden behind the order? But we had no choice but to obey, despite our darkest forebodings, and to prepare ourselves for a possible disaster.

JOSEF GITLER BARSKI

Josef Gitler Barski was a member of the PPR – a communist organization – and one of the ghetto fighters in the uprising of January, 1943. Source: Yad Vashem Archives.

. . . After the armed ghetto uprising in January, 1943, I decided, in agreement with my comrades, to go over to the "Aryan" side. I didn't know whether I would succeed. For the time being, we began to construct a shelter in the basement of our house, 44 Muranowska Street. Our most urgent need was to get in touch with Adolf.*

I took advantage of the telephone left in the empty office of Centos on 56 Zamenhof St. After several attempts, we managed to make a connection.

I was given, in code, an address in Praga where I might place my wife, Celina, and our little girl. The landlady was afraid to accept a man. I was, however, assured that they would arrange a room for me as well. And indeed, in our next telephone conversation, I was told to come to the same address. Using the same

*Dr. Adolf Berman was then the representative of the ghetto underground on the "Aryan" side, and secretary of the Jewish Coordination Committee.

method Celina had used ten days earlier, I joined a group which was leaving the ghetto for the Ostbahn working group, on the eleventh of February, 1943. As soon as I got away from the group, I was stopped on the street by a man who was walking with two Volksdeutsche. They took me to the nearest gate and demanded a high ransom. After long bargaining, the criminals robbed me of everything I had, including a briefcase with all my personal papers, and left me alone.

Pani Helena Szabtowska, the landlady of my hiding place, awaited me in the apartment in which Celina and the child were hiding. She took me right away to her apartment on 2 Grajewska Street in Praga. I stayed there without the knowledge of the owner's neighbors or acquaintances. When there was a visitor, I locked myself into the last room, and some time later, in a specially camouflaged hideout in the foyer.

In the second half of March, Celina and the child had to leave their rooms, and they came to me. Conditions worsened, particularly after our landlady took in two young Jewish women who had escaped during the deportation of their small town in the Warsaw district. The situation became still more dangerous when I had to make room for my brother-in-law with his daughter who had run away at the last moment from the burning ghetto.

The gathering of so many people in one apartment couldn't remain a secret for long. Only one week after my brother-in-law's arrival, two Gestapo agents came to search the apartment. At the sound of the bell, we all locked ourselves into the small closet which separated us from the foyer with a thin wall, and in front of which was a long clothing rack. We could hear the agents making threats. They searched the apartment thoroughly, but couldn't find our hiding place. After more threats and curses, they left promising to return soon. In spite of this, and the fact that our landlady was summoned several times to the house administration on suspicion of harboring Jews, she allowed us to stay on. The reason was simple — all our attempts to find another apartment were unsuccessful. But we lost the relative peace we had enjoyed during the first three months of our stay on Grajewska St. We arranged a nightly watch at the window to see if someone wasn't coming for us. We were prepared for the worst.

This state of anxiety lasted until July 7, when our landlady was once again summoned to the house administrator, who told her that he had received a copy of an anonymous report to the Gestapo, which charged that "Pani Szabtowska was hiding Jews." In addition, it contained a description of our closet in which we hid when someone came to the apartment. We considered all this and concluded that we must leave the apartment immediately.

For me, to leave the apartment meant certain death. We had literally nowhere to go. The streets were full of blackmailers. We had no money. I didn't know any address, neither Adolf's nor anyone else's, from the underground. I had once arranged with Adolf that in case of such an emergency, we would go to the Hotel Polski and communicate with David Guzik about further help. I had known for some time of Guzik's presence in the Hotel Polski. Adolf, who visited us several times on Grajewska St., had told us that Jews in possession of citizenship papers of neutral countries were concentrated in the Hotel Royal on Chmielna St. for "exchange purposes." Together with Adolf, we thought that these people's lives were exposed to danger. It was incomprehensible that the Nazis, after their terrible liquidation of the inhabitants of the ghetto, would allow witnesses of their horrible crimes to go abroad.

When the Hotel Polski, in turn, became the gathering point of those who qualified for exchange, David Guzik, himself in possession of Argentine documents, remained in that hotel, maintaining contacts both with Jews hidden on the "Aryan" side and with representatives of the underground. I therefore took a chance that fatal day when we found ourselves in a hopeless situation, and sent first my wife and daughter to the Hotel, and then followed them.

I walked the entire distance from Praga to Dluga St. on foot, because riding the tram would expose me to blackmail. It was a sunny morning. The appearance on the street of a man with such Semitic features must have drawn people's attention. Everyone turned to look at me, but no one stopped me.

I arrived at the hotel without any misadventure. Guzik was there. I asked him to find us a new place and also to get me in touch with Adolf.

However, it appeared that according to Guzik's information,

79

there wasn't the slightest chance of hiding anywhere. The Germans had put up posters threatening with collective responsibility the inhabitants of the entire house containing an apartment in which a refugee from the ghetto was found hidden by a tenant. As a result, more and more people were losing their hideouts, and it was impossible to find new ones. We had no choice but to legalize our presence in the Hotel. Guzik did this by registering us on the so-called exchange with Palestine.

That evening there was a rumor that the next day everyone would be sent to a camp in Germany. There was a state of great anxiety, particularly among those people who had no documents of foreign countries and who were in the hotel illegally. People had the most sinister premonitions. There could be no thought of leaving because the danger on the streets was immediate.

The next morning, the hotel was surrounded by Germans. We were all ordered to be ready within an hour and to come to the courtyard with our luggage, where a number of trucks stood ready to leave. When everyone was gathered together, the gendarmes began to call out the names of those who had documents or promesas of South American countries and of those who were on the Palestine list. The rest had left the hotel. We learned later that on that same day, they had been taken to the Pawiak and, with a few exceptions, shot.

HENRYK ZAMOSZOWSKI

Henryk Zamoszowski of Radom lived in Warsaw at 16 Pulawska Street at the time he gave his testimony. Source: Yad Vashem Archives.

People began streaming to the Hotel Polski, having been told that from there they would be sent to America.

The leaders of the Hotel were Lolek Skosowski and a certain Adam, both agents of the Gestapo, in which they held important posts. They even had a car at their disposal. They were frequently seen in the ghetto carrying briefcases and armed with guns. One day they began telling everyone that they wished to save the lives of the surviving Jews by sending them out of the country.

Since the Gestapo possessed a large number of promesas of Jews who had perished during various deportations, the two

80

agents planned to counterfeit passports for surviving Jews in the names of those who were already dead.

A promesa is a written promise distributed by the consulate of a country — for instance, by Paraguay, Uruguay, and the Central American States — from whom one could obtain, for a bribe, the necessary papers.

And why did the promesas enjoy such success? First of all, the Germans were interested in getting their citizens from foreign countries in exchange for Jews. And secondly, some of the Jews on the "Aryan" side were fantastically wealthy, and the Germans wanted to lay their hands on these fortunes. And finally, the Germans wanted to create an impression in the world that they were a normal state which behaved decently and let out its foreign Jews.

The above-mentioned two Gestapo-collaborators wanted, with the aid of that affair, to rehabilitate themselves and play the role of benefactors. They would stop Jews on the "Aryan" side and say to them: "We want to give you documents so you can leave as foreign citizens."

The Jews knew very well that they were dealing with Gestapo men, but they had no choice and were forced to agree. These men would give the documents for free to well-known Jewish personalities or ghetto fighters, demanding in return signed letters that they were saving Jews from death. From others they took colossal sums of money, which they shared with the Gestapo officials. And so they approached Natan Buksbaum, leader of the left wing of the Poalei Zion organization, the famous writer Joshua Perle, and me. We three refused to give them such letters of thanks — we wouldn't even give them receipts for food cartons we received through them. But others did. For instance, a group of Revisionists who were partisans, along with their leader Lopata, wrote a memorandum that they regretted having become partisans, that they had been seduced into that role. They even returned their arms — six guns Later, in the Bergen-Belsen camp they were tried by an inter-party court which consisted of Natan Buksbaum (Poalei Zion, left); the witness, son of Joshua Perle (a member of the PPR, Communist); Minzberg from the PPR, son of the Orthodox leader, Yekhiel Minzberg; Rabinovitch, a representative of the Bund; Eliezer from Hehalutz; and Grzybowski of Hashomer Hatzair. The

81

sentence was as follows: Social and personal boycott of the re-visionist group for giving up their arms, which should have been destroyed instead of being handed over to the Germans. The Hotel Polski was always full of Jewish dealers who made fortunes by mediating between the hotel leaders and the Jews. One of those who came to the hotel in order to register on a foreign passport, a certain Lusternik, was naive enough to give Adam a letter to his relatives in Switzerland, asking that they should send papers to his relatives in Poland. Adam had also obtained a letter from a Jewish editor testifying that Adam was saving Jewish souls from extinction. The editor appealed to Jews all over the world to help Adam in his treacherous work. Lusternik was later put on trial in Bergen-Belsen, and the sentence was: social boycott. This occurred shortly before the camp was liquidated.

A large number of promesas and parcels arrived addressed to the Joint director, Daniel Guzik,* who, being an Argentine citizen, could move and ride freely. Guzik would give those documents to prominent and distinguished Jews. But the documents had first to be legalized by the Gestapo and he was obliged to bribe the German officials and the Jewish Gestapo collaborators. The witness knows of many instances in which Guzik not only gave documents away free of charge, but also gave money to some of these people so that they could cover their necessary expenses. One such family, Shurman, survived thanks to Guzik. Skosowski and Adam demanded letters praising their conduct in return for their parcels.

ANNA SZPIRO

Anna Szpiro was born in Lodz in 1914. In 1936, she married Dr. Maximilian Herzog. When in 1940 the Germans began deporting Jewish professionals, the couple went to live in Warsaw on 52 Leszno St. In the last stage of the ghetto uprising, the Germans discovered their bunker, on 45 Mila St. The husband, together with the other men, were shot, and the women were taken to the Umschlagplatz, and from there, on April 29, 1943, to the labor group on the Eastern Railway (Ostbahn) station in Warsaw. Source: Yad Vashem Archives.

*In some accounts David Guzik's first name is mistakenly given as Daniel.

. . . I worked very hard, loading coal and potatoes. One day I heard about the existence of the Hotel Polski from one of the women in the group, who had managed to smuggle herself there and promised to send more information. She sent me a card through a Polish woman, telling me that there was a possibility of leaving Poland and advised me to come to the hotel on 29 Dluga St. the very next day at 10 A.M.

I began to make preparations to escape the camp. This, it appeared, would be very difficult, because the commander of the group, himself a Jew who also planned to escape with the help of the same woman, declared that he wouldn't let me go. After long talks, he agreed to send me to work the very next day especially early, at six. We lived in a barrack four kilometers from the place of work. The commander of the station was a Volksdeutsche who behaved towards me in a friendly manner because he had seen me crying when we heard about the burning of the ghetto. I had once told him about how my husband had been shot. He had then promised me that if I ever needed a favor, I should turn directly to him.

Since I could arrive at work so early in the morning, I immediately approached him and told him about the Hotel Polski and about this chance to go abroad. Maybe he could help me? He answered that, with the arrival of the first freight or passenger train, I should take some rags, go to the train, and start cleaning its windows. He personally would stand at the gate and start a conversation with the Ukrainian guard. He would signal me by raising his cap, which would be my signal to leave the train and pass through the gate. He also told me to ignore any shooting, for the guard would only shoot into the air.

I began to clean the windows, watching the man all the time, and when I saw him raise his cap, I boldly left the train and went towards the gate, for I had nothing to lose. I went through in spite of several shots — the Ukrainian was indeed shooting into the air.

I possessed only 150 zlotys, and had no documents whatsoever. To return to the Ostbahn was impossible. The working place was on the outskirts of the city, and the problem was how to get to Dluga Street. I approached a droshky driver and told him to take me there. He demanded 100 zlotys, but as soon as I got inside he asked for 150, for he had guessed, from my destination, that I was a Jewess. Sure as I was that he would take me not to the Hotel but to a police station, I agreed to his price, for I was lost anyway. However, the driver was apparently a man with some scruples for he brought me to the hotel.

When I arrived, the whole building was surrounded by Germans, armed with bayonetted rifles. Having nothing to lose, I went straight to one of the Germans at the gate and told him that I was an *Ausländerin*, a foreigner, and he let me in.

Inside the courtyard, I saw trucks full of people who were, so they were told, going to be exchanged. I noticed among these people a former patient of my husband's, a Pole named Skosowski. I went up to him and told him in short that I had three months ago lost my husband and that I was now in a desperate situation, for I had just escaped from the camp and had no papers which I could use on the "Aryan" side.

He replied that I had unfortunately come too late, and that all he could do was to give me some money with which I could live in the hotel until the next transport.

At that moment, the Germans who were sitting behind the table not far from us looked in my direction and smiled.

Encouraged by this smile, I approached them and they asked where I would like to go. I looked at the sheet of paper that lay on the table and saw the word "Palestine" written there. I replied unhesitatingly, "To Palestine." They asked my name and I almost said, "Herzog" but at that moment I heard Skosowski whisper into my ear, "Brande" and therefore I said, Brande.

They asked for my first name and I hesitated, waiting for new directives, but there was silence, and I said, Anna. I was then asked why I had no luggage, for everyone else was loaded with suitcases, bundles, and also with money and jewelry. I couldn't tell them that I had just escaped from the labor camp and that my entire possessions consisted of my handbag. I therefore replied that my luggage had been stolen. Finally, they asked why I had come so late, and I replied that I had been sick. After that, they told me to get into one of the trucks. Skosowski came up to me and told me to remember that my name was now Brande. He promised to come to the railway station and bring me some food parcels, for the journey was to take four days and three nights.

At the station, the Germans began to call out our names and I heard them call Brande, but I was too nervous to remember and

I didn't move. They called the name a few more times until I became aware that they meant me, and I went over to them. One of the Germans said to me, "It isn't enough that you were robbed and that you're sick. You're also unconscious." I entered the train car. A few hours later, Skosowski came with a four kilo food parcel. He ran from window to window shouting "Brande" until he found me and handed me the parcel, saying, "You're lucky. May you come out all right."

But we weren't sent to be exchanged with German foreign nationals. We arrived at a camp in the middle of the night and were taken off the train.

It was the camp of Bergen-Belsen.

ELLA SENDOWSKA

Ella Sendowska lives today on 23 Arba Artzot St., Tel Aviv. Ella was born in Lodz in 1909. After finishing high school, she studied music. In 1928, she married Jacob Rolnik. After the Germans occupied Lodz, the couple escaped to Warsaw before the ghetto was created. Later, she went, together· with her husband and two children, Artur aged 11, and Danusia aged 4, to the "Aryan" side, where they hid in four different places. Tempted by the prospect of getting foreign documents, the husband went with their eleven-year-old son to the Hotel Polski.

After her husband and their small son arrived at the Hotel, he wrote several letters to her depicting the mood, the situation, and the people, who were deceived by the perfidious hope of being sent abroad, only to be robbed of their possessions and then shot in the Pawiak prison. Both father and son were shot the day after their arrival. Source: Yad Vashem Archives.

. . . It's well known what role the Hotel Polski played in the martyrdom of the Jews. I shall therefore tell only how my husband and son, who had excellent hideouts, came to that hotel. It was a result of the treachery of the Nazis, who, with the help of vicious people, pulled Jews from safe hiding places, and who, for large amounts of money, gave them the false hope of going abroad. In our tragedy, a remote relative of my sister's, whom I shall call Michael, took part.

At that time, we were all hidden on the "Aryan" side, and when our little Artur was writing cheerful letters that he was

85

fine, that he felt quite well with the Polish family of Mr. Czeslaw, Michael started pestering us. He said that he had contacts with a certain young woman, Ewa, who was known to be the mistress of the famous Jewish traitor, Lolek Skosowski, who was later sentenced to death and shot by the Jewish underground. Michael promised that with the help of Ewa, he would obtain foreign documents for my husband and we would then be able to go abroad. The price for these papers was one kilo of gold per person. The only people who could afford this were of course, the very rich. Michael knew that before the war we had been very wealthy, and wanted to take advantage of us.

The whole affair seemed simple. Many relatives of Warsaw Jews who lived abroad had sent genuine exit visas to the members of their families, but in most cases, these relatives had already been murdered during "actions" or sent to extermination camps. Therefore, the documents remained unclaimed and it was possible for others to use them after changing the names and the photos. This little swindle of course, carried a high price. It was said that the Americans would exchange one German for three Jews. Such were the rumors.

At first, my husband wouldn't listen to Michael's persuasions. But Michael, who was eager to carry out this transaction, assured my husband that as soon as he came to the hotel, he would himself meet the woman, Ewa, who would hand him the documents. I, in the meantime, was to stay in my hiding place and await news from my husband. Before leaving, my husband took along our son, Artur, whom he had brought with him from his hiding place.

The Hotel Polski was on Dluga Street. It was considered a temporary site from which people would be sent away. Before going to the hotel, my husband had already heard that three transports had been sent away and that they were in a camp near Hanover.

That same evening, after my husband and son had gone to the hotel, I received letters from them through my Polish friend, Pan Franciszek, which had been written in the courtyard of the hotel. I answered them but by then, it was too late. The next morning, driven by terrible anxiety, I left my hideout and went to Krasinski Square, which was close to the hotel. Hidden behind the gate of a house, I saw two trucks packed with people going in

86

the direction of the Pawiak prison. This was the last group of about 600 people who were shot. Among them were my beloved ones. That was the end of the Hotel Polski. After that, no one was deceived anymore by the German murderers.

This is a letter which eleven year old Artur wrote to his mother:
Dear Mum,
I feel well but terribly nervous. No wonder. Everything is so scary. I am afraid that they will take all of us and . . .
(here follows an erased word which could read as "murdered." Evidently, after writing the letter, the boy didn't want to worry his mother. It is also possible that the word was erased by his father.)

The following is a letter written by Mr. Rolnik to his wife:
I am in the courtyard of the Hotel Polski. Hundreds of acquaintances, among them people waiting two or three weeks and don't want to go. They think that here is the best asylum. There are people who only three or four days ago left the hospital (the ruins of the ghetto).
Pani Ewa promised to call you tomorrow morning and meet you. You'll be able to come here and stay a few hours with us.

That same afternoon, Mr. Rolnik wrote a second letter to his wife.
Send me the thirty notes. . . . Artur says that they are too good to us. People are celebrating and arranging parties. . . . Isn't it all one big swindle? . . . I am inclined to believe that all this is a bald lie. Pani Helena has a scrap of some Palestine paper — another lie.

That same evening, he wrote still another letter:
I'm more and more convinced that all this is a fraud. For God's sake, wait for my letters! Pani Ewa was here and assured me that our transport is certain, but personally I doubt it.

The letter contains a few lines added by a friend, Pani Hela.
Tomorrow I am to leave for the unknown . . . I regret my decision against the advice of my protector . . . but I was spiritually and physically at an end. The mood among the people here is not too cheerful. . . .

Now the further notes of Mrs. Rolnik.
The woman, Ewa, was well aware of the fate that awaited the people at the hotel. In spite of this, as long as the collaborators

managed to drain the people of everything they possessed, they cheated them in every possible way. Pani Ewa was later sentenced to death and was executed by the underground.

HELENA GOLDBERG

The same Jacob Rolnik is also mentioned by another witness, Helena Goldberg, who saw him at the Hotel Polski. Helena was born in Lodz, studied in Cracow, and married Lazar Goldberg. When the war broke out, she and her husband and their daughter went first to Lodz, and then, in July, 1940, came to Warsaw where they remained in the ghetto until 1942. The husband was deported during the great "action." She and her daughter lived on the "Aryan" side where she learned of the Hotel Polski, to which she went, and from where she was sent to Bergen-Belsen. She remained there till the spring of 1945. She was evacuated with a group and liberated by the Russians. She later emigrated with her daughter to Palestine.

While on the "Aryan" side, she and her child wandered from one hiding place to another until she found a secure bunker for a relatively small rent in the apartment of a decent Pole. Her father and sister were deported. She was unable to leave the hiding place because of her "bad" features. For this reason, she couldn't receive a Kennkarte, but was given a false birth certificate under the name of Helena Isabella Kowalska.

One day, she was forced to leave that last hiding place, for German gendarmes had come looking for someone else in that building. She began leading the life of a hunted animal. She managed to place the child in a children's home, but the child couldn't stand how the other children spoke abusively about Jews. Once, when she defended them, the children suspected that she herself was Jewish and shouted, "Bella, back to the ghetto!" Then the mother learned about the Hotel Polski. (Source: Yad Vashem Archives)

. . . I decided to go there with Bella. I'd heard much about it. They said that the Nazis were sending the Jews to Vichy in France. Was this perhaps a trap? My brother-in-law was against my decision. He tried to dissuade me, insisting that this was a snare to catch Jews. But I thought, let it end . . . there is no room for me anywhere. The Germans put posters up on the walls: "Death penalty to anyone hiding Jews."

In order to leave the Hotel Polski alive, one had to convince the Nazis that he had relatives in Palestine or in America, and that they had sent the necessary documents. I had no such papers, but while in Cracow, I learned that my husband's sister, who lived in Palestine, had sent ship tickets for us to the Lloyd Triestino company. However, we didn't manage to get them, because Italy had joined in the war in the meantime, and the Italian consulate in Warsaw closed. Much later, I heard that an Italian consulate had been opened in Katowice, but by then it was too late. I decided to mention all this in case there was an investigation. In the meantime, trade with the Palestine certificates was blooming. Most of those who had received these certificates from relatives in Palestine were no longer alive. They had been killed in "actions" or murdered in the camps. Gestapo agents, taking advantage of this situation, sold these certificates to rich Jews. In July, 1943, I crossed the gate to the hotel. Nobody prevented me from entering. No one asked me from where or why I had come. The gate stood open, unbarred.

The hotel and its entire courtyard were filled with people roaming about. I saw a number of Poles who had come here to do business. They circulated among the Jews, buying gold and diamonds. A few acquaintances I met there suggested that I get American papers, saying that my brother-in-law could pay for them. I was told that the next day the hotel would be shut down and all the inhabitants sent away.

I met Mr. Jacob Rolnik and his little boy in the courtyard. He was terribly nervous. He told me that he had a bad premonition. He knew that tomorrow some of the people would be sent to the Pawiak and he was terribly frightened. He told me that we must escape from here, that we could not believe the Germans' assurances. They only wanted to cheat us out of our money and valuables, and then kill us.

At that moment, Ewa, a Jewess infamous for her contacts with the Gestapo, entered. She instructed Mr. Rolnik what to say to the Germans during the investigation. He was confused and absent minded, and hardly listened to her. That same evening, he decided to leave with the boy, and not to return.

I met a man from Lodz who told me that in one of the rooms, a Mr. Engel sat preparing a list of those with Palestine certificates. I went to see him. There was a long line in the corridor to his room, but I finally reached him. It transpired that he knew my name from Lodz and was willing to help me.

Down in the courtyard, Mr. Rolnik was still restless. "Let's leave together," he suggested. "Perhaps we'll find a place to stay for at least this night." He was convinced that we were all in danger, and we left the hotel. But we looked for a place to sleep in vain, and returned to the hotel.

I spent the night with my little girl on the stairs — there was no place in the rooms. In the morning was the announcement: "Get up. We're leaving." A few German trucks rolled into the courtyard. The Germans called out names. I later learned that Mr. Rolnik and his little boy were shot at the Pawiak prison.

But most of us, including myself, rode in the trucks to the railway station, and then travelled in a train whose cars were sealed shut. In the middle of the night, we stopped in the middle of a forest. There was an order: "Aussteigen!" The Germans began counting us. There was panic and screams. Before the Germans had arranged us in rows, one woman swallowed poison. Her body was left on the road.

HELENA SLAWA CITRYNIK

Helena Slawa Citrynik, whose maiden name was Zeldowicz, was born in Warsaw in 1905. After she was graduated from high school, she married a physician, Tadeusz Citrynik (Marszalkowska 139).

She lives today in Tel Aviv, on Shderot Hen 8.

At the outbreak of the war, her husband was mobilized, then taken prisoner by the Russians and sent to Siberia. Mrs. Citrynik lived in the Warsaw Ghetto with her mother and her brother's wife, Dr. Fiszhaut Zeldowicz, on 17 Sienna Street. She worked in "shops" (factories), first in Ostman and then in Schultz. She went over to live in hiding on the "Aryan" side. On learning that a group of Jews with South American papers had been sent to Vittel, she decided to go to the Hotel Polski on Dluga Street which had become the gathering place for "foreign" Jews, after the Hotel Royal. Here is what she wrote in her notes: (Source: Yad Vashem Archives)

. . . The papers were sent from Switzerland or America and sold for large amounts of money. The documents came from Paraguay, Uruguay, and Ecuador to people who had already been murdered by the Germans. Jewish Gestapo agents who collaborated with the Germans began selling the documents to Jews hiding on the "Aryan" side who could pay. In 95% of the cases, these Jews later left Warsaw under assumed names. When they started the Palestine list, registration was much cheaper. Not having much money, I decided to join that list. At that time, the Palestine list contained the names of fifty people only, but there was still room for over two hundred. My Polish landlady accompanied me to the hotel, and there I waited for the transport.

Nobody believed that the Palestine list was worth anything. Even Zionists who were in touch with the Jewish Agency preferred American papers. The Joint director himself, Guzik, provided his family with American papers. One of the main Jewish Gestapo men told me that the Palestine list was a swindle, that they knew nothing about it in Berlin.

Many of my acquaintances whom I met in the hotel tried desperately to change their Palestine papers to American ones. A few succeeded. Some had certificates to Palestine under their true names from before the war, while the American papers were counterfeit.

. . . I left on July thirteenth with a transport of 2700 people. A week earlier a previous transport had left and we had heard no news from it. We travelled in a passenger train. Everyone had a seat. We arrived at the station of Zelle and from there marched seven kilometers to a camp. Among us was a group of young ghetto fighters. Nearly all of them later perished. The only one of their group to survive was a young woman, an underground courier who carried arms between Warsaw and Cracow. She was saved because in Bergen-Belsen she had changed her papers. She refused to do this but her comrades begged to choose Palestine instead of America. They called a special meeting and convinced her to agree. This way, they argued, in case those on the Palestine list would survive, there would be at least one witness to tell the story of the ghetto fighters.

STANLEY OSINSKI

Stanley Osinski was a frequent visitor at the Hotel Polski. He came not with the purpose of obtaining a visa for himself and going abroad, but to carry out commercial transactions with the "foreign" Jews who needed to exchange their valuables for money. He afterwards began coming to the Hotel daily when his own father, sick of living on the "Aryan" side, decided to join the "foreigners."

Stanislaw Osinski was born in Warsaw in 1920. After finishing a vocational school, he spent the fall of 1939 in a military preparatory camp near the town of Suwalki. In the first days of the war, the Germans surrounded the camp and carried out a "selection" among the recruits, separating Volksdeutsche from the Poles and the Jews. For the first time in his life, Osinski made a fateful decision. He declared himself to be a Pole. Later, when the Germans began moving the prisoners in the direction of East Prussia, he escaped together with a few others, first to the town of Mlawa, and from there, on foot, to Warsaw.

His family – his parents and two brothers – lived at that time in a small town near Warsaw, Minsk Mazowiecki. On the 21st of October, 1942, the mother was "resettled" to the death camp of Treblinka. Osinski had by that time established himself as a Pole on the "Aryan" side in Warsaw, and managed to bring his father, brothers, and one of their wives to Warsaw, where he found them hiding places.

Thanks to his "good looks," flawless Polish, and courage, he moved freely about town, wearing the uniform of a Polish railway worker. He smuggled great quantities of food into the ghetto by bribing the German and Polish guards. He also had access to an illegal printing shop where Kennkarten (I.D. cards) for Jews in hiding were manufactured. He rented numerous hideouts for Jews who had escaped from the ghetto during the great deportations. In one of these places, on 5 Brzeska Street, in the suburb of Praga, thirty Jews were at one time hiding in the apartment of the Polish Skalski family.

Despite his "good appearance" and composed behavior, he was on two occasions stopped by Polish blackmailers. He managed to get away from them. After the war, he caught these blackmailers in liberated Warsaw. He had them arrested, and they were tried and sentenced to long prison terms.

The story is based on several personal interviews with Stanley Osinski in New York.

In the meantime, the situation of the "illegal" Jews on the "Aryan" side was constantly deteriorating. The Germans had pasted posters all over the city threatening that Poles caught hiding Jews would be killed together with their entire families, and the entire building would be razed. Many Poles, in their fear, refused to keep these Jews any longer. At that time, after the final destruction of the Warsaw ghetto, news began to reach the illegal Jews about the Hotel Polski, about the affair of the foreign documents and the possibility of an "exchange."

Osinski became a frequent visitor to the Hotel. Most of the Jews there possessed gold, diamonds, or foreign currency, and needed money to pay for their accommodations at the Hotel — if they could get a room — as well as to pay for food in the restaurant and for acquiring clothing, suitcases and other necessities for the trip abroad. Osinski was one of the many — some of them Gentile Poles — who took part in these commercial dealings.

He usually arrived at the Hotel in the morning and spent many hours there. He came as a Pole, but once inside the courtyard became a Jew. This was the only territory in the city, miniature as it was, where a Jew was not arrested or shot on sight. The danger came later, on leaving the Hotel, for the streets were full of Polish blackmailers who would fall on their victims and rob them or hand them over to the Germans. On leaving the Hotel, Osinski would run to the nearby Miodowa Street, jump onto a moving tramway and again assume the identity of a Pole.

The Hotel was packed with Jews. They filled the courtyard, the stairs, every corridor and corner. There were always long lines to the Jewish Gestapo men who were in charge of the whole passport scheme — Adam Zurawin, Lolek Skosowski, Pawel Wlodawski, and Kenigel. Most of the Jews in the Hotel were wealthy. They occupied all the tables in the restaurant where Polish waitresses served their most exotic foods, bought especially in the town. But there were also other Jews who had only recently escaped through sewers from the ruins of the ghetto, and those who, sick, exhausted, and destitute, had nowhere else to go. Some of the Jews made the dangerous trip to the Hotel in the company of their Polish friends. Some came in rickshaws, others in the most fantastic disguises, wearing the uniforms of forest rangers and firemen. Osinski once witnessed how an entire family came out from inside a wardrobe which had been delivered into the Hotel courtyard by a furniture truck.

Osinski's father, Menachem, who at that time lived in hiding on Sliska Street, was completely exhausted and a nervous wreck. He felt unable to bear the nightmarish conditions any longer. When he learned from his son that one of the people in the hotel who was helping provide foreign documents was the JDC director, David

Guzik, he asked his son to take him there. He had known Guzik from the times when he himself had been a town councillor in Minsk-Mazowiecki, and had had dealings with the Joint.

Osinski went once more to the Hotel to investigate the "affair." Among the people there were two cousins of his and a great number of acquaintances. He spoke to every one of them. Nobody had complete faith in the affair. Most saw in it another German trap to lay their hands on the surviving remnants of the Jews and their money — but the conditions on the "Aryan" side were unbearable and they had decided to take the risk.

The belief that this affair might be a true means of escape grew, particularly after several transports of Jews who held false Latin American or Palestine papers were now reported to be in the transit camps of Vittel in France, or Hanover in Germany.

Lured by these illusory prospects, Osinski's father, brother, and brother's wife decided to take the risk and went to the Hotel. Both the brother and sister-in-law decided to give up after a few days and returned to their hideouts. His father remained. Osinski now tried to buy foreign documents from the Jewish "leaders" in charge of selling them — Adam, Lolek, Pawel, Kenigel, and a young Jewish dancer named Franciszka Mann. But it wasn't easy to get to any of them, for they were beleaguered with applicants.

And then, the affair ended in the feared catastrophe. One day, on July 13, 1943, when Osinski came to visit his father, who still had no foreign documents, the building was suddenly surrounded by German police, and all the Jews — about six hundred — were loaded onto trucks and taken not to the railway station, but to the Pawiak prison a few blocks away. On the way, Osinski attempted to jump from the truck, but his father wouldn't let him. "Don't, they'll shoot you."

(One of those present in the Hotel Polski at the time of that final round-up, was Benyomen Miendzyrzecki [Benjamin Meed], husband of Wladka Peltel, whose book *On Both Sides of the Wall* we quoted earlier. Benyomen Miendzyrzecki came to the Hotel to investigate the possibilities of saving some members of his family. When the Hotel was surrounded by the Germans, he managed with a few others, to hide in the attic of the building. He thus avoided being taken to the Pawiak prison where, having no "foreign papers," he would have shared the fate of the majority.)

The trucks drove into the courtyard of the prison. There, be-

94

hind a table, sat several German officials of the *Auslandstelle* with their secretaries, and they began to make selections—first separating the Jews from the non-Jews (for there were several Poles who had come to visit their friends, or on business). Stanislaw Osinski went over to the small group of Poles. Next came the identity check of documents. Those in possession of foreign papers, only a small part of the six hundred, were sent to "Serbia," the women's section of the prison. The rest, Osinski's father among them, were kept for two days in the courtyard and then led in groups of five across the street from the prison, to the ruins of the ghetto. There they were ordered to strip and were shot. Their bodies were later burned by a group of Jewish sonderkommando.

Stanislaw Osinski remained in the prison for several weeks until he managed to escape. He later took part in the Polish Warsaw uprising.

He lives today with his wife and two sons in New Jersey, USA.

BARBARA RUCINSKA

Barbara Rucinska was born in Lublin in 1913. She lives today with her family, all Orthodox Jews, in Israel. (Source: Yad Vashem Archives)

. . . My husband, our child and I lived in a hiding place behind a wardrobe in the apartment of an Aryan family called Lipski, in Lublin. Their children were unaware of our presence. We could often hear them talking about Jews without their knowing that a Jewish family was hidden a few steps away. One of them once said, "This is the time for us to get rich." I asked my husband to provide us with cyanide, but he, being religious, refused. Our hiding place behind the wardrobe became insufferable. We decided that the child and I would go to Warsaw.

The Polish woman, Lipski, accompanied us for protection. I found a room on 18 Leszno Street in the Warsaw ghetto, and planned to bring over the rest of the family. But this wasn't easy. All the men in my family were Orthodox, had beards and wore long black Hassidic coats called "kapotes." The women wore wigs. And Jews were forbidden to ride the trains.

I became very active. I managed to get a travel permit for a sum of money and brought my husband and my family to Warsaw, and then brought the children of my deceased sister to

Ostrowice. I spent much time outside the ghetto. I would go over to the "Aryan" side by way of the Polish Courts Building on Leszno Street, where the police were bribed. When I got to the "Aryan" side, I took off my armband and changed into an "Aryan."

In July, 1942, the Germans began the mass deportations. On the very first day, I was dragged to the Umschlagplatz, but managed to get away. I knew by then that there was no escape from death except on the Aryan side.

I told my husband, "Ksyl, you must become a *goy*." His whole family laughed. He wore a *kapote* and had a beard . . . but I was determined.

It was decided that I would leave first with the child and try to find a hideout for my husband.

I bribed the guard of the Courts to let me through together with my child. I told him that I was a Christian and intended to save a Jewish child. I waited in the Court building and my husband brought our little boy, waved his hand and said in a loud voice, "Lady, I wish you luck."

I prepared two hiding places — one for myself and one for our child. My husband remained three more weeks in the ghetto. I visited him every day in a café there. He said that the German ring was getting tighter and that it was becoming more difficult to avoid deportations. There was no other way — he had to leave. He shaved off his beard and put on a "European" suit. One day, he joined a gang of Jewish workers who worked outside the ghetto, taking along his *tallis* and *tefillin*. His father sat "*shiva*" in mourning, because his son had shaved off his beard and taken off the *kapote*.

My husband came to stay with me. My landlord and his wife already knew I was Jewish.

In the beginning he never left the apartment because he had no documents, but later I provided him with an Aryan passport.

I was accosted many times by *shmaltzovniks*, blackmailers, and by Polish policemen, and I had to bribe them in order to save my life. My Polish landlady, Kowalska, stole all we had and said that our things had been taken by the Gestapo. I had to look for some way to earn money.

It was at this time that I was in touch with a Jewish woman, a Swiss citizen who managed to acquire a safe "arrangement" on the "Aryan" side. She manufactured documents for Jews on the Aryan side. Once, while I was travelling on business by train to Lublin, I was arrested by Germans and imprisoned for possessing a false identification Kennkarte. I denied being Jewish, saying that I had received the Kennkarte from an unknown man on the train. After spending eight months in the Lublin prison, I went before a German court, Sondergericht. The judge believed my story and I was freed.

I returned to Warsaw. Only a few members of my entire family were still alive, and they had gone to the Hotel Polski. Among them were my sister and her child. I decided to join them. My husband, however, didn't believe in the whole affair. However, he didn't unequivocally say "no."

There were rumors that one transport which had left the Hotel Polski was now interned in the French resort of Vittel. My husband was of the opinion that we should register for Vittel. But talk began that the next transports would be sent to a camp near Hanover. My husband now became convinced that the whole thing was a trap. He didn't trust the Jewish Gestapo men who prowled the hotel. One of them was called Adam, and the other was Lolek Skosowski. They declared that the list was closed.

I stood in line waiting for these two men and tried to "charm" them into adding our names, but they refused. I intended to stay in the hotel overnight, to say farewell to my sister before her departure. My husband had been obliged to go home and had left the hotel. But a while later he returned and said to me in a firm voice, "Get dressed, you're coming with me."

I asked him what had happened. I didn't want to go. I wanted to stay with my sister for at least that night. But my husband was unbending. After getting home, he told me that he had heard one of the Poles in the hotel tell another that the Jews were stupid to let themselves be trapped like this.

That same night, the hotel was surrounded and all those who had no papers were taken to the Pawiak and shot. The others who were on the list were taken to an unknown destination — none of them survived. Among them were my sister, her child and relatives, the Frenkiels from Bielsko and the Rapaports.

During the entire occupation, my husband strictly observed all the religious commandments — he ate only kosher food and never parted with his *tefillin*. Before Passover, 1944, I cleaned the kitchen and, with the help of our little son and a cousin who also lived with Aryan papers, baked matzot. Two days before Passover, our house was surrounded by German gendarmes, Polish policemen and Polish firemen. I was at that moment returning home from town. Seeing the blockade, my first thought was, "Is my husband home?" But at that moment I saw him coming from another direction. He too had been in town. Thank God! But our landlady was in danger, because if the Germans would enter our apartment they would find the matzot and the *tefillin*. In the meantime I found that they were looking not for Jews, but for a clandestine printing shop.

I went into the apartment and with the help of the landlady ground the matzot into flour and put it in a sack. But what was I going to do with the *tefillin*? I returned to my husband. "What shall I do?" He replied, "Do as you wish, but be careful not to damage them." I got angry. "You can have either a wife or *tefillin*!" But I went back home, put the two phylacteries in my blouse, and so, with a large bust, returned to my husband. His treasure was saved.

NIUTA GUTKOWSKI

Niuta Gutkowski was born in Suwalki and came to Warsaw before the war to study law. She was married to a young lawyer, also from Suwalki, now a renowned lawyer in Israel. They lived in Warsaw, on 13 Leszno Street. The story is based on several interviews with Mr. and Mrs. Gutkowski in Tel Aviv.

After the outbreak of the war, her husband, following an order of the Polish government, left the capital with tens of thousands of other young men, "going east" to join the no longer existent Polish armed forces. He finally arrived at the city of Vilno, which had been "liberated" by the Russian army and turned over by the Soviet government to the Lithuanians. Having been an active Zionist, Mr. Gutkowski received one of the few Palestine certificates which had arrived in Vilno, and he left by plane for Palestine.

Niuta Gutkowski remained in the ghetto together with her five-year-old son, her mother and her mother-in-law. Having lived most of her life among Poles and assimilated Polish-speaking Jews, and possessing "good Aryan looks," she left the ghetto in January of 1942 with a few close friends, to live on the Aryan side. Her child had earlier perished in one of the "actions." On the "Aryan" side, she engaged in the underground work of the Delegatura, the clandestine homeland arm of the wartime exiled Polish government in London. One of her missions was to find hideouts for Jews who lived in the ghetto. Her underground work took her once or twice to the ghetto, where she also visited her mother and mother-in-law. After entering the ghetto, she would remove her hat and put on the armband with the Star of David. During one of her visits to the ghetto, she was told that there were some letters for her at the Jewish post office on Zamenhof Street.

One of the letters contained a *laissez passer* Palestine certificate for her boy and her. The other envelope contained a letter from Istanbul, Turkey, in which she learned that her husband was living in Tel Aviv. The letter, written on a Red Cross form, said briefly, "Regards from your husband. Take the child and go to the Gestapo because you are on the exchange list." She took the two envelopes to her apartment on the Aryan side where she lived with a Polish woman whose husband was a prisoner of war.

One evening, towards the end of December 1942, she sat with several of her Jewish friends in a clandestine apartment, waiting for some telephone call. Some time later, Niuta left the apartment with a friend and went to a cinema. That same evening, the meeting place was raided by the Gestapo which took six people to Pawiak prison. Afraid that her own position was now in danger, she burned the two papers — the Palestine certificate, and the Istanbul letter — for they both proved that she was Jewish.

Her main worry at that time was to find a way to free her imprisoned friends, who were in danger of being shot. It was then that she heard of the Hotel Polski, that it was run by a few Jewish Gestapo agents who had close connections with the Germans; and she believed that she would perhaps succeed by bribing these shady characters to free her imprisoned friends.

That same day, she set out for the hotel, but not like the so many others who had gone with the hope of becoming "foreigners," and thus eligible for an exchange.

After entering the hotel, which was packed with hundreds of

people, a man who had received a Palestine certificate with her at the same post office, ran towards her and said that it was fortunate that she had come, for the Hotel Polski "administration" was just now registering people for Palestine. She hesitated, but people all around assured her, "We're all here for the exchange." They directed her to a Mr. Engel who was indeed in possession of a "Palestine list" which contained the names of those eligible to go to Palestine. When she told him her name, he looked at the list and exclaimed, "That's right! Your name is on the list. You're one of the very few, of just eight or ten people, who have authentic certificates."

When she saw her name on the list, she was convinced that this affair was genuine, for it coincided with the *laissez passer* and the letter she had received from Istanbul. She decided to take a chance.

But she hadn't forgotten the original purpose of her visit, which was to free her friends from Pawiak. She went to see the hotel "leaders" — the Jewish Gestapo men, Lolek Skosowski and Kenigel. She had previously known both. After the establishment of the ghetto, she had worked for some time at a place called the "Melody Palace," a dance club which belonged to her parents' close friends, the Hirszfelds, who owned restaurants and delicatessen stores over Warsaw. She had first worked there as a cashier and then as a waitress. Among the performers in the club was a young Jewish dancer, a woman who was suspected of working for the Gestapo, Franciszka Mann; another performer was the popular singer, Vera Gran. The club was frequented by wealthy Jews and by Jewish Gestapo agents and German collaborators. Lolek Skosowski and Kenigel used to go there and amuse themselves, usually at night, and often in the company of Germans.

Now that she was in the hotel, Niuta Gutkowska approached them and gave one of them (she doesn't remember whom) a large sum of money for promising that the prisoners would be freed. It later appeared that only one left the prison, and was a few hours later shot in the street.

Niuta spent one more night in her room on the Aryan side. The next day she returned to the hotel with a five-year-old Jewish girl, who had been handed into her trust by her parents, who themselves later perished in the Poniatowa camp.

Most of the people in the hotel held various South and Central American papers. Only 270 were on the Palestine list. The atmosphere in the hotel was excited and anxious. Everyone was busy preparing for the trip — packing his belongings, putting on a hat, a coat. Before the transport left, the Germans for the last time checked everyone's documents. When Niuta's turn came, something unexpected occurred which required quick presence of mind. The slightest false step would mean death for the little girl. The German conducting the check of the documents looked at the list and then at the child, and asked, "It says here that you have a boy Abram, but this is a girl." Niuta Gutkowski promptly replied, "It's a mistake. The child's name should be written as Abrama." The German added an "a" to the child's name and the girl, who today lives in Israel, and is herself the mother of a girl, was saved.

The transport was taken to Bergen-Belsen. Some time later, all the "foreigners" holding Latin American papers were taken to Auschwitz. The name of the young Jewish Gestapo woman, the dancer, Franka Mann, came up again when it was later reported that upon arriving in Auschwitz, she grabbed a gun from one of the SS men, shot him dead, and then wounded two others.

Niuta Gutkowski, along with most of those who were on the Palestine list, was liberated on April 13, 1945, by an American soldier named Abraham Cohen from Chicago, a few miles from the German city of Magdeburg.

JOSHUA PERLE

Another victim of the Hotel Polski was Joshua Perle, one of the most brilliant Yiddish writers of the period between the two wars.

Rachel Auerbach, a writer who was active in the Warsaw ghetto, caring for the Jewish intellectuals, survived the war on the "Aryan" side. She wrote a book of memoirs in which she described the circumstances under which Joshua Perle and his son were lured into the Hotel despite their both having exceptionally good chances to survive as "Aryans":
Rachel Auerbach relates:

101

Joshua Perle lived with his son on Franciszkanska Street. Between the two waves of deportations, he wrote a book about the first great "action" which took the lives of 300,000 Jews. After the war, the manuscript was found in the dugout of the Ringelblum archives, and published under the title of *The Destruction of Warsaw*.

Perle's apartment on 30 Franciszkanska Street bordered a candy factory in which I worked, and visited him frequently. He told me that shortly before the outbreak of the war, in September of 1939, he had just finished the second part of his great novel, *Everyday Jews*. He left the copy with friends when he escaped to the Soviet Union during the first month of the war. He retrieved it after returning to Warsaw. "Do you want to see it?" he asked me. He bent down and pulled out a suitcase from under the bed, and handed me a heavy typewritten manuscript. I carried it to 37 Nalewki Street and began reading it with great fascination. In the meantime, a new "action" came which lasted from January 18th to the 20th [1943].

Following the new deportations, a rumor spread together with the news about Stalingrad that the rest of the Jews in the ghetto were to be resettled in a small quadrangle between Niska and Stawki Streets, a few steps from the Umschlagplatz. Perle and his son had moved to the Toebbens shop on Leszno Street. Then came the order that all those employed at the Toebbens factory would be transported to the Poniatowa camp. In the course of his moving and packing, Perle's manuscript was lost.

The third chapter of Perle's attempt to escape his fate came now. And somehow, as it sometimes happens, he committed his greatest error in his attempts to save the dearest and most beloved person in his life — his son.

One of Perle's close friends, who had known him for many years, told me that after his young wife's tragic death in 1926, he had developed a morbid anxiety about the life of his only child. This anxiety remained with him to the last moments of his life.

After leaving the ghetto to live on the Aryan side, I learned that Perle and his son had left the ghetto in March, 1943. The young Perle had Christian friends (he was a member of a communist organization) and they provided father and son with the necessary Kennkarten, and a place to live. They called the father "Pan Stefan." They quickly established more connections and

102

would have most certainly remained alive to this day, were it not for the accursed "dead souls" affair of the Hotel Polski. The Perles acquired South American papers which had arrived after the deportations, addressed to someone who had perished in Treblinka. In July, Perle, his son, and a large group of others left under an escort to an internment camp not far from Hanover. It was said that the camp was under the auspices of the Red Cross and that Jews would be exchanged for Germans interned in Allied countries.

A few months later, the news arrived that none of the "South Americans" from Hotel Polski were still alive. They had been murdered in Auschwitz.

I cannot understand how a wise man like Joshua Perle would allow himself to be cheated in such a way, and to willingly allow himself to be led into the devil's jaws.

After the war, I learned that the camp not far from Hanover was Bergen Belsen. None of the holders of American documents came out alive. Only those registered on the Palestine list survived.

One of these survivors, Slava Cytrinik, later told, in her testimonial for Yad Vashem in Jerusalem, of the joy which overtook the "American nationals" in the Hotel Polski when they were ordered to pack in order to be sent away. A kind of euphoria, a mood of happiness which is felt by sick people who are about to die befell those preparing for the transport. Many "Palestinians" would have given away all they possessed at that moment to change places with one of the "Americans." One of the girls, who didn't want to separate from her beloved, actually agreed to such an exchange, and survived.

I recently found a beautiful essay in a book devoted to the memory of the Jews of Radom, Joshua Perle's native town. Written by Joshua Lender, it describes Perle, "the painter of the Polish landscape." He quotes the words of a survivor from Bergen Belsen that Perle was in a constant state of nervous breakdown, depressed and crying.

I'm overtaken by a great sorrow when I think of Perle's last days and nights. I feel the burning tears of the father who, with his own hands, brought his only son to the altar to be sacrificed, as Abraham. But no miracle happened. No angel turned the knife away from the child's neck.

103

The Hotel Polski in Fiction

The Perishing Daniel
by Adolf Rudnicki

Between July 22 and September 7, 1942, the Germans deported 300,000 Jews from Warsaw. The Germans said that "they
were being taken for soap" which in effect meant that they
planned to turn their prisoners into soap. It must never be
forgotten that this phrase originated with the "German nation of
thinkers and poets."

The extermination continued between September, 1942, and
the Passover holiday of 1943, although on a much smaller scale
than previous so-called "actions" (the executioners forced their
terminology onto their victims). On April 19, the Germans
began the final liquidation of the northern part of the city. They
burned and destroyed one building after another. The number
of those trapped between those walls during that ultimate attack
was estimated at 30,000. These people suffered a most terrible
death. A few managed to save themselves, in various ways. Some
broke through the walls of the guarded buildings or dragged
themselves through sewers. Others managed to escape from the
transports carrying them to the crematoria. Most of these people
were relatives of Jewish policemen who engaged in dealings with
the German gendarmes. For a fee, these gendarmes would pull
the victims from their bunkers and carry them in covered wagons to the "Aryan" side. After escaping, these people continued
their life under the shadows of the death sentence. The German
governor, Fischer, appealed to the Poles to hand over those Jews
who were hiding in the Aryan section. Many hideouts were
"burned" at this time, which meant that they had been discovered or become suspect. There were rumors that in some parts
of Warsaw, on Mokotow, Zoliborz and Wspólna streets, the
Germans had captured and executed not only Jews in hiding,
but also the Polish landlords who had provided them with shelter. As a result, a great number of Aryans refused to rent out

apartments to any prospective tenant who evoked the slightest suspicion. They preferred to forgo the rents they might have received. In those days, no one felt the vital necessity for housing as did the Jews.

Following the liquidation of millions of people, the Germans' technique was refined. They were aware of the tactic of dividing the opponents among themselves to make their elimination easier. Nothing could help those who had been burned alive in their houses. However, they still designed how to trap those Jews hiding on the Aryan side who were daily begging their landlords for a little more patience until they could find a new place to stay, for they couldn't possibly sleep in the street. One day, the word was gotten through to them that they were by no means lost — that they had an unusual and genuine chance to save themselves. And so those who lived in hiding were given new hope.

Those who had survived the ghetto deportations remembered well the growing preparations preceding the "action" of the summer of 1942. The Germans had limited the number of gates in the ghetto wall to two or three; the Christian clergy were ordered to leave that quarter which contained a few churches, and the Jews were left alone. Those holding foreign passports were then ordered to the Pawiak prison for internment. Oskar Bronstein, a Swiss citizen, asked for a few days' delay as he had a sick child, but he was told that it would be better in the Pawiak for the sick child as well. He didn't ask a second time, but went straight to the prison.

There, the "foreigners" were immediately divided into two groups: citizens of those countries engaged in war, and citizens of neutral countries. Oskar Bronstein belonged to the second group, all of whose members were immediately shot. Those of the first group were put in the small rooms of the old prison administration, which had small, unbarred windows overlooking Dzielna Street. From these windows the internees could see the great masses of people being driven to the *Umschlagplatz* where cattle trains awaited them. These people walked in utter silence; the crowds no longer believed in the value of human speech. The internees heard neither the sighs of old men nor the crying of children. In the midst of these events, the internees continued to be treated well. They could get food unrestrictedly from the Aryan side and were addressed by the Germans as "Sie." Some of the women, moved by the politeness of the Gestapo men, even contemplated buying them presents.

The internees remained together in Pawiak from July to January of 1943. The possession of foreign passports made Jews and non-Jews equal. In January, they were taken for two days to the Hotel Royal on Chmielna Street, from which they were taken away. Everyone was convinced that this was a new German trap and that they would never be heard from again. However, four weeks later letters began to arrive on prisoner of war forms. These weren't simply letters, but panegyrics — they were living in a famous European spa, in luxurious hotels . . . Nuns were teaching their children English, and life was as beautiful as a vacation on a yacht during a fantastic sea voyage. This place, called Vittel, slowly became legendary among the condemned who remained in the Warsaw ghetto, living like rats in their hiding places, or daring to step out at the risk of their lives. At the time of the Passover uprising, a second transport left for Vittel.

People were being burned alive . . . and there was Vittel. We had constant expectations of death . . . and there was Vittel. We were in perpetual fear of blackmail, of suspicious landladies . . . and there was Vittel.

Here were *shmaltzovniks*, blackmailers with eyes like knives at every street corner . . . and there were nuns teaching English. Here was the ever present fear of running out of money which even the richest did not escape . . . and there people lived in elegant hotels receiving American food parcels.

Here we were in the pit of hell . . . and there was Vittel. It isn't difficult to understand the temptation..

When the ghetto was aflame for the last time, passports began to arrive in large quantities from overseas. Henryk Goldman had tried to obtain a passport for an entire year, sending imploring letters through various channels: "You have no right to peace until . . ." Word was finally sent to him that he had received foreign citizenship, a so-called "PROMESA." But by the time this communication arrived, he was no longer alive. There were many more like Henryk Goldman who were poisoned, cremated, or beaten to death. Neither their streets nor their houses existed any longer. The news spread that one could buy a passport or be included on one together with other members of the family for a certain sum of money. It was clear that over there, in the foreign country, it would make no difference if a Goldfarb or Goldstein arrived instead of a Goldman. What mattered now was the Germans' attitude, and this time they seemed willing to help. The Jews reasoned that the Germans would sell them the passports for they were always eager for money, and in addition, they had their own political motives.

It was at that time that Daniel received a registered letter from Switzerland sent c/o a friend who soon afterwards left Warsaw. Daniel was notified by the Honduras consulate that he and his family had been granted Honduran citizenship, and he was requested to supply some necessary information together with photos. The promesa had arrived just in time.

The day before, Daniel's landlady had come into his room and looked around, gazed at each piece of furniture as if seeing it for the first time. "That little desk," she had said, "is so fragile. Don't you think that you write too much on it? It cannot bear the heavy hand of a man like you. And look here, the desk has marks! Do you think it's so easy to get furniture nowadays? Do you suppose that I can afford to buy a desk with the rent you give me?" She walked over to the table. "Don't you open that table too much?" she asked, pointing to twelve thin little legs on wheels which resembled a wooden centipede. "I can't replace it because it belongs to someone else."

"I'll be careful," said Daniel.

But as far as the landlady was concerned, this was only the introduction. "You are a very handsome man," she continued. "The whole street praises you. They say that you are polite, delicate, well bred — please don't deny it, you are very handsome." Here she smiled as a 60-year-old woman would to a man half her age — coquettishly but with dignity. "When you first came here, you presented yourself as Mr. Kowalski. Later you gave my daughter-in-law a document under the name of Dzikowski and wished to be registered under that name. So what is your real name, Kowalski or Dzikowski? Do you see this little girl?" She stroked the black curly hair of a child who had accompanied her into the room. "Poor darling, she too is something of a Dzikowska. Her father changes his name every three months — a very nice man! I'm really sorry, but I must ask you to move out as soon as you can. When the political situation changes, it will be all right, but not now . . . If you are indeed a Kowalski, you'll have no trouble in finding a room. People search high and low for a quiet, handsome young man like you who pays his way. But if you are a Dzikowski — also a nice name, very nice — then you must admit that I have behaved honestly. I risked my life for twelve months. Do you know how many sleepless nights I had because of you? I fulfilled my Christian duty. The time has come for others to take their turn. I strongly ask you to move out. I hope that you don't want to kill an old woman like me and have my house set afire."

The woman's arguments were uncontestable. Daniel knew that the chances of finding another room were non-existent, and convinced her with great difficulty to wait another few days. When the promesa arrived just in the nick of time, Daniel did not feel relieved. He couldn't decide whether to get the Germans to authorize it. One would have to be both blind and deaf, he kept saying to himself, not to see that the entire affair was a fraud. Deportations usually started with a suggestion that people were to go "east" to labor camps, "zum Arbeitslager Treblinka." Daniel repeated that this was another one of their tricks, realizing with terror that he would soon be without a roof over his head. The decision was finally made by someone else.

As with so many others, his friend, Dr. Kaliski's life was permeated with two emotions — a feeling of danger and of a horrible vacuous boredom. All those who lived in hiding were like grains thrown into a vacuum. It was a life without work, without women, with no attractions but that of awaiting death. As a principle, people did not reveal their addresses, and received no visitors. Everyone stayed with two or three people who had to suffice for one's entire world. By nature very active and energetic, Kaliski suffered much more than others from the boredom. He had some money, a relatively good apartment, and his needs were therefore more sophisticated. He visited Daniel, drawing him into endless discussions concerning war strategy about which neither had the slightest idea, but which both conducted passionately. Kaliski would interrupt occasionally with an aria from Don Juan, and proceeded to mutter through his badly

108

filled teeth that he would go mad if something didn't change in his life.

When he learned of the promesa that Daniel had received, he immediately adopted it as something that belonged to him as well and began to act. He used all his energy to force Daniel to arrive at a decision. He behaved like a hero. He moved about town disregarding the Germans and the *shmaltzovniks*. He even went to the Hotel Royal and brought back news from the Vittel front. Daniel strayed close to madness in his inability to make a decision. It came to the point where he wouldn't open the door for Kaliski. He was terrified by his savage will to live at any price, by his energy. One day Kaliski came with the news that tomorrow was the last day — that they were about to close the list. "The Germans said that there were too many people, that the rich were paying any price for a place. One day more might be too late. There were no lack of passports there — Adam had bought an entire sack of promesas. Tomorrow they might refuse to authorize ours. My landlady has been asking the strangest questions, my money is coming to an end . . . If you have no intention of going, then I'll buy your place! I'll turn to Adam."

The case was a delicate one. The promesa was actually written in Daniel's name, but Kaliski was close to the R. family which had sent the promesa. Besides, Kaliski had trouble with his mother and sister who were in hiding somewhere. Daniel, who had no family, could save them all. But if he were to take the Kaliskis, he too would have to go. And he kept on repeating to himself that it was a trap. He could, of course, give the promesa to the Kaliskis, but this wasn't so simple. He didn't want to go, but he wasn't willing to give up the promesa, which was, in a sense, a ticket to life. Should he fall into the Germans' hands (a likelihood at any moment) it might save him. He therefore consistently rejected all proposals. (Janka W., the wife of a well known politician, who was a prisoner in the Pawiak, offered him half a million zlotys for the promesa. Someone else wanted to give him a deed for half the property on Chmielna Street in exchange for the document.)

That morning, when Kaliski came with the news that the list was about to be closed, Daniel told himself that he wouldn't go, that the world was sick, and that in such a world one must move about as little as possible. But directly before Kaliski's arrival the landlady demanded that he leave the premises as the Germans were going to search her place that night. That same day, he went to the Hotel Royal.

Over 2,000 people had gathered near the Hotel Royal on Chmielna Street, and from there been taken to Hotel Polski on Dluga Street. The trap had worked.

Among those 2,000 was not a single person who did not understand that it was a trap, and that the Germans had once more cast out their nets as they had countless times before. But these people had nowhere else to go. Yesterday they had lost their roofs for the hundredth time with no prospects of finding another. Among those who came were old people who felt they had not much to lose, and youngsters whom nobody wanted, neither the forests nor the city. The wise came together with the stupid.

During the endless debates on whether or not this was a trap, some said that the Germans wouldn't bother with a special hotel in order to liquidate another 2,000 people. But everyone was skeptical and counted on no more than a one per cent chance of survival. Once outside the hotel, they realized that even this one per cent didn't exist. There they found *shmaltzovniks* waiting to rob them before handing them over to the Germans.

Daniel didn't go. A week later, when a rumor spread that the people were to be transferred to another hotel, he was convinced that it would be a Majdanek, and he disappeared. This man, for whom the move to Chmielna Street had been so difficult, who went to sleep with one resolution and awoke with another, whose inability to make decisions made everyone around him unhappy, packed within five minutes. He was "lighter" than the others, having no family to be responsible for.

Daniel's suspicions appeared to be groundless. The second hotel turned out to be Hotel Polski on Dluga Street. People mocked him. The Kaliskis laughed at him. The next morning, after escaping from the hotel, Daniel accidentally found a little room where sandals were manufactured during the day. The German field-gendarmerie, who closed the door before the curfew, was stationed in that same house. Whenever Daniel came home, a uniformed gendarme opened the door for him, wishing him a good night. This discovery of a place to sleep created new doubts in Daniel's mind. Had he behaved like a fool in giving up his chance at the hotel? In actuality, he hadn't given it up completely. Every day he returned to the Hotel, always putting off the final decision.

Four weeks later, when it appeared that the transport was going not to Vittel but to Zelle in Germany, Daniel decided to remain where he was.

About 1,400 people left on the first transport, among them the three Kaliskis under the name Dzikowski. The entire transport was detained for some time in a camp next to Hanover, and from there they were taken back to Poland, to be annihilated in Auschwitz.

A man named Rafal Ochock, had lived together in hiding with Kaliski, his mother and sister Ewa. As soon as the chance to leave arose, both women immediately chose to go. Rafal committed an act bordering on folly. Living in hiding, he had no right to go out, for this compromised everyone's safety. But, ignoring the fact that he was destroying his hiding place and risking death, he left home and searched the entire town for the hotel — and Ewa. He had burnt all his bridges behind him, as the landlady forbade him to return. But on reaching the hotel, he discovered that the young woman was already interested in someone else. Relations were easily formed in those catastrophic times, and women weren't very strict about their virtue.

The hotel held three kinds of people — those whose status was secure and who thus belonged to the privileged caste; those in the process of gaining a place through the payment of large sums of money; and the poor, who had come simply because they had nowhere else to go.

Rafal at once fell into that third, most miserable group. Madly in love with Ewa, he noticed that she had given away the last of her money for a place on a passport marked "Dzikowska," whose owner had remained behind.

Although many of these people had already heard of the death camps, they nevertheless walked into the German trap. Why? One reason was that the Germans had the support of several Judases, traitors who believed that in so acting they would save their own skins, and in the meantime, collect enough money and jewelry to be able to escape to Switzerland. Without the help of those Judases, the Germans wouldn't have succeeded in pulling so many Jews out from their hideouts.

Daniel had given his passport to the Kaliski family; he had sent away eighteen people and taken their money, but himself remained behind.

Walking around the Hotel Royal and then the Hotel Polski, Daniel kept on repeating to himself, "If an old man who doesn't know the language, if a mother with her child who have no strength left to struggle, allow themselves to be sucked in, they have their right. But you? Wouldn't you suffocate under the camp conditions, even if it were a peaceful camp? Would you be able to be fed by the hands that built Treblinka and Auschwitz? By the hands of those that drove your dearest to the ovens? Would nobody understand that one mustn't negotiate, even at the price of one's life? And even if you did manage to survive, wouldn't you be ashamed of the price you had to pay? And what about those who remained on the Aryan side? Had they perhaps also decided to stay behind because they realized that it is forbidden to receive life sustenance from the hands of the executioners?"

Standing in the hotel courtyard, he struggled with himself, full of disgust for the crowd which had allowed itself to be ruled by spies and by prostitutes. He saw in that crowd not a trace of contempt. On the contrary. "Adam's come! Lolek's come! Pawel's come!" He saw the piety with which people pronounced these names. He saw how everyone made way for them. He saw the pride on the faces of those with whom the turncoats were willing to shake hands. Spies and prostitutes were the royalty of that crowd. When he confided his thoughts, he was told that he understood nothing, that he didn't consider what they had all been through. They had arrived from bunkers, from the sewers, from a hundred ways of dying, spat upon, humiliated, finding their only defenders in those informers and in that whore who lived with a German. He was told that he saw the mud but was incapable of perceiving the reasons behind it — like all anti-Semites.

And yet, while walking over the courtyard, torn inside, he pondered, "They shall leave and be cremated. I shall remain, and maybe I'll survive. Afterwards they will ask, How? Every survivor will be under suspicion. What shall I tell them?"

Chapter Two:

VITTEL, THE FRENCH RESORT

VITTEL

Before the war, Vittel was (and remains today) a small town in southern France, with fewer than seven thousand inhabitants. But it was famous as a spa which attracted patients from all over the country and abroad who suffered from kidney troubles, arthritis, obesity and other diseases.

But Vittel was still better known as an exclusive tourist resort for the very rich, with a number of luxurious hotels, posh restaurants, a casino, a hippodrome, tennis courts and an opera house. Two of the most famous guests at Vittel were the legendary playboy and multi-millionaire, Ali Khan, and Egypt's King Farouk. Their presence attracted scores of film actresses, dancers, courtesans and adventure seekers.

The Nazis chose this elegant French spa as an internment camp for British and American citizens probably in the hope that the United States and Great Britain would reciprocate and treat their German nationals similarly.

It is easy to imagine the impression this site made on the "foreign Jew" from the Hotel Polski who had traveled from the ruined and blood-soaked Warsaw, through the entire German Reich, and who now arrived at the Vittel station and was led to a magnificent hotel which stood in the midst of a beautiful park.

The first to arrive from the Hotel Polski, at the end of June, 1943, were taken to the Hotel Providence, where they were greeted by fellow-Jews who had arrived earlier from the Pawiak and the Hotel Royal. All that reminded them of the past nightmare was the barbed-wire fence which separated them not only from the outside world but also from the other hotels, which were still more elegant, and where the "real" Americans and British were interned.

This chapter will begin with the diary of the Jewish girl, Mary Berg, whom we quoted in the Introduction. She was a genuine American and therefore lived in one of the luxurious hotels reserved for United States and British citizens. Her diary depicts how these privileged internees lived in contrast to those who arrived from Poland with South and Central American papers.

We also quote extensively from Dr. Hillel Seidman's descriptions of life in the ghetto and the beginning of the "foreign" affair in the Pawiak prison. Dr. Seidman was one of the very few who managed to avoid deportation from Vittel by hiding in a bakery oven in the internment camp. Another witness in this chapter on Vittel is Mrs. Miriam Novitch, who later became co-founder of the Kibbutz of Ghetto Fighters in Israel. This kibbutz was set up in the name of Yitzhak Katznelson, the Yiddish-Hebrew poet who went through Vittel where he wrote his shattering poem, "The Song of the Murdered Jewish Nation." Excerpts from his Vittel diary are included.

This chapter also contains a full list of names of the inhabitants of the Hotel Providence, who, with a handful of exceptions, were deported in two transports — first to the French camp, Drancy, and from there to Auschwitz. The subsequent history of some of the survivors is also recorded.

Ber Baskind, already introduced in Chapter One, who went through the Hotel Polski and the Pawiak prison, and was then sent to Vittel, managed to avoid the deportations, and he lived to see the camp liberated by the Allies. This chapter contains longer excerpts from his Vittel diary.

MARY BERG

In the Introduction we already met Mary Berg, author of the *Ghetto Diary*. Her mother was a genuine American citizen and so her father as well as herself and her sister were recognized by the Germans as real Americans. Mary Berg has told the story of the Jewish foreign internees in the Pawiak, who had been assembled there a few days before the Nazis began the great deportation of Jews from the Warsaw ghetto. The internees were kept in the Pawiak for almost half a year. In her diary entry of January 17, 1943, she describes how the group was taken to a train supposedly traveling to an exchange camp. The internees were brought to Vittel, where the few real Americans were separated from the others and were placed in separate luxurious hotels. The others, holders of South and Central American documents, were put in another hotel, separated from the rest by a barbed-wire fence. Several months later, in May, 1943, the first transport from the Hotel Polski arrived at Vittel. These people held South and Central American papers and promesas. In June, a second and last transport arrived from the Hotel Polski. Mary Berg's diary, which she continued through these days, is of particular importance because it describes the greater part of the camp, to which the Jews from the Hotel Polski had no direct access, as their Hotel Providence was separated from it by a fence.

The train which left Warsaw's Central Station carrying Mary Berg and the internees from the Pawiak traveled all day long across Germany, detouring in order to avoid passing through Berlin. In the afternoon they reached Saarbrücken, where they saw ruins caused by Allied bombs for the first time.

At six o'clock that same day the train stopped at Metz, where the German Red Cross gave the passengers a plate of "good tomato soup." Late that night, they arrived in Neuburg where they were given a "good meal on tables covered with a white tablecloth." The train then passed Nancy and twenty minutes later, stopped in Vittel.

This is the girl's first impression of the camp, noted down three days after their arrival.

> We are fenced off with barbed wire, but we are living in paradise as compared with our three years in the ghetto. We have a separate room on the fourth floor of an elegant hotel. It is clean, and each one has a bed for himself. What more could one ask for? . . .
>
> This is a large camp. In the park there are three hotels: the Grand Hotel, the Vittel Palace, and the Ceres. Two thousand Englishmen are living in the two latter — they were interned immediately after the capitulation of France. At first they were kept in the military barracks at Besançon, but for a year now they have been at Vittel. These two hotels are very comfortable, and in the Ceres there is a fine library with books in many languages. The Vittel Palace has been transformed into a hospital, and the medical service here is excellent. The doctors are French war

115

prisoners. On the ground floor of the Grand Hotel are many stores. One of them, the *Bon Marché*, has wooden shoes (rationed), needles, thread, old-fashioned dresses of 1920, collars, artificial flowers, and similar dry goods. In another store can be found brooches, pins, and boxes with the inscriptions, *"Souvenir de Vittel"* and *"Nous Reviendrons"* ("We Shall Return"), which has become a patriotic badge which almost every Frenchman now wears.

On Saturdays and Sundays there are moving-picture shows, mostly of old French films. During the week the screen is pulled up and the cinema is changed into a theater. Excellent plays, revues and concerts are given here.

The three hotels are connected, and all together they form an enormous block situated on a hill. From the Grand Hotel stairs lead to the park in which are situated the mineral water springs. They are being operated even now. The park is surrounded by three barbed-wire fences, and outside, armed guards walk back and forth. In the middle of the park there is a little lake with the inevitable swan. There is also a little pavilion in which several shoemakers are working. They, too, are internees, and each of us is entitled to have his shoes repaired by them once a month. Behind the pavilion is a church and the magnificent villa of the camp commandant. To the left of the commandant's building is a narrow path leading to the Hotel de Source, which is also inhabited by English people. Beyond is the Hotel Continental for people over sixty. The English and American nuns, too, are staying there; they take care of the old men.

On the other side of the camp is the Hotel Central, reserved for the Americans, whose number is not very large. They arrived in Vittel in September, 1942. Only women are here; their husbands are at Compiègne.

Everything indeed sounds like paradise except for the wire fences and the armed guards outside, but even this doesn't sound menacing. However, the girl complains about the food from the very beginning; it was insufficient and the internees would have starved were it not for the Red Cross packages. Otherwise, everything was perfection: entertainments, drama circles, sports competitions, educational groups, and so on.

The camp also had a number of Polish Americans and they began to openly demonstrate their anti-Semitism. When a few Jewish girls intended to prepare a Polish dance for one of the artistic evenings, the Polish gentiles were "offended by the idea that Jewish girls were to dance Polish dances" and boycotted the performance. But a few gentile women did attend the evening and "even applauded the Jewish girls."

116

From a letter received by one of the interned American nuns, the Jews in Vittel learned about the uprising in the Warsaw ghetto and the death of the last 40,000 Jews. Later, the internees received the full story from a group of Jewish foreigners who arrived from the Hotel Royal. All the new arrivals were put in the Hotel Providence, and separated from the rest of the camp by a fence. However, the internees could see and talk to each other from the windows.

> On July 15, 1943, a certain Mr. R. arrived from Warsaw. There is a suspicion that he is connected with the Gestapo. He came all alone, without any police escort. He says that nearly two thousand people who had foreign passports were recently sent to the camp of Bergen-Belsen near Hanover. According to him, the last internees of the Pawiak and the Hotel Polski are there.

On August 6, 1943, Mary's father finally arrived in Vittel from the camp of Titmoning, where all the men from the Pawiak had been kept separately from their families. Similar transports also came from Compiègne and Kreuzburg.

In November, 1943, the first exchange of prisoners between England and Germany took place. About one hundred people left Vittel, mostly the sick and those over sixty.

In the following weeks, the camp internees and even the Americans lived through days of great panic. On December 18, the Germans suddenly ordered Americans and British of Jewish origin to register.

> We do not know what this means, but various rumors are circulating. Some say that the Jews will be sent to Palestine in exchange for Germans interned there. Others maintain that we will be sent back to Poland. The Jews sit in their rooms in despair and do not know what to do. It looks as though something serious were afoot, for a special commission composed of high officials from the German Foreign Office has arrived in camp. The Gentile internees sympathize with us, especially the nuns. Mother Saint Helen declared that should we be sent back to Poland, she would not permit the children to go. "I will not give them the children," she said resolutely. "I will hide them in the church, and I defy them to go there."

This time it ended with only a scare. The Nazi Commission disappeared, and Jews and non-Jews breathed with relief.

117

A month later a new wave of uneasiness surfaced in the camp. A rumor arose that in Vittel, too, the Jews will soon be isolated in a kind of ghetto. Many Gentiles are indignant and declare they will not permit it. But, strange as it may seem, even here there are "Aryans" who are pleased at this prospect, who maintain that the Jews should be separated from the Gentiles, just as they were in the camp at Titmoning. It is possible that the same anti-Semites are responsible for these rumors.

After six more weeks of nervousness and anxiety, after several false alarms that the Jews were to leave, all "apparently for the sole reason of torturing us," the day finally arrived. "We are in the train!" writes Mary on March 1, 1944. "We are going despite everything."

> During the last twelve hours we have been through the most heart-rending experiences. Every half hour there were changes. At 6:00 P.M. the camp administration called out, over the loudspeaker, the names of all those who were not on the list. A few persons were lacking to make up the transport, so we hoped that we, too, would be taken. My mother rushed to the commandant, but soon returned with a downcast face; it was too late. But she did not give up hope, and kept praying that something would happen at the last moment.
> And it did happen. At 10:00 P.M. transports arrived from Titmoning and Liebenau, and it turned out that there would be room for some more internees. The administration summoned the native Americans, and my mother was accepted at once. At first my father was supposed to remain in Vittel.
> At seven in the morning my mother went to the camp administration office and, a few minutes later, she came running back, crying: "We're all going!"

The train took them to Biarritz, through Spain to Lisbon, Portugal, where they boarded a Swedish ship, the "Gripsholm."

> I was awakened by the sound of the ship's engine. The "Gripsholm" was on the open sea. I went out on deck and breathed in the endless blueness. The blood-drenched earth of Europe was far behind me. The feeling of freedom almost took my breath away.
> In the last four years I have not known this feeling. Four years of the black swastika, of barbed wire, ghetto walls, executions, and, above all — terror by day and terror by night. After four years of that nightmare I found it hard to enjoy my freedom at first. I constantly imagined that it was only a dream, that at any moment I would awaken in the Pawiak and once again see the aged men with gray beards, and the blooming young girls and

proud young men, driven like cattle to the *Umschlagplatz* on Stawki Street to their deaths.

I even fancied sometimes that I heard the cries of the tortured, and the salty smell of the sea suddenly changed into the nauseating, sweetish odor of human blood, which had often entered our windows in the Pawiak.

By nightfall of March 14 the outline of the American coast began to emerge from the mist. The passengers went out on deck and lined the railings. I was reminded of the Biblical story of the flood, and of Noah's ark, when it finally reached dry land.

All that day I felt completely broken, as though I had to bear the burden of many, many years. I did not take part in the entertainment that night. I lay in a corner of the deck, listening to the sound of the waves that were growing stormier and stormier. On March 15 our ship approached New York.

BER BASKIND

. . . After a moving farewell with David Guzik, my heart filled with darkness and death, and I went with the engineer to Vittel.

We left Warsaw, and after an uneventful 36 hour journey arrived in Vittel on a Saturday, November 13 [1943]. After the customary formalities of registration and luggage checks, I was assigned to live in the Hotel Continental.

Next morning, after a night-long rest from the trip, I began to look around to contact some of my new companions in misery. Guzik had given me letters to bring to his friends in Vittel: Y. Katznelson, the director of the Hebrew gymnasium in Lodz, and Alexander Landau from Warsaw. I found that they were living in the Hotel Providence, and went there immediately to give them Guzik's letters.

We had many things to talk about. They asked me many questions about Warsaw, and the experiences I had undergone. In return, I asked them about conditions in Vittel.

At the end of 1943 there were about 200 Polish Jews interned in Vittel, possessing the legal status of South American citizens. Most of them had received their American passports either before the establishment of the Warsaw Ghetto or before the great deportations. Since July, 1942, they had been imprisoned in Pawiak prison and had come to Vittel in January, 1943.

None of them had faced the nightmarish experience undergone by those whom they had left behind. They knew very

119

remotely, in a distorted way, of the real history of the Jewish sufferings. They lived an artificially sequestered and quiet life, and as a result were unaware of the horrible dramas that had been taking place for so many days, months and years.

I was painfully impressed by the peaceful surroundings. I saw myself living through the nightmare of recent past days. At every moment of the day and often at night I relived these terrible memories, and it seemed that the surrounding reality was a dream. But it was not a completely beautiful dream — it too was filled with fear and uncertainty. Was it possible that in this peaceful place, guarded by Nazis, these criminals who tortured and slayed human beings like us throughout Europe, would spare Jews? That we would indeed continue to walk freely, without being forced to perform harrowing labors and undergo threats and beatings? Was it possible that, to the contrary, we would be able to continue to remain well-fed, receiving weekly packages from the American Red Cross, be able to promenade in a marvelous park and even amuse ourselves at a cinema, play various games, sing and dance? This all seemed a false freedom and false joy. In these seemingly worry-free conditions, everyone went around tortured by his own doubts.

Most of my companions had been here since January; the others had come in after May, 1943. It seemed wonderful to me that they could communicate with the outside world, that they could send and receive letters.

There existed, however, an area of silence which made us anxious: we had still received no news from Bergen-Belsen. It was known — or so believed — that about 2,000 Jews who possessed American passports had been sent there. Many attempts had already been made, both officially and illegally, to get information from Switzerland about these people who had disappeared. We had so far learned nothing.

At last, in January, 1944, we witnessed the arrival of a group of Jewish-Russian women from Bergen-Belsen. We learned from them that a great number of Jews possessing "war documents" had been interned in that camp since the arrival of the last transport on October 22, 1943. There they had been assembled, and then, with the excuse that they were being transferred to an open camp, sent to an unknown destination. Those who were left behind in Bergen-Belsen believed that they had gone to Bergau. But there had been no news from them, and nobody had ever heard of a place with that name.

The Swiss delegation which visited us from time to time knew nothing about those who had disappeared. We grew more and more anxious about the fate of our brethren, who were perhaps the last survivors of Polish Jewry. And of course everyone at the same time was filled with the unexpressed fear that their fate would also overtake us.

And, indeed, the feelings of insecurity with which we lived suddenly changed to a new fear when we one day learned that a German commission, one which specialized in checking documents and identities of Jews, had arrived from Berlin.

Shortly afterwards, in March, the camp commander ordered the South American Jews to leave the camp and to move into a specially-designated hotel. The reason given was that since America refused to accept us in exchange for German nationals, we could no longer remain together with the other internees. As a result of that order, 230 of our group of 280 were immediately transferred, while the rest remained, temporarily, at the original site.

Once more I witnessed the spectacle of migration, which painfully reminded me of similar resettlings in the Warsaw Ghetto. In our new quarters, the gate remained closed for a week, after which we were again given the right to go out.

Everyone was anxious and fearful. Everyone wrote alarming letters asking for help, but the days passed and nothing happened. One Sunday our fears were justified as the Germans staged new tragic scenes.

The hotel was suddenly closed and surrounded by a double cordon of guards. The commandant announced that he had received orders to transfer us to another group. He immediately selected 200 of us in the hotel to be transferred, as well as some of the people who had remained in the camp. Everyone was overwhelmed with fear about the meaning of this transfer. Some of us were overcome with the same great terror that had overtaken the Jews during the deportations, and we saw a repetition of scenes similar to those that had then taken place.

A few people threw themselves down from high floors — others poisoned themselves. The wife of Prof. Szor, a well-known scholar in Warsaw where he had been chief rabbi of the

121

Great Synagogue, took poison together with the entire Baumgarten family. They were buried at the cemetery of Vittel.

Others were only wounded or fell ill and were taken to the hospital. And two internees managed to escape during the night: Szulim Dudelzak and Ajzensztadt. We later learned that they had managed to reach Switzerland, and a month after their escape they were able to send us some news.

On April 18 a group of 180 people were sent away. A week later we found out that they had been taken to Drancy, from which they were to be transferred back to Poland. We knew very well what that meant. All we could do was wait for the second transport to which we, no doubt, would be consigned.

We clung to the slightest hopes, and kept sending out SOS letters to various countries, but all ways were cut off. Four weeks later, on May 16, the second transport took place. This time, seventy people were sent away, among them sick people from the hospital.

As if by a miracle, 35 people managed to avoid the transport. They were all that remained of the Polish Jews who had managed to transform themselves into American citizens. But the German perfidy was set upon eliminating even the last Jew.

That small group of survivors consisted of a few gravely ill people, several women in advanced stages of pregnancy and a few others who were just lucky. But all of us too were scheduled to be sent away in a third transport, which was to follow soon. From that day on we lived in a state of constant terror, convinced that one of these days no tricks would save us from deportation. Every time we saw railroad cars at the station, we didn't sleep in our rooms, for we were sure that they were for us.

At that time I suggested that we escape and join the French partisans in the forests. But this wasn't possible because nobody among us spoke French. Some of us looked for a way to escape to Switzerland, and Hillel Seidman had already prepared such a plan of escape. Five of us began to prepare to attempt this escape in a few days. But before then, an official letter arrived from Berlin which stated that all those who had South American documents — even if they were acquired during the war — had the same rights as the North Americans. That official letter came as a result of numerous interventions of various figures overseas to whom we had been writing alarming letters since March. The

Germans here followed their usual method: first they deported all Jews whose foreign naturalization was obtained during the war, and then they favored a handful of the survivors.

From that moment on, our situation seemed to have improved, but our long experience had taught us not to trust the Germans. And while events were occurring which would lead, in a few weeks, to the liberation of France, we lived under constant strain right up to the very last moment.

I will not describe the unforgettable feelings we all had when we saw, on September 1, the Germans pack up and leave. But although we realized that we had at last been saved, we also knew that we were only a handful of survivors of that great number of people who had perished before the day of our liberation.

It is worthwhile to record what followed.

Between our liberation and the arrival of the American army, we were cared for by an American authority. But none of us knew what had happened to those who had been deported, and to this day I have not been able to obtain any news about them. And so the long nightmare ended for me personally. The camp of Vittel was quickly liquidated toward the middle of October, 1944, and those who, like myself, had relatives in France, were free to look for them. Others, who could not return to their native countries, such as those from Poland, went to La Bourboule. I went to Paris to seek my brother, who had lived there since 1925. But I didn't find him, for, as in the East, the Nazis had ruled there too. My unfortunate brother had been deported with all of his family.

HILLEL SEIDMAN

... The Germans surrounded the hotels of that famous French resort with barbed-wire fences and brought British and American citizens of all the countries in occupied Europe and North Africa. They also brought 173 Jews from Poland and some from Belgium, who held American passports. The internees received food packages from the American and British Red Cross and were permitted to write letters to all countries with which the Red Cross had access, including the United States and

123

Great Britain. Compared with conditions in the Warsaw ghetto, those in Vittel were, generally speaking, satisfactory.

We were recognized as Americans and treated like the other, real American citizens.

We spent the first few months in relative peace. I say "relative," for every one of us had lost a part, or, like myself, all of his family, and many of our dearest loved ones and friends. We were all experiencing great suffering. Many of us still had close or more distant relatives in the ghettos or camps, and we did all we could to rescue them. The only way to save them was to obtain foreign documents for them similar to ours.

We bombarded Jewish organizations and personalities and acquaintances in Switzerland and England with letters. We wrote in code because of the German censorship. We also sent letters through secret emissaries of the French underground (Maquis), whom I managed to contact. There was also another method: using paid smugglers. In addition, letters were sewn into the clothing of American, British or Palestine citizens who left for the exchange. In all our letters we alerted the world to save the remaining Jews in Poland and in the German camps.[6]

I sent such letters of alarm to my cousin, Anshel Fink in New York; to Mr. Harry Goodman in London; to Dr. Abraham Silberschein in Geneva;[7] and to Chaim Israel Eis in Zurich. I also sent lists of prominent Jewish personalities who still lived in the ghetto.

A number of Jewish personalities were in Vittel: Rabbi M. Rotenberg from Antwerp; Rabbi Shabtai Rapaport from Pinchev; the Hebrew poet, Itzhak Katzenelson; the wife of Professor Moses Shorr, Tamara; Rabbi Chaim Leyb Berglas; Rabbi Josef Frenkel from Bielsko; Dr. Nathan Eck and his wife; the writer and pedagogue, Guta Eisenzweig; and others.

A number of interned Catholic nuns organized a school. Most of their pupils were Jewish children, and the nuns used the classes for missionary purposes. The rabbis and Mrs. Shorr convinced them to establish courses of Jewish subjects and I became the teacher of Jewish boys. Guta Eisenzweig organized a Beth Jacob School for girls, where she taught Yiddish and Hebrew.

The discipline in the camp was not very strict. I even got special permission to leave the camp and travel to Nancy to get a pair of glasses.

This "idyll" lasted until December, 1943. Some of us managed to get foreign documents for our closest relatives through Switzerland. But this wasn't enough. We also approached the Spanish government — which represented some South American countries such as Paraguay — with a request that it protect the possessors of such passports who were still in ghettos or camps by interning them.

But the Spanish consul in Berlin notified the German commandant of the Vittel camp that our passports weren't recognized by the government of Paraguay.

This was a terrible blow which greatly endangered our lives. And very soon the Germans started a series of identity checks,[8] investigations and inquiries in Berlin. We realized that we were in danger and began sending SOS alarms to all parts of the world: "Save the last remnants of the Warsaw Jews!"

In January and February, representatives of the international Red Cross and delegates of the Swiss consulate arrived at Vittel. Switzerland was the protecting power over the North African and British subjects. The rabbi from Antwerp and I asked them to place us under their protection, at least until our passports would be recognized. But they received us very coldly, showed no interest in our pleas and answered briefly, "That doesn't fall under our jurisdiction."

I explained to the Swiss delegates of the consulate and the Red Cross that we only wanted to be left here in Vittel. I was sure that the Jewish leaders in the United States and Great Britain would "shake the world" to save us. Besides, I had news from Switzerland and my friends in the United States, Josef Eis and Rabbi Shabse Frenkel, that we had been recognized by the South American countries.

The shadow of death hovered relentlessly over our heads.

On March 18, 1944, the Germans "resettled" us, the 173 Polish Jews, to a separate hotel, Beau Site. One month later, on April 19, 1944, on exactly the first anniversary of the Warsaw ghetto uprising, the last surviving Jews of the Warsaw ghetto were deported from Vittel to Drancy and from there to Auschwitz.

When our hotel was surrounded on April 18 by the Germans, we were engulfed in a sea of panic. We who had come from the hell in Poland knew well what this meant. Many committed or attempted suicide: Mrs. Tamara Shorr; Joel Bauminger and his wife; Dr. Natan Ek; Guta Eisenzweig; Wladyslaw Natanson; the painter, Tadeusz Rozanykwiat; the daughter of Professor Shorr, Dr. Felicja Kohn; Dr. Fakler and others. Mrs. Shorr and Joel Bauminger and his wife died after swallowing poison.

Four of us, amidst this panic, hid in an oven in the basement of the hotel, where the Passover matzos were baked. We remained there for 24 hours. Next day, we were found, half-choked and unconscious. Guta Eisenzweig, who had drunk a whole bottle of poison, was taken to the hospital in critical condition and the doctors gave her up, but she recovered after two weeks. The Germans, this time, allowed the sick to stay while they deported all the others.

But one month later, on May 16, 1944, they carried out a second deportation. This time they also took the sick with the exception of those who weren't "transport-fähig." The French doctors in the hospital, especially Dr. Figach, Dr. Manthit, Dr. Levi and Dr. Marc Andrien Weil, pleaded with the Germans to allow at least a few of the sick to remain — Mrs. Felicja Kohn, who broke a rib after jumping from a window on the fourth floor, Miss Guta Eisenzweig, and I, remained.

And so I was once again saved, at least for the moment.

I remained over three months in the hospital and recovered against my will. I tried to eat little — I didn't eat anything cooked in the non-kosher kitchen — but I slowly grew better. It was clear that we couldn't remain in the hospital any longer and that we would be taken away with the next deportation. I began hiding in the camp in empty rooms or in hotels which the internees had left. Sometimes I was hidden by interned Christians or Jews born in England. Among other places, I hid in the rooms of Mrs. Miriam Kastel-Novitch; Madame Skipvitz (an English writer); Mr. Salomon (an Iranian Jew); and Mrs. White. We spent each night somewhere else.

In the meantime, we received news from the Va'ad Hatzala in New York that our passports had been recognized by the South American countries. The German commandant of our camp officially announced that the remaining internees would not be deported. But we no longer trusted the Germans. We kept hiding during the night in various places, for the deportations usually took place in the early morning.

At the same time, I contacted the Maquis, the French underground and we received Aryan identity cards. I planned to escape together with a few other Jews to Switzerland. We had already written to Switzerland for a guide to help us safely cross the border. Madame Miriam Kastel-Novitch gave me a pair of shears to cut the barbed wire. Together with Guta Eisenzweig, we cut the fence in several places, and were now waiting for news from Switzerland. (Several interned British officers escaped through the cut fences.) In the meantime, the Allied armies landed, the front was approaching and the borders with Switzerland were strongly guarded on both sides.

On the night of September 1, 1944, exactly five years after the outbreak of the war, the Germans abandoned Vittel. Several days later the Americans came and — miracle of miracles — I was alive and free. Saturday morning I quickly ran to the *shul*, which had been opened the day before, and recited the *Gomel* prayer.

But I said no *"shehekhiunu,"* because *"shehekhiunu"* is plural and means, "You have given us life," but I couldn't say "us," because I remained alone, alone without my family, my friends, without the community with which I had been so closely tied throughout my entire life.

MIRIAM NOVITCH

Miriam Novitch was born in Poland and emigrated before the war to France, where she was married to the painter Kastel. She was active in leftist student circles in Paris and after the Germans occupied France, was interned in Vittel.

There she became a close friend of many of the Polish Jewish internees, in particular, Itzhak Katznelson and his son. Thanks to her devotion and courage, she brought help and consolation to the Jewish internees and was instrumental in saving the lives of a few. She also helped Itzhak Katznelson to hide his manuscripts and then smuggle them out from the camp. After the liberation she left for Palestine, where she became co-founder of the Kibbutz of the Ghetto Fighters, which was named after Itzhak Katznelson. Here are excerpts from her account of Vittel (Archives of the Kibbutz of Ghetto Fighters):

127

Right up to the 8th of September, 1943, this small community of South American nationals in Vittel felt that they were already out of danger, although from time to time some doubt would creep into their minds.

Their fears were heightened when rumors reached them that some Warsaw Jews possessing similar passports, who had been interned in Bergen-Belsen, had been deported back to Poland. In order to disarm those Jews in Vittel who were in possession of these South American passports, the authorities decreed that all the internees must give up their documents to the special Commission of Investigation sent from Berlin. Not an eye was closed in the entire camp on the night of the 17th-18th March. . . . On the following day it befell me to witness with my own eyes the typical scene which had been enacted with sickening monotony in the ghetto.

Groups of men, women and babes, surrounded by German soldiers armed with guns and with drawn swords, making their way through the barbed wire fence of the camp to keep their appointment with death. . . . There, trudging along, was Chief Rabbi Rothenberg of Antwerp, with head bowed, his long white beard fluttering in the wind and bearing his bundle upon his stooping shoulder. There, too, were dispatched Rabbi Rappaport, Dr. Goldberg, Alexander Landau with his wife and saintly child. So also, Pinczov and his family who managed to escape from the Warsaw Ghetto, Nathan and Clare Eck with their little daughter, Dr. Fackler, Avramele Wingart, a charming person and great friend of Katznelson, the Zucker family, Nathanson, Shire, Bauminger, Gehorsam, the Ticzman sisters, Hillel Seidman, the journalist, and many others. There I stood by the barbed wire fence as if nailed to the ground, weeping tears of utter despair, as I watched Katznelson and his son moving further and further away. . . .

On the following day, another ghetto scene was enacted! The deserted rooms of the Hotel, the forlorn playthings and toys of the children, pieces of bread, plates, bowls, and old clothes! In the deserted room of the poet I found an old map of the Russian front. I took it away as a souvenir.

It was many days before we could make any contact with those people, who were now imprisoned in the Hotel Beau Site, a kilometer away from the camp. Some time later special passes were issued to allow them to stroll in the park. Katznelson resumed Hebrew lessons and talks on Hebrew culture. We were a class of three, two young Halutzim — Avraham Shlomo from Antwerp, Yitzhak Yacobovski from Brussels — and myself. The final tragedy, however, was soon to come.

Our final meeting with the poet was on Sunday, the 16th of April. He read Bialik's poem, "The Slaughter," and two of his own, explaining them as he went along. Thereafter, I accom-

128

panied him, as usual, to the gate that led to the Hotel Beausite and returned to my room without suspecting anything amiss.

Early on Monday, the 17th of April, our two companions, Shlomo and Yacobovski, who were deeply attached to Katznelson, came and told me that the Hotel Beau Site was surrounded by the SS, that the park was closed and all communication with the internees in that Hotel was forbidden. The Camp Commandant and chief of "Abwehr" in Vittel announced that the group of Jews would be transferred to some unknown destination. Many attempted suicide and some actually made their escape from the claws of the Nazi beast in this way.

On the 18th of April, one hundred and seventy-three people, amongst whom were Katznelson and his son Zvi, were sent to Drancy which served as a concentration camp for French Jews prior to their dispatch to the East.

Early in May, 1944, a group of Jews from Eretz Israel arrived in Vittel from Drancy. They reported that Polish Jews possessing South American passports were regarded by the Germans as stateless and sent from Drancy on the 29th April, 1944, to the furnaces of Auschwitz. The poet had sent his greetings to me together with a photograph of himself and his son taken while they were still in the Warsaw Ghetto. They said that he was in good spirits, and that immediately upon his arrival at Drancy he had instituted Hebrew classes for the children. He conversed freely with the other Jews in the camp and told them everything about the horrors of Poland. At dawn on the 29th April, ten days after their arrival at Drancy, Katzenelson and his son, together with a group of about sixty Jews, were surrounded by a German squad and directed to a reserved cattle truck. They were bound for the same final journey that millions of Polish Jews, including the poet's wife and two sons had made before them. Yitzhak Katzenelson drank to the dregs the cup of bitterness, like the rest of his people.

* * *

Madam [Miriam] Novitch further relates how they hid "The Song of the Murdered Jewish Nation." After much deliberation they decided to hide it in the grounds of the park. "The poet placed the writings in three small bottles. I produced a knife and a small cinder rake. We chose a pine tree that had a cleft in it — actually the sixth in a row of pines, near the football field. Katznelson stood guard while I dug up the ground, but as soon as anyone appeared he signalled to me, whereupon I would throw my coat over the hole that I had made and we both seated ourselves and pretended to be reading the newspaper. In this way I was able to hide the bottles deep in the ground beneath the roots of the pine tree. After I had heaped soil over the roots, I scattered some dry leaves over the top. Little did I conceive that the day would come when I would be the one to unearth the treasure."

Mrs. Novitch managed to get the writings of the poet along with his diary smuggled out of the camp and brought them to Palestine.

In 1980, the Kibbutz of the Ghetto Fighters published Katznelson's "The Song of the Murdered Jewish People" in an edition including the photos of the original manuscript with an English translation and annotations by Noah H. Rosenbloom. We reprint here the first and last stanzas of the poem:

> Sing! Take your light, hollow harp in hand,
> Strike hard with your fingers, like pain filled hearts
> On its thin chords. Sing the last song,
> Sing of the last Jews on Europe's soil.
>
>   *   *   *
>
> Woe is unto me, nobody is left . . . there was a people and it is no more. There was a people and it is gone . . .
> What a tale. It began in the Bible and lasted till now . . .
>   A very sad tale.
> A tale that began with Amalek and concluded with the far-crueller Germans . . .
> O distant sky, wide earth, vast seas. Do not crush and don't destroy the wicked. Let them destroy themselves!

YITZHAK KATZNELSON (KATZENELSON)

One of the internees in Vittel was the great Yiddish and Hebrew poet, Yitzhak Katzenelson (later deported to Auschwitz, where he died). Katzenelson, who was born in Minsk in 1886, was a leading modern Hebrew educator and a prolific and versatile, bilingual poet and playwright. He was an active Zionist and had visited Palestine several times, where his brother, Abraham, had helped found the Kibbutz Shuaim, near Herzlia. Katzenelson had visited Palestine shortly before the outbreak of the war, and returned first to Lodz and then to Warsaw, where he joined his wife and their three young sons, Zvi, Ben Zion and Benjamin.

In the ghetto, Katzenelson belonged to the category of the so-called "unproductive" elements, who were among the first to be deported. Luckily, Katzenelson was provided by friends with an Ausweis, an official identity card, indicating that he had been employed in a German factory in the ghetto. On August 14, 1942, his wife, Hanna, and their two young sons, Ben Zion and Benjamin, were deported to Treblinka. This disaster crushed Katzenelson completely and his sole consolation remained his oldest son, Zvi.

The great ghetto uprising erupted on Passover Eve, April 19, 1943. Despite his eagerness, Katzenelson was 57 years old and could hardly be a military asset. He and his son, Zvi, were therefore smuggled out of the ghetto to the "Aryan" side prior to the outbreak of the revolt. They lived in hiding in the same underground bunker with Emanuel Ringelblum and 35 other Jews on Grojecka Street, in the suburb of Ochota. He stayed there with his son three weeks.

Soon, however, an opportunity presented itself which rekindled a faint glimmer of hope in the heart of a few of the survivors including Katzenelson: The Hotel Polski Affair. Katzenelson and his son were provided by their friends with Honduras documents and in May, 1943, were despatched with the first transport to Vittel.

Upon his arrival at Vittel, Katzenelson and Zvi were given a small private room with the barest furnishings and were also provided with food, elementary comforts he had not enjoyed for a long time. There was no harassment and, most significantly, there was the glimmer of hope that he and his son might be exchanged for Germans held in Allied prisons. Nevertheless, as evident from the first entry in the *Vittel Diary* of the first day, he was extremely distraught and agitated. The sight of barbed wire evoked in him painful memories, despite the obvious fact that it was far less foreboding than the tall massive walls of the Warsaw ghetto. Minor incidents became major sources of irritation. Zvi's smoking, calmness, sleep, the garrulity and normal curiosity of some young Jewish girl internees provoked him to inordinate outbursts of anger. The girls' make-up repelled him, and he thought them to be "painted like whores," their Polish speech grated on his ears and the sound of a violin caused him to explode: "If the murderers of my wife and sons will not kill me, this violin will."

Katzenelson wrote in his diary on May 22, 1943:

131

My son Zvi and I are now in Vittel. We came with a small group of Jews, all of whom were nationals of different northern countries of South America. Zvi and I are nationals of Honduras. We were sixty in number, men and women, and all of us had left Warsaw together. We were brought into a spacious hall in the Hotel Providence, and after we had been directed to one side of the room, our bags and pockets were searched. They asked our names, place of birth and where we had lived until now. They enquired about my wife and sons, who were not with me. I told them that they were dead. . . . Actually, I do not know for certain whether they are dead — Yes, they died! . . . Shall I tell them that the mother and my two sons were taken away to a place from which they never returned? These interrogators are Germans, on the lookout for Jews who spread "Atrocity Propaganda." We arrived today and I have not yet been outside, nor have I even made any attempt to do so. My son did venture out but came back. It is really impossible to go out today, and we shall also remain in our room all day tomorrow because another group is expected to arrive here from Warsaw. I looked out of the window and saw a barbed-wire fence all along the length of the opposite pavement. Beyond this stood the blocks of buildings which housed many of our brothers and sisters. Although I have come from Warsaw, this fence creates a painful impression. A similar fence is being erected by local labor along the pavement and houses on our side.

A crowd of young girls, mostly Jewesses, peered out of the windows on the opposite side. As soon as they saw that we were new arrivals, they stormed out and bombarded us with endless questions. They whistled and yelled raucously; so much so, that we could not make out what they said. They spoke a coarse Polish. It was the language of a country to which they would never return. Their people are no longer there and their homes are burned to the ground. Not a single one spoke Yiddish or Hebrew. These few remaining girls were painted like prostitutes. The rouge, like their voices, spoke a language of its own. Both were quite unnatural. They spoke a Polish that Poles despise. Had these women, peering out of the window, not yelled so much, the mere sight of them would have caused me to burst into tears. I am indeed depressed, but my feeling of revulsion exceeds my depression which at this moment reaches down to my very soul. At first, I could not understand the presence of this "women's enclosure." Where are the men? I have just been informed that the men have been sent to a "labor" concentration camp. Perhaps by way of punishment? Some are of the opinion that it is not true that our status vis à vis the different governments is not yet clarified. Henceforth, we, prisoners in Germany, will be treated as German prisoners would be treated in the Land of Israel. The men who have been sent to labor camps in Compiègne and Titmoning will shortly return. I have heard that the interested parties have come to some understanding on this issue. I arrived here today without my wife and my two dear sons. The world around me here, without them, is dark and dreary. If only Hannah were with me here! Oh, if only Benzikel and Binyamin were here! Together we would bemoan the destruction and annihilation of the whole of our people. Here in this tiny room in Vittel we would all wring our hands at this calamity. Alone, I cannot do this! It is my first day here and I am afraid that my loneliness will drive me mad. The presence here of just Zvi alone does not suffice.

In this great catastrophe, I need all four of them. During these last ten months I have not had such a roomy apartment, nor such a bed to sleep on, yet I am conscious of an oppression much greater than any I experienced before.

How I envy some of my companions who have rooms which face a quiet court. These wretched women jabber with their mouths and hands. One of them has a husky violin and she keeps strumming away on it! Oh my God! My God! What is to become of me! If those who murdered my wife and two sons will not kill me, this violin will definitely finish me off."

* * *

Katzenelson himself seemed to have realized the paradoxicality of his mood. "During these last ten months I have not had such a roomy apartment, nor such a bed to sleep in, yet I am conscious of an oppression much greater than ever before." However, his reaction, in the context of his experiences, was not strange at all. Living in the abysmal conditions of the ghetto, in a perpetual state of tension, in constant danger for his life, struggling to survive, tormented by hunger, thirst, sleeplessness he had no chance to think and reflect. The sudden fortuitous change in the new surroundings which seemed to give him a new lease on life presented him with leisure and concomitant opportunity to recollect, ponder and brood. It seems as if all the pent-up fears, anxieties, suppressed traumas, and sufferings suddenly surged and surfaced to his conscious mind. The lid of his mental pressure . . . so tightly held by the extraordinary conditions, under which he lived in Warsaw, suddenly sprang open in Vittel, overwhelming him with his own agonizing memories. . . .

On October 3, 1943, two days after Rosh Hashanah, Katzenelson began to write his most famous poem, "The Song of the Murdered Jewish People," which he completed three and a half

133

months later, on January 18, 1944. This poem, which became the jeremiad of the Holocaust, Katzenelson dedicated to the memory of his wife and his brother, Berl.

Exactly two months after completing his poem, "The Song of the Murdered Jewish People," Katzenelson and his son Zvi, together with other internees, were removed from Vittel to the transit camp at Drancy near Paris. After a brief stay there they were deported with other Polish Jews, who had Latin American passports, to Auschwitz.

Most agonizing and ironic is the fact that two weeks after Katzenelson was deported from Vittel, on May 31, 1944, the German authorities recognized the validity of the passports he and his fellow internees possessed. Similarly regrettable is the fact that Katzenelson was granted a certificate by the British Mandatory Government to emigrate to Palestine but the German authorities or camp commander refused to inform him or recognize it. Thus, in spite of all efforts by his friends in Europe and in Palestine, Katzenelson was destined to share the cruel fate of his people.

A short time before his deportation, Katzenelson succeeded in concealing his Vittel manuscripts with the help of another internee, Miriam Novitch, who survived.

Transport Lists
Jewish-Polish Internees in Vittel

On August 1, 1944, the office of the American Joint Distribution Committee in Lisbon, Portugal, sent the following letter to the Joint in New York:

American Joint Distribution Committee
242 Rua Aurea
Lisbon, Portugal

August 1, 1944

To: AJDC, New York

For your records and information we enclose herewith a copy of a list of names we received of internees in Vittel, France, as of July 10, 1944. You will note that those persons whose names are followed by the numbers "1" or "2" were deported. Should we receive any additional information, however, we shall let you know.

Robert Pilpel

On December 18, 1944, the same Lisbon office wrote another letter to the AJDC in New York, this time including the list of names.

American Joint Distribution Committee
242 Rua Aurea
Lisbon, Portugal

To: AJDC, New York

Re: Deportees from Vittel

For your information and records we wish to advise you that on October 10, 1944, the British Embassy in Madrid sent a note to the Spanish Ministry of Foreign Affairs concerning certain Jewish internees, holders of Latin-American passports, who were formerly interned in Vittel and who were deported in April and May to an unknown destination.

The note pointed out to the Ministry that the persons referred to were eligible for exchange under the auspices of the International Red Cross and that they should, therefore, be interned in one of the exchange camps under the inspection of the International Red Cross to await exchange. Special reference was made in the note to Rabbi M. Rotenberg, the former religious head of the Jewish Community in Antwerp.

The note requested that the Spanish Foreign Ministry bring these facts to the attention of the German Government. Attached to the note was a list of the people who were deported from Vittel in April and May. We enclose a copy of these lists.

The following persons were deported in the first transport:
FIRST TRANSPORT
Paraguay

Bauminger	Leon	Blumenkopf.....	Wolf
	Lea		Helene
Berglas	Chaim Leib		Krystina
	Rita Hinda	Blumenkopf.....	Chaya
Blumenkopf.....	Aron		
	Rywka	Blumenkopf.....	Yuda Leib
	Rozia		Stella

Frankel ....Yosef	Rapaport ....Israel Rywen
Perla	Dvorka Malka
Mathilda	Jacob Binem
Doris	Rapaport ....Szapsa
Frankel ....Alexander	Gitla
Yochwed	Matla
Ruth	Estera
Perla	Rapaport ....Simon
Leib	Rywka
Pinkus	Rapaport ....Jacob
Frankel ....Mendel	Annie
Goldberg ....Henryk	Rapaport ....Rosa
Malka	Sabina
Koller ....Frederick	Rapaport ....Saul
Halina	Mina
Landau ....Leib Alexander	Josef
Jerzy	Rottenberg ....Marcus
Poznanski ....Yacob	Sara
Mariem	Naftali
Rapaport ....Aron	Rottenberg ....Rosa
Rywka	Naftali
Rapaport ....Aron	Lasar
Rapaport ....Genia	Herman
Rywka	Wolf
Mozes	Rottenberg ....Szila
Rapaport ....Szapsa	Estera
Malka	Naftali
Rywka	Natan
Bela	Franz
Perla	Weingart ....Abraham
David	Mathilda
Rapaport ....Wolf	Rosi
Pola	
Miriam	Wolf.................Sami
Israel	Rosa Ruchla
Moses	Zygmunt
Rapaport ....Symcha	Leon
Golda	Erna
Israel	Wolman ....Henryk
Moses	Chaja Hena

136

Zieber ....Josef
            Frymeta
            Henryk
            Frajala

Guatemala
Osiek ....Sara

Ecuador
Fleischer ....Estera
Wentland ....Malka
Wentland ....Judith
            Noemi
            Adam
            Krystyna
Tylber ....Rosalia
            Salomea
Micmar ....Estera
            Jerzy
Haiti
Muszynski ....Leon

Venezuela
Malcowsky ....Saul
Malcowsky ....Sara
            Maurice

Chile
Frumkin ....Anna
            Hermina Rosa
Gorlin ....Eugenie

Costa Rica
Lichtman ....Oskar
            Anna Rosalia
            Regina
Mandelbaum ....Sylvia Helena
Rosshandler .....Henryk

            Charlotte

Wetstejn ....Mieczysław
            Stella
Schein ....Izaak

Nicaragua
Pasowoder ....Boris
            Cypa
            Aleander
            Miriem
Trucht ....Amalia

Honduras
Horenstein ....Abraham
            Estera Sara
Kacenelson ....Itzchok
            Zwi
Brinman ....Marie
            Yetty
            Erica
            Helena
Schonberg ....Ella
Schonberg ....Samuel
            Estera
            Bella
            Jerzy

Peru
Ajzenstadt ....Felix
            Rouana
            Marcel
Dudelzak ....Szulin
            Tyszla
            Jerzy
Dudelzak ....Rachmil
            Rachela
            Ital
            Arcadius
Garsinski ....Enrico
            Helena

137

Goldstein..........Nachman
　　　　　Sara
　　　　　Lea
　　　　　Szyja
Zemsz...............Leon
　　　　　Cecylia
　　　　　Blanca

SECOND TRANSPORT
Paraguay
Bauminger ....Kalman
　　　　　Marta
Blumenkopf.....Nuchim
Eck...................Natan
　　　　　Clara
　　　　　Raja
Frankel.............Rosa
Gehorsam........Abraham
Geller...............Konrad
　　　　　Stella
Landau.............Bronislawa
　　　　　Estera
Poznanski........Yenta
Rozanykwiat.....Tadek
　　　　　Gerda
　　　　　Richard
Weingart..........Leo
　　　　　Estera
Weinstein........Lea

Costa Rica
Fackler.............Szyja
　　　　　Stefania
　　　　　Henryk
Natanson..........Wladyslaw
　　　　　Stefania
　　　　　Jadwiga
Schein..............Salomon
Zucker..............Salomon
　　　　　Regina
　　　　　Bernard

138

Schapu..............Samson

Honduras
Kadysz..............Iccu
　　　　　Rachmil
　　　　　Aviva
Krystenfreind...David
　　　　　Ita
　　　　　Szajndla
　　　　　Ruchla
　　　　　Aron
Zurawin............Adam
Skosowski........Cecilia
　　　　　Izidor
　　　　　Lucina
　　　　　Jadwiga
Heyman............Berek
　　　　　Cecilia
　　　　　Sasza
　　　　　Stefania
　　　　　Wladyslawa
　　　　　Lidia

DIED IN THE CAMP
Bauminger.......Yoel
Schorr..............Tamara

SURVIVED
Paraguay
Bretstein..........Bernard
Eisenzweig.......Szyja
　　　　　Gina
　　　　　Gitla Mariem
Gehorsam.........Helene
Geller...............Erna & baby
Joskowicz..........Moszek
　　　　　Chana
　　　　　Alma

Kuropatwa......Yosef	**Costa Rica**
Felicja	Schein...............Eleonora & baby
Richard	Zucker..............Malka
Henryk	Bronislawa
U.S.A.	Schwarzbard.....Chiel
Rapaport.........Aron	Perla
Feiga	Martin
Beila	Suchelow.........Ella
Chuna	Adela
Benny	Branel..............Letty
Hager...............Malka	
Hersz	**Nicaragua**
Lusa	Kon...................Felicja
Netty	Jacek
	Peter
Uruguay	Stefan
Schwarzman.....Zipa	
	Honduras
Panama	Zurawin............Lea & baby
Neuman...........Fanny	Szeinbaum........Lion
Haiti	Sophie
Muszynski........Leon	Szeinbaum........Nehemia
Lily	Cina
	Szeinbaum........Mayer
Bolivia	Szeinbaum........Marian
Spinadel...........Miriem	Szeinbaum........Stefan

It should be noted that not all of the names on the above list are authentic. Many persons belonged to artificially-constructed families and so assumed the names of the owners of the passports or foreign documents under which they were registered. Those owners, in many cases, had long been deceased.[9]

A few of those mentioned, who were sent to Auschwitz with the first and second transport, managed to survive: Dr. Natan Eck escaped from the train when it approached the camp Drancy; his little daughter, Raja, was hidden in the camp by Miriam Novitch; Adam Zurawin jumped from the train not far from Auschwitz. Also, Shulim Dudelzak and Felix Ajzenstadt escaped from Vittel and managed to reach Switzerland.

Chapter Three

BERGEN-BELSEN, BETWEEN HOPE AND PANIC

Bergen-Belsen, called an *Aufenthatslager* (internment camp), was established by the Nazis in 1943; it was in part a prisoner-of-war camp, but was mainly intended for Jews, whom the Germans allegedly intended to exchange for Germans in Allied territories.[10]

The camp was run by the SS and there were three consecutive commanders: Adolf Haas, Siegfried Seidke and Josef Kramer. The Jewish inmates possessed Latin American passports or documents, Palestine certificates, or promises to receive Palestine entry visas.

Between July, 1943, and the end of 1944, over 9,000 Jews from Poland, Greece, Holland, North Africa, France, Yugoslavia, and Hungary passed through that camp. Most of the Polish Jews, holders of Latin American papers, were deported to Auschwitz. Some were exchanged — 301 were sent to Switzerland (165 were detained on the way, and only 136 arrived) and 222 were sent to Palestine. During 1944, conditions worsened, food rations were reduced below minimum, and the treatment of the inmates became more brutal, particularly under the rule of the sadist, Josef Kramer. At the time of the retreat of the German armies, more deportees and prisoners of war were sent to Bergen-Belsen. In December, 1944, the number of inmates had risen to 15,000 and, in March, 1945, it exceeded 41,000. During the last weeks of the war, there was a great influx of new prisoners from the East.[11]

Our account of Bergen-Belsen contains the diaries and reports of witnesses whose personal experiences in the Hotel

Polski were given in the first chapter. They are: Josef Gitler Barski, Mrs. M. Tomkiewicz, Simcha Korngold, Helena Goldberg, Anna Szpiro and also Mrs. Roza Goldberg, who was taken to Bergen-Belsen not from Warsaw but from Lodz.

MIECZYSLAWA TOMKIEWICZ

This section continues Mrs. Tomkiewicz's report and tells how she was taken together with her five-year-old boy to Bergen-Belsen from the Hotel Polski in the third transport.

... We were travelling. At the last moment, the Germans who were standing in front of the trucks added Ania to the list. She was my neighbor from Leszno Street, and had managed to come from the work group Ostbahn. Our open-topped trucks drove through the streets of Warsaw. People stood and gaped. "Jews are being taken to die. Look how they're dressed! Where have so many of them come from?" I was a little moved, because we were leaving, and cried a little, in a womanly fashion.

The train was waiting on a railway siding somewhere on the outskirts of the city — second and third class passenger cars. Well, that was a relief. People were gaining courage. The Germans arranged us in the cars, eight people to a compartment. And we waited. They counted us several times, checked some suitcases, explained and reassured. The ever-precise Germans. We waited. Various great ideas came into my head on how to recover my things, but, naturally, I didn't move. After all, I'd lost so much already that these two suitcases of Bobush would simply be an addition to the list.

During that last year of deportation I had learned to hold things in contempt, to treat them like an unnecessary load which hampers any movement, hindering and entangling those who are in love with things. I had seen so many things in empty apartments, to which the owners would never return. So many things had I seen lying in the street not tempting anyone. So many things. I had thrown down from my balcony the most expensive porcelain and cobaltware, and had broken valuable crystals with a stick. In that period I had lost all respect for material things.

My brother Stasio lay on the grass outside the train, flirting

141

with young ladies. He exchanged a roll for a cigarette. For the first time since his two months in a cramped hideout on the Aryan side, he gladly inhaled fresh air and freedom. He talked very loudly as a contrast to those two months of subdued life. Before the train left, Adam and Lolek distributed food parcels, as well as candies for the children, with nobility and fine manners.

At 6:30 the train began to move, carrying nearly a thousand people. The journey was uneventful. We talked. Everyone spoke about himself. The other would pretend to sympathize and then soon began to tell his own stories, adventures and misfortunes, the history of his miraculous escapes thanks to his inborn talents or courage. At the stations we tried to get drinking water and talked to railway men. Some of the people started up their tricks. Two such people pretended to represent the *ausländer* train and exchanged thousands of Polish zlotys for German marks. This way our money completely lost its value, for we had no more chance to exchange it. But this was unimportant.

What was important was that we were passing German towns which hadn't been damaged, where life was settled and absolutely normal. And yet I had expected destruction, for the rumor existed that the war would end in a few months.

In the next compartment an elderly woman was complaining in a tearful voice that she had let herself be drawn into this trap — why had no one dissuaded her from taking that mad step? When the other passengers delicately suggested that if she wished to continue croaking of that sort she should go elsewhere, she replied with pathos, while chewing on a sausage, that she should have had the right to say farewell to her dearest ones before her death. That tragi-comic scene illustrated the mood of the majority of the travellers. And no wonder. Most had no documents or were in possession of doubtful "promessas" under false names. Most had been dragged from their hiding places on the Aryan side by German collaborators, and pushed into that train which was hurrying to an unknown destination — everyone felt uncertain. And we'd all had enough experiences of that kind.

As for myself, I thought little of these important problems, faithful to the principle that "it will work itself out." Besides, I had already seen how little one could achieve in a life which is

142

controlled by the most bizarre forces, by accidents, without our knowing how and why. Our train passed green meadows and wheat-covered fields. I recalled how during all my years in the ghetto I had been longing for nature, for space. Now, in my present state of nerves, it didn't impress me. Bobush was gay, pleased with the journey. He played with a small companion and with Jurek, although Jurek, who was a bigger boy of about six, demonstrated aggressive tendencies. "Bobush, don't lean out, Bobush, you'll fall out. Will you eat something, my treasure?" I spoke like any normal mother on the most normal journey to Otwock or Piotrkow.

One night passed in the train, then another, and finally a third. We began to have our first little quarrels. One person couldn't sleep a wink; another took up too much room; another wasn't making an effort to get water. At last, in the middle of the night the train stopped and we were ordered to get out.

The night was pitch black, lit only by the flashlights of the SS men, and the night's silence was broken by their shrill orders. Conversations were whispered among our people. "This is the end. . . . gas chambers . . . We are lost . . . It was your idea. Didn't I tell you it would end like this? . . . Why did you drag me here, you fool?" For the time being the SS ordered the men to separate themselves from the women and children. This was an ominous sign.

"Are you from Lodz? Because at the last moment I would like to be with somebody from my town! Could you give me some courage? I am a terrible coward and you seem to be so brave."

The other woman attempted to comfort her: "Did you say farewell to your husband? I'm glad that my husband died and didn't live for this moment."

I had no time to think of death, for some of my badly wrapped packages kept slipping from my hands and I had to search for one in the darkness while I was losing another one. Bobush moved around my legs. He was sleepy and uncategorically demanded that I give him one of the flashlights of the SS men. I was also terrified, but was ashamed to admit this to myself.

The Germans counted us over and over again. They ordered us to stand in rows of five, then without the children, and then again with the children. They couldn't stop counting. Our restless company seemed to double and triple in the officers' eyes.

Their flashlights glared. Women kissed their children, some cried softly, afraid of the Germans; some even began to quarrel. "Can't you stand still? You're bringing misfortune on everybody. It isn't fair!"

"Quiet! Line up! These are real cattle, not people."

It was generally quiet. We changed from one row of five people to another and we moved around, we sent our children with "last instructions" to relatives and friends who stood further up. There was an atmosphere of great uncertainty and suspense. Every few minutes we were lit up by a blinding blaze of light.

The men had already left. At least the officers finished counting, or perhaps gave up, and ordered us to board a number of tarpaulin-covered trucks which stood in a row. "This is what they did in Treblinka," a woman said to the crying, cowardly woman. Inside the trucks it was pitch black, terribly stuffy and uncomfortable. The children whispered and their mothers, themselves terrified, tried to calm them. Suddenly a loud, fearful voice came from the back of the truck: "Say good-bye for me to Zygmunt — I've had enough." Everyone was involved with her own thoughts, and no one paid attention to these strange words. But later, when we were ordered to leave the trucks it appeared that one of the women was dead — she was a young nurse from Lublin who had poisoned herself with cyanide. She couldn't stand it anymore — her nerves had given out only a few minutes before our situation was resolved. As soon as we jumped down from the truck we were welcomed by loud, cheerful voices of people who called out names and reassured us.

In the meantime, we remained in the middle of a large square which was full of bundles and suitcases, pelted by a sharp irritating rain. I wrapped Bobush in a dirty, abandoned blanket. There was no sign of Stasio. I was worried about our food parcel which he was carrying, because we had been warned that there was little food and that people stole.

We learned that we were in a camp, one with many barracks where the people were treated well and were fed from foreign parcels, and that we should in the near future be sent out on the *Austausch* (exchange). Maybe in a few days or weeks ... All right, but in the meantime we were very sleepy.

"Who is in charge? Who should I approach? The child is terribly tired."

"Go over there, to that gang; the commandant is a young guy, a kapo and Gestapo man called Włodawski."

This Włodawski was always surrounded by a few shady characters who shared a common trait: they all stole, doing all they could to radically reduce the already small food rations. It would be pointless to complain to the camp leaders. One had to rely on oneself.

All this was told me as I sat in the darkness in the rain, and it hardly penetrated my consciousness. I was only concerned that Bobush not catch a cold. But this admonition that I help myself evoked in me a sudden determination to act, and I set out on an exploring mission around the camp.

After coming upon the barbed wire fence a few times, and tripping on the uneven ground several times, I discovered a barrack in which some of the newcomers had already arranged themselves and lay down on straw spread on the floor. It wasn't very comfortable, but I managed to fall asleep; as for the child, he slept as if in his own white little bed.

The first news that reached me the next morning was that Stasio had been robbed, his food parcel stolen. I was savagely angry, but also had the satisfaction that I had foreseen that sad possibility. Besides, I was now rid of a worry: I was no longer obliged to worry about being robbed!

That morning, despite that tragic event, and after the gloomy night, was bright and sunny. I had never before seen so many barracks. They were made of wood and painted green. In each building stood rows of bunks with gray military blankets and straw mattresses.

Social Life

Many women wore dresses of silk and velvet. There were of course others who were not so elegantly dressed, but I was struck by the sight of these women who against the background of a harsh camp in Germany looked so chic. It made me upset, for I realized that I had nothing to wear — but such is life: people are more impressed by velvet and silk than they are by plain cretonne and cotton.

I met a woman who had lived in the same house with me before the war. She took me into her barracks and presented me

145

to the commandant. Her name was Rubin and she was a lawyer. She immediately gave me a bunk because we were of the same profession. This was a great favor, since most of our transport slept for the next few weeks on the floor. My ex-neighbor of pre-war times treated me to a piece of sausage. I was so moved that I began to cry. I felt ashamed at how tears at that time came to me so easily. I felt like a sponge filled with tears, which overflowed at the slightest touch.

As soon as I put my huge pillow encased in blue crepe-satin on the bunk, I felt at home. I arranged all my bags and handbags in the corners of that single bunk (which I of course shared with the child) and then had a pleasant chat with the neighbor from "upstairs." She admonished me not to be angry if I found some of her belongings on my bed and that I shouldn't let my child awaken her in the morning, and also that I should empty the pot immediately after arising.

Then I went for a stroll across the grounds. Of all the arrangements, I was most impressed by the latrines. Those collective toilets were for a long time a source of amusement to me as I sat there in the presence of dozens of others. I always had a proud impression that I was some heroine of Remarque or Barbusse. Besides, all the gossip and all transactions took place there. However, the common washroom made me feel at first ill-at-ease — but I grew quickly accustomed even to this. The distribution of food, which was the climax of the day, originally didn't impress me to the same degree that it did later, for the simple reason that I was rarely present when it occurred.

As for the social life in the camp, it blossomed and prospered, as in the good old days from before the war. I too had a lot of acquaintances — Piotr's friends and neighbors from the ghetto — and I ran all day from barrack to barrack or else from bunk to bunk. They deplored Piotr's fate and shook their heads — terrible, unbelievable. But, although it may sound unethical and not very nice, this listening all day to praises for the past and seeing so many acquaintances alive with their families, didn't put me in an especially good mood. Additionally — when I looked around at who comprised the society of the camp, and realized who had saved himself and who survived, my mood became even gloomier. Beneath well-known family names were often hidden renowned and less-renowned Gestapo collaborators, scoundrels and hooligans with lots of money and few scruples. But there were also ghetto-fighters, and many who belonged to the intelligentsia and who were mostly silent and depressed, feeling lost in that noisy crowd.

Everyone without exception went through horrible times and developed a primitive attitude to solving various problems: rough, pitiless and selfish. They defended themselves with tooth and nail and saw nothing beyond their own existence. With the preservation of their own lives as their guiding star, they trampled everyone who would stand in their way and allow himself to get trampled.

These traits became more pronounced as our stay in the camp lengthened and our condition worsened.

But this reflects the inner aspect of life in the camp, which I didn't grasp for some time. On the surface life was colorful, calm — almost gay. There were many beautiful and beautifully dressed women, and a good deal of flirting. There were musicians, singers and dancers. There were lectures on painting, literature, architecture and Biblical subjects. All these undertakings were equally successful: crowds attended both the lectures on Nietzsche's philosophy and dance recitals of *Miss Mann*, a well-known Gestapo collaborator. I must admit that, in view of our general condition, I was much impressed by this Jewish interest in scientific and cultural matters. Jews like to study, always and everywhere. Besides, they didn't want to think — they wanted to forget.

Since the Germans were so liberal, our commandant, Włodawski approached them with a request for permission to set up a tennis court. He also requested that a piano be provided, because the accordion we had couldn't express the properly subtle musical nuances. We needed it absolutely! And why not? Are we or are we not *Ausländers*? The tennis court, though, was especially important because Włodawski's wife, a Gestapo collaborator, owned a pair of tennis shoes which she wanted to show off in the proper circumstances. It was as simple as that.

Food and Trading

Our daily food ration consisted of cabbage, turnip or beetroot soup, thirty decagrams of black bread and one decagram of butter, as well as a weekly spoonful of marmalade. Little children who belonged to that category later to become famous: "up to six years" — received half a liter of hard-to-get groats with some milk substitute. Bread was measured out with a centimeter tape. Most people had some spare food — there was still no hunger.

In the canteen one could buy for Polish zlotys tall bowls of crabs, which some smart women knew how to cook, fry, chop and stuff. One could on occasion buy there as well beer, large straw hats, photograph frames, beads, and other items which may have had some use for natives of Haiti or the Congo but not for false *Ausländers*. But people were buying them simply to spend their worthless zlotys. Some, though, knew how to make use of these items. They used the straw hats as handbags or as sacks to gather branches for fuel.

I too stood on the line to the canteen to buy things which Bobush immediately broke, tore or lost. At first I didn't buy crabs, the sight of which nauseated me. I wasn't yet hungry enough. Later I bitterly regretted having lost such an opportunity. Even at that late hour, when crabs had become a rarity, I neglected even to buy enough bread, which was very stupid of me. I could as well have easily bought clothing for myself and the child, for trade in the camp was blooming.

For the price of bread or cigarettes one could buy the most beautiful clothes, as well as gold, dollars and furs. A kilo of black bread cost thirty dollars or, as they were known, "hard ones." Some of the inmates were so stuffed with dollars that they didn't know what to do with them. They were afraid of being robbed and of searches and, since they were hungry, no food was too expensive for them to buy.

One such millionaire complained to me, "I'm very rich. I have loads of money, and I'm still hungry — I can't stand hunger."

The very idea that one could buy a dress or bracelet for the price of a several-days' fast drove some women crazy. They would pay six portions of bread plus two portions of marmalade. They would sell a portion of salt bacon for a bottle of French perfume or a necklace. They bartered bread for soup, soup for butter. They couldn't eat what food they received — they couldn't resist any temptations. These women were usually the first to succumb to starvation. An acquaintance of mine, Anna, never ate her entire food ration. At last she was so swollen that we didn't think she would survive. But she couldn't behave differently — to the very end she had to have her lipstick, cream, powder, and a new blouse or dress. There wasn't a single person in the camp who in one way or another didn't participate in that craze of trading. Even Stasio one day triumphantly brought chocolate for Bobush, which he had bought with vodka and cigarettes.

The most acute shortage in the camp were shoes. The ground was muddy, and, when dry, gravelly. Our shoes tore like paper. I remember how the commandant of our barrack appealed to those who had stuffed suitcases, "You don't know if you'll be able to use all the shoes hidden in your trunks. Better to give them to those who have nothing to wear."

Mrs. Rubin was right. They didn't have a chance to wear them. That kind, clever Mrs. Rubin. Behind her mask of a smile she hid one of the greatest tragedies in the camp. She worked from morning till late at night in order to forget. She aided everyone with her advice or help, tactfully and with all her heart. She helped in the way that only a person who had suffered so much can do. But sometimes an empty, haggard look in her eyes opened the gate to the world of her sufferings. Sometimes, in the middle of the night, she would talk to her husband whom she had adored, to her two small children, all of whom she had lost during the deportations.

She wasn't the only one who had been deeply wounded. Many of these elegantly dressed and seemingly calm people, playing cards or attending lectures, had lost their closest and dearest. One could often hear subdued sobbing in the middle of the night. Other people spent entire days on their bunks, apathetic, depressed and recalling: "Last year they took away my child. . . . Today would be my husband's birthday. We would go together to a restaurant. I saw him shot. . . . Today is my parents' wedding anniversary, they used to have splendid receptions. . . ." And then to sleep. But the next day, as if everything were fine, again there were laughter, lectures, food distribution and trading. This is how it was — how it had to be. And next to these lonely, broken, empty people were entire families who had miraculously survived, who sat together around a table and celebrated some anniversary or holiday. With all its contradictions, with inhabitants spanning the range from the best to the most evil, from the poor to the rich, from the honest to the criminal, with all its contrasts of fortune and misfortune, joys and sadness, Bergen Belsen was a microcosm of the world, a deformed small cosmos where the extremes were magnified to absurdity. All the differences between human beings which in normal life are blunted by the four walls of personal life, here lay open and exposed. Nothing was hidden. In the course of a week every individual became an open book displaying all his virtues and vices.

Slowly and with great effort I began to adjust to the life of the camp. Above all, I couldn't suppress my sufferings. Earlier, before all this had happened, I was unrestrained in expressing joy and happiness. Now I became unrestrained in pain. Pain was caused often by some insignificant detail, which now assumed an insufferable importance. It weighed upon my conscience that my father had not been buried — he had been religious and had liked "nice funerals." I promised myself that I would arrange a magnificent funeral after the war. My loneliness and longing pressed on my empty heart like a stone.

In the meantime life in the camp went on with its usual monotony. Around six A.M. the barrack commandant and her assistants began shouting, "Please get up! Make your beds, there may be an inspection and they'll take away the marmalade rations." If breakfast consisted merely of coffee, these shouts rarely helped. However, if breakfast included soup, the ladies jumped up quickly to be first on line to get soup and then, by slipping again onto the line, to receive second helpings.

After that we returned to the bunks and began conversing on general themes. In the morning our topics were very prosaic: that some ladies urinated in front of the barrack instead of going to the latrine; others peed on the floor. "That's terrible; unheard of; it's worse than murder . . . These ladies should be taught a lesson." And they listed a long list of punishments which would have horrified everyone even if committed by the cruelest Gestapo man. "Pigs! Insolent criminals!" The violent conversation then took a more concrete turn: how to catch these vile women "in flagranti," who was going to clean up after them, and whether this job should be specially rewarded.

Sometimes this morning conversation centered on more serious matters, like stealing bread. Usually these conversations

150

were interrupted by the appearance of "the man with the cane," whose task it was to see to order. His appearance was greeted with squeals, confusion, swift jumping from the bunks which were hurriedly covered with blankets. The "man with the cane" marked down the name of the nearest victim who, for that offense, was deprived of her marmalade ration.

The day began for me with washing, arranging the bunk, dressing myself and the child, breakfast (if I had some bread left) or waiting for dinner, if I had no bread. Afterwards people lay in the sun either on their blankets or on the sand. The women wore shorts or bathing suits, and the gentlemen wore shorts. Some read books and others learned languages, especially English, since, as Auslanders looking to be exchanged to Palestine or America, we had to know that tongue.

Then came the day's climax: Dinner, with a capital D. Would it be cabbage or turnip soup? With potatoes? Thick or watery? A full liter, or, heaven forbid, less? Will those who give out the soup be careful not to spill the cauldron? One of the kettles had turned over! Catastrophe! How much does soup cost today? Do you know anyone who wants to sell? I heard that X has diarrhea, he won't be able to eat.

In our barrack we sat around a table and the woman on duty carried the bowls around. Other barracks used other systems of distribution since ours facilitated abuse. Each barrack had its own ideas on how to more efficiently portion out the soup. There were always quarrels around the kettle, sometimes accompanied by vulgar insults and even fights. "I always get the more watery portion." "That one got a larger measure." "This whole week I haven't gotten a bit of meat while my neighbor . . ." Since each day a different person was in charge of giving out the soup, everyone was accused of swindling.

After dinner some people went to sleep, or to sew, wash, or visit neighboring barracks and play cards. Cards were played for food or money, sometimes for hundreds of dollars. The "Americans" had brought along fantastic sums of cash and gold. That group was indeed ready to travel overseas; they were sure of themselves and their documents. They believed in their survival and in light of that belief organized their way of life.

The "Palestine list," on the other hand, consisted of "refuse," the most desperate beggars and poor wretches who had taken

151

this route in utter despair for they had no other way. They were popularly known as the "fourth class passengers."

Mondays and Thursdays were food allocation days: butter, jam, bread and sometimes blutwurst or cheese were distributed. On other days "concerts" were arranged, either general or for separate barracks, featuring such camp stars as Miss Mann, Rutowski, or more modest local actors. The performers weren't always of the highest caliber, but they were received with such good will and enthusiasm that they began to believe in their own talent. At any rate, everyone tried to enjoy himself! Romances blossomed and couples multiplied. The guardhouse searchlight beam often disturbed these twosomes, to whom darkness gave the illusion of aloneness. Once the Germans discovered several men in a women's barrack. The men were taken away and the next day were paraded before the entire camp while the Germans ordered everyone to mock them. And there were indeed those who roared with laughter. The names of these perpetrators were written on a blackboard. Among them were a few who had visited their wives, seeing no reason for abstinence.

From time to time some important event took place in the camp, such as the arrival of new people. The first transport came from Warsaw, from the Hotel Polski. These people were even more frightened than we had been, for they had gone through a real hell directly before leaving the hotel. The same guards who had helped us leave arrested all those who remained in the hotel and took them to the Pawiak Prison. There a nightmarish game of "papers" took place. The Jews were divided according to some unknown criteria. After several days of tragic uncertainty the Germans recognized one part of the group as *Ausländers*. The other people were shot in the prison courtyard.

These *Ausländers* came to the camp traumatized, exhausted, as if they had returned from the other world. They brought some news, that the war would soon end; that we, the first transport to Bergen-Belsen, were considered to be dead because no one had received any letters from us, and that we would shortly be leaving. We sighed over the fate of many of our friends who had been murdered in the Pawiak, and returned to our normal daily life. I reflected that had I waited for Bobush's suitcases of clothes he would never have had the opportunity to wear them. So, long live impetuousness!

A second group arrived in the middle of the night. They were brought via Warsaw from the concentration camp in Lublin. These people were mostly families of Gestapo collaborators as well as people who had bought documents belonging to others. (In truth, nobody lost anything by this, for most of the real owners were no longer alive, and others couldn't be reached.) The Gestapo collaborators had full sacks of foreign documents which had arrived too late to save their owners.

The new arrivals told most horrible stories about Lublin, that the people walked barefoot and wore striped paper uniforms, that they were beaten and tortured. I knew that the train in which my family had been taken had gone in the direction of Lublin. I forced myself to ask some of the arrivals if they hadn't seen any of them — my parents, my husband, my sister-in-law. Very often I couldn't tell my own name — I had some inner blocks which I couldn't comprehend. I was ashamed to ask if they had seen my mother or father or husband in the concentration camp barefoot, in stripes, dying from hunger. I was ashamed, or, perhaps, frightened. Maybe I didn't want to imagine such possibilities. I defended myself against them. My mind was teeming with images of my dearest ones in paper clothes, with shaven heads, starving and beaten. Perhaps the Germans had killed them before all that? God, grant that such was the case.

Later came more transports from Bochnia and Lwow, whose people had possessed absolutely genuine documents of American and Palestinian citizenship. That transport brought an enormous quantity of luggage. The people were tremendously sure of themselves. They pretended, even to each other, that everything with them is 100% kosher — which later proved to be false. They looked at us with disdain, pointing out the phoniness of our papers. They believed that they were suffering because of our sins, that because of our swindle in the hotel they were being prevented from going immediately to Palestine, Chile or Guatemala. That group contained many physicians, lawyers and other professionals.

With these new arrivals our number rose to approximately 2,700. Bergen-Belsen, of which we were the first wards, began to take on the look of a miserable barbed wire camp. Next to us, on the other side of the fence, the Germans put a group of Greek Jews. They were thought to be a band of kapos and policemen who as a reward for their services to the Germans had been sent here. They were a handsome, healthy, cheerful and song-filled people. But they were soon taken to work — to build new barracks, to dig trenches, to the kitchen and to the saw mill.

Then came a very large group of Jews from Holland, from the camp in Westerbork. This group consisted of several thousand people with children, baby carriages and luggage. They were cultivated, "better" people, also in possession of foreign documents. They were put together with the Greeks and they too were set to work.

That large Dutch-Greek camp section went through a period of a power struggle. There were two gangs, each of which wanted to grab all the power. It was a man named Albala who finally won and sent his rival to do the dirtiest and heaviest kind of work.

The Greek Albala, with the approval of the Germans, became the ruler of life and death over his people. He robbed them of all their possessions and mistreated them. We learned all this because we saw the people from that camp daily — we talked across the fence and even did some trading.

And so passed July, August, September, October.

Bobush fell very sick with pneumonia and I carried him to the hospital. I had to warm the hospital room with some miraculously-obtained coal and wood, and I became a specialist in tending a small oven. It was ironic when one of the greatest thieves from the Kommandantur once caught Stasio carrying some coal to the hospital and accused him of theft and even wanted to put him on trial. Fortunately people intervened. I won't forget how Stasio worried over that handful of coal which I wanted to use to warm up the hospital. Bobush's sickness used up a lot of my own health and nerves, so frightened was I about the only human being I really loved who still remained from my family.

Before he had completely recovered the Germans announced the date of the so much looked-forward-to departure. But the immediate great wave of enthusiasm subsided considerably when we learned that we would not go directly to Palestine (or Nicaragua or Chile or Guatemala . . .) but for the time being to an allegedly better camp, in Bergau.

The enthusiasm changed, in fact, to depression when we

154

learned that not everyone was going. We began comparing documents, but nothing became clearer, because the Germans separated families who held identically legal papers. We analyzed time and again the investigations which each of us had undergone in the office of the political chief of Bergen-Belsen, Dr. Seidel.

At first it was announced that the first to depart would be the people on the Palestine list, and we had already prepared our bundles and suitcases. I taught Bobush how to walk, for after his sickness he could hardly stand on his little feet. But at the last moment, a few hours before we were to leave, an order arrived delaying the departure of those of us on the Palestine list. I was very glad that I didn't have to drag along the child so soon after such a serious illness. The joy of the others, the American citizens, who believed that in a day or two they would go to Vittel or to the direct exchange didn't penetrate my mind. I didn't believe in my lucky star. I was no longer used to being happy. And it appeared that because of that I avoided the disappointment which became the lot of the others.

About 1,800 people departed. All those whose names weren't on the posted lists sat the entire day next to their luggage on the other side of the gate undergoing formalities and countings. The camp commander, Haas, flirted with the beautiful Hanna and told her how beautifully placed the camp in Bergau was, not far from Dresden, and that the living conditions and food over there were much better than here in Bergen-Belsen.

All those who departed were dressed beautifully: everyone put on the best that he or she had, thinking that the Auslanders should look very chic. Some women wore overcoats with foxes, or minks, and large velvet hats in the fashionable manner of the Aryan side, with gauze stockings and special travelling shoes. They carried pigskin handbags and English plaid blankets thrown across the shoulder.

In the evening the Germans began to load them into the trains — cattle cars with bundles of straw. The cars had small barred windows — not windows, really, but twenty-centimeter openings. They left, and we who remained had a great ball because we received a great portion of soup.

Several weeks later Yanka M., who had remained behind because she was about to give birth, went to the hospital in the neighboring town of Zelle. There she received a very strange postcard from one of those who had left, written several days after he had departed from Bergen-Belsen. Since this man was an Aryan Pole who was married to a Jewish woman with whom he had come to Bergen-Belsen, we guessed that he had jumped from the train. We also deduced other things. Since the postcard was mailed from a railway station close to Auschwitz — but we were afraid to verbalize our deduction even to ourselves. Besides there were in our camp parents whose children had travelled on that train — and people had brothers, sisters, relatives and friends on that train which was supposed to travel to Bergau. We didn't want to poison their lives with unnecessary and after all unconfirmed deductions. We also didn't want to poison our own mood. We didn't know who was going next.

Only two years later did we learn about the fate of the transport to Bergau. The people had been taken directly to Auschwitz.

JOSEF GITLER BARSKI

. . . Our transport, consisting of 625 people, was taken from the Hotel Polski on July 15, 1943. We were brought to the Gdansk railway station and put into passenger cars. On the way, our escorts treated us fairly well. We were told that we were going to Germany, where we would stay in a transfer camp near Hanover until our exchange.

I later learned that the camp, Bergen-Belsen, had originally been planned by the Germans as a camp mainly for Jews in possession of citizenship papers of neutral countries — in particular, of South and Central America. Those Jews interned in Bergen-Belsen who belonged to that category (numbering about 10,000 Jews from occupied Hungary, Poland, Yugoslavia, Holland, Spain and other countries) were to be exchanged for foreign Germans after the necessary negotiations.

During these negotiations, German offices in Poland began to receive citizenship documents from neutral countries, or promises for such citizenship (so-called *promesas*), for a number of Jews. Some of these Jews were kept in the Hotel Royal on Chmielna Street in Warsaw, from which they were taken, in small groups, in January and May of 1943, to a transit camp in Vittel (in occupied France). As a result of the hopes raised by this action, Jewish organizations in Poland began, through various channels, to notify Jewish organizations abroad about the urgent need to send more documents of that form. In the first half of 1943, such papers issued by South and Central American consulates in Switzerland indeed began to arrive in German offices in Poland. But the majority of the Jews in whose names these documents were written had in the meantime shared the fate of many other Jews and had been murdered or deported to the death camps.

It was in this situation that the initiative arose to take advantage of these documents and use them for persons hiding on the "Aryan" side, or for those who had just escaped the burning ghetto. Among those who took part in getting these documents out of German offices, was a certain Lolek Skosowski, who was known for his suspicious contacts with the Nazis. Skosowski bought these citizenship documents or promesas, which kept arriving for no longer existing Jews, from the German offices. He then sold them to representatives of the Jewish Committee of Help (ZKP). The Committee, in turn, handed the documents over to persons who came — usually with their families — to the gathering point for "foreign Jews" in the Hotel Polski. Apart from these holders of American papers were also persons who, finding no additional such citizen documents for them, claimed that they had close relatives in Palestine who had promised to send them so-called Palestine certificates. These were instrumental in their exchange for German citizens interned by the British in Palestine.

Altogether, 2,533 Jews arrived from Poland to Bergen-Belsen between July 7 and October 21, 1943. Most of them, numbering 2,039, were Jews from Warsaw. Shortly after the arrival of the last transport, most of the Polish Jews were deported from the camp. A senior official of the German security office came to the camp and ordered the immediate deportation of 1,800 Polish Jews from Bergen-Belsen. The Jews were told during the roll call that they were being sent, temporarily, to a transfer camp named Bergau, near Dresden. That large transport included among its number the political activists, Nathan Buksbaum and Czerski; Joshua Perle, the Yiddish writer; Grzybowski, the ghetto fighter; daughter of the well known labor leader, Galka Leszczynska; the physicians Dr. Chorazycki, Dr. Przedborski, and Dr. Weintal; and many others. This transport was sent, not to the fictitious Bergau, but to Birkenau-Oświęcim, to the gas chambers.

It became known after the war that the people of that transport began a revolt on arriving at Oświęcim. They threw themselves at the SS men, tearing their weapons out of their hands and tearing down the fences. This was later verified by the commanders of Oświęcim, Rudolf Höss, during his trial.

The large transport called "Bergau" wasn't the last to be sent from Bergen-Belsen to Oswiecim. Another 350 people were later sent, in two smaller groups. Of the more than 2,500 Polish Jews, no more than about 400 survived.

The journey from Warsaw lasted from 9 A.M. until 11 at night. We left the train on a siding track, surrounded by a great number of SS men. Brutally, and with savage shouts, they pushed us away from the women and children with rifle butts. The latter were loaded unto trucks, and the men were all lined up to march. All our illusions vanished. Under the impression that we were being led to a death camp, one of the women swallowed poison and died instantly.

The men's march to the camp, a distance of about twenty kilometers, lasted the entire night. At last we saw the silhouettes of wooden barracks in a dim light. At the sight of the barbed wire fences, towers, and savage faces of the armed SS men, we were overtaken by despair. We didn't know what had happened to our women and children. We were soon chased into the unfurnished barracks. Straw mattresses with dirty blankets were spread on the floor. Beastly tired, we lay on the mattresses in our clothes and covered ourselves with our coats. We had the worst forebodings.

In the morning, we went out and received a surprise — we met acquaintances. It appeared that there were people in the camp who had left Warsaw with the transport of July 7. I met my school friend, Marek Wasserman. He told me that our situation wasn't as tragic as it had appeared the previous evening. There were about 1,000 people in the barracks, the men separated from the women and children.

In the barracks, people slept on bunks stacked one on top of the other. The Germans appointed a certain Paweł Włodawski, the son of a Warsaw dentist, as "leader" of the camp. Paweł had been suspected of collaborating with the Gestapo while in the ghetto.

I walked around the camp. It was an enormous terrain enclosed on all sides by barbed wire. On both sides stood barracks. In the distance was a thick forest. On the other side was a road leading to another field, which, as I later learned, was a camp for Soviet prisoners of war; and, next to it, a camp for Argentine and Spanish Jews. The entire terrain was studded with watch towers manned by SS guards with searchlights who were armed with machine guns.

We spent the first day in the camp settling into the barracks and arranging ourselves. We were told to bring bunks from the depots to the barracks. Everyone tried to place his bunk close to a window in order to have his own "corner" and some light. The Germans allowed us to help our families settle themselves in the women's barracks. The depots supplied us with straw mattresses, a cup, bowls, and spoons. We were informed of the camp rules: 5:30, reveille; 6:00, roll call; breakfast consisted of some ersatz coffee; after this, cleaning and sweeping the barracks and the entire general area. At 12:00 soup. During the day, various types of jobs; in the evening, another roll call and soup or "coffee" for supper. Besides this, we also received 30 dkg of bread each day, and a cube of margarine or marmalade. Although food was scarce and living conditions in the barracks primitive, life at first gave some measure of relaxation after the continuous nervous strain on the Aryan side.

A few days after our arrival, the above-mentioned Paweł, who had been appointed by the Germans as leader of the camp, tried — in obvious collusion with the Germans — to organize a "self-governing committee." He drew up a list of all the social activists in the ghetto and invited them to a meeting in the administration barrack. At that meeting, Paweł declared that all those in the camp would shortly go abroad, but, since the date of departure wasn't as yet fixed, life here must be organized in the interim. He added that he didn't want to take the entire responsibility on his own shoulders, and had therefore called this meeting. He further said that although he had been promised the aid of the German administration, he would like to have the collaboration of the committee of camp inmates. Several of Paweł's "aides" agreed to his proposal, but the group of social activists remained silent.

Paweł once more underscored that he was counting on everyone's cooperation. I quickly consulted my neighbors, the well-known pediatrician, Dr. Przedborski, and Rabinowicz, who had been one of the leaders of Jewish self-help in the Warsaw ghetto. Then I spoke up and said that I saw no need for the formation of such a committee, and would definitely not participate in its workings. After I finished my speech, all the social activists present made similar declarations. Paweł reacted by saying that this attitude would only harm the camp inmates and that he would therefore act alone. Paweł's rule, however, didn't last very long. He was shortly removed by the Germans as a result of a number of thefts carried out by his "associates" among the new camp prisoners.

Following this incident with Paweł, we set out to organize life in the camp illegally. A month after our arrival, in August of 1943, we formed a group of PPR members (communists) which was comprised of myself, Pinchas Mincberg, the engineer Perle (who was in the camp with his father, a well-known writer) and a few others. At the same time, a wider prisoner committee was also formed, which was comprised of Henryk Zamoszkowski and Natan Buksbaum, from the "left" Poalei Zion; Yehoshua Perle, the writer and Rabinowicz of the Bund; the former members of the command of the ZOB (Jewish fighting organization in the Warsaw ghetto): Eliezer Geller; Ari Grzybowski; Helene Sziper, wife of the ghetto fighter Lutek Rotblat; and Mincberg, Perle and Josef Gitler-Barski of the PPR. Later we also added the ghetto fighter, Kanal. Under the initiative of the formal Committee, we developed cultural and self-help activities in the camp.

Despite stern prohibitions, we established contacts with the neighboring camps. In the last stage of the camp's existence, when we heard the first news of the collapse of the German front we formed so-called "militant groups of five" whose task it was to disarm the Germans in case they would, in the last moments before the capitulation, try to murder the prisoners.

We also started a newspaper called *Tramway*, edited by me, Henryk Zamoszkowski, Yozef Rozencwajg, Dr. Bernard

Grynblat, the engineer Solowiejczyk, Maurycy Bojman and a few others. Individuals would write articles which we read aloud to one another — from here it derived its nickname, the "spoken newspaper." It contained news items from German newspapers accompanied by our editorial comments, as well as the contents of lectures delivered by some of our members. The *Tramway* was in existence for the entire period of our internment in Bergen-Belsen, despite the growing hunger, disease, and continuous dangers.

* * *

Gitler-Barski kept a diary while in the camp. Excerpts of a few of the more important sections are presented here:

10.20.1943 The first three months in the camp demanded constant adjustment to the deteriorating conditions. I refused to participate in a camp committee recognized officially by the Germans. Instead, we organized a clandestine group of political activists who hold discussions in the barracks. There are also groups to study foreign languages.

10.21.1943 A sensation — a list was published yesterday of people selected to leave. The list contains 1,800 names. They are to go through a temporary camp, Bergau, near Dresden, before being exchanged. The people were today arranged in rows and led out of the camp. We bid them farewell with mixed feelings.

10.27.1943 Our group has shrunk to 700 people. We were therefore moved to the Greek camp, and the Greek Jews moved to ours. Some of us fear for the fate of those who left. Others envy them.

11.7.1943 We placed a guard before the barrack and I gave a lecture on the 26th anniversary of the October Revolution.

11.14.1943 A woman was brought from Vittel. The Germans carried out selections there of those supposed to be going abroad.

11.16.1943 A representative of the *Auslandstelle* in Berlin has arrived. There is excitement in the camp — we expect decisions to be reached about further transports.

12.30.1943 A group of religious prisoners — 34 of them — is trying to organize a kosher kitchen.

1.6.1944 We discussed with Zamoszkowski the problem of "Social changes in the Jewish population since the outbreak of the war."

1.11.1944 For the first time, there has been an air strike against the camp. There are again rumors of a transport to take place between the fifteenth and twenty-fifth of the month.

1.12.1944 1,150 Jews from Holland have arrived at the neighboring area.

1.26.1944 Several days ago, 286 Greek and Dutch Jews who hadn't the necessary papers from neutral countries were sent to Theresienstadt.

2.3.1944 180 Spanish and 11 Soviet Jews have departed.

2.7.1944 Snow and frost. 200 Spanish Jews have departed.

2.22.1944 63 African Jews have left the camp — they are said to have held English citizenship.

2.24.1944 A group of North African Jews, British citizens, arrive from a camp in Italy.

3.5.1944 Yesterday, one of our inmates, Hollander, was slapped twice in the face because he didn't take his cap off before an SS man.

3.6.1944 Today a group of 7 Soviet Jews left.

3.9.1944 Purim — a children's performance.

3.17.1944 Mrs. Szop has returned from the hospital in Zelle, where she gave birth to a child. She brought back heartening news from the front.

4.1.1944 There is talk of organizing a Passover seder. A list has been made up of all those who would like to receive flour instead of bread and vegetables instead of soup during the holiday.

4.5.1944 There have been repressive punishments as a result of the "affair" of Mrs. Szop. Before going to Zelle, she took a few dozen post cards with her to mail to addresses given her by inmates. While in the Zelle hospital, she even sent a telegram to an "Aryan" daughter of a prisoner from Leipzig. The Germans have investigated the matter. Now they have forbidden the baking of matzot and increased work levels. The religious Jews organized a *seder* in the sick room for the "elite." We didn't take part.

4.8.1944 At 4 P.M., Bergen-Belsen was strafed by American planes.

162

4.15.1944 The children gave a performance on the occasion of the last day of Passover.

4.16.1944 The arrival of a representative of the *Auslandstelle* has brought new anxiety. Some of our people react with fear — others, with hope.

4.26.1944 Another of the *Auslandstelle* has arrived. We expect new transports to go out.

4.27.1944 An unusual event — a German guard in one of the watchtowers lowered a loaf of bread on a string together with a slip of paper in which he expressed, in Polish, his wish for peace.

4.30.1944 We organized six groups to study foreign languages.

5.1.1944 In the evening, we celebrated Mayday.

5.5.1944 Seventy women from Paris and a new transport of seven Hungarian Jews has arrived.

5.9.1944 Eleven people who held British citizenship papers have left the camp — are they going for an exchange to Palestine?

5.14.1944 A general commotion — we may be departing. A special order has been issued: 145 people with American citizenship are to prepare to leave within the next few days.

5.17.1944 The 145 people have left.

5.20.1944 We expect the departure of the other people still in the camp who possess American citizenship papers.

5.23.1944 A special roll call was announced. Those who are to leave have been segregated. The Germans called out the names of 147 people who hold South American documents.

5.24.1944 Today, early in the morning, another group left. Our camp now has 267 people registered to go to Palestine, 44 with U.S. documents, 49 with documents of South American countries, 28 Argentines, and 174 Spanish "nationals."

6.19.1944 Another German commission arrived two days ago.

6.23.1944 About 400 Jews from Yugoslavia have arrived.

6.28.1944 The African Jews have left; 220 Dutch Jews have left for an exchange with Palestine.

7.5.1944 The wife of a French prisoner of war told us that a great number of Jews have been sent from Vittel back to camps in Poland.

8.15.1944 Several thousand Polish women and children have arrived at Bergen-Belsen.

8.18.1944 About 2,500 Polish women and children who recently arrived have been sent back to the trains.

8.23.1944 A group of Hungarian Jews is leaving for the "exchange." They have taken letters from us to mail once they are abroad. This was discovered by the Germans and they deprived us of bread for three days.

9.19.1944 The Germans have made a list of prisoners according to citizenship and promesas. Despite the cold and the hunger, we continue our cultural activities. I gave a lecture entitled "Prison walls."

9.27.1944 Yom Kippur. Last night the religious Jews organized the *Kol Nidre* prayer. Zamoszkowski spoke on the origin of Jewish holidays.

9.30.1944 Dr. Salomon and his daughter cast lots between themselves for their potatoes and sugar — an ugly sight.

10.1.1944 Mrs. Miecia Tomkiewicz has written a beautiful poem, "My Warsaw."

10.15.1944 It is fifteen months since we have arrived at Bergen-Belsen. The camp discipline has been tightened. Haas, the camp commander, walks around carrying a machine gun. Heavy evacuation trucks have arrived in the camp. We don't know whom they have arrived for.

11.7.1944 Our oral *Tramway* issue is devoted to the anniversary of the October Revolution.

11.19.1944 A delegate from Berlin has arrived. Those holding South and Central American papers were registered.

11.19.1944 Further deterioration of the food situation.

12.4.1944 1,200 Jews from Hungary have departed, allegedly to be exchanged in Switzerland. They wrote our names down on their underwear to pass on to the Red Cross.

12.7.1944 A new group of Hungarian Jews has arrived.

12.9.1944 There is rejoicing in the camp. The Germans have given us food parcels which arrived for the Hungarian Jews who already left.

12.10.1944 The first Hanukah candle.

12.13.1944 Seventeen months after our arrival, we are for the first time permitted to send letters. I wrote three cards: to relatives in New York, to the Schneersons in Palestine, and to Dr. Silberschein in Geneva. Will these postcards reach them?

12.20.1944 Goldberg received a postcard from Vittel — this

164

means that the mail has begun functioning.

12.21.1944 Eugeniusz Braude (Wasserkop) died yesterday of starvation.

12.23.1944 Food parcels have arrived from Stockholm for 21 people. Rabbi Szapiro had written down their names in a Pentateuch and taken it with him when he left the camp.

1.4.1945 Dr. Matzner has received a letter from S. Wortman and Solowiejczyk has received a postcard from Dr. Silberschein, both from Geneva.

1.25.1945 A group of prisoners from Auschwitz has arrived.

1.27.1945 There have been more deaths. Several days ago, Mrs. Naftal died, and today, the 76-year-old Jacob Grand from Mexico passed away.

1.31.1945 There is a great commotion. For the first time, the Swiss Red Cross has sent food parcels to the prisoners in our area of the camp.

2.8.1945 The Russian armies are said to be 20 kilometers from Berlin. The total number of people in the entire camp is about 40,000.

2.19.1945 The children ran around shouting joyfully, "The war is over!" They probably heard this from one of the German soldiers. Unbelievable!

2.27.1945 There have been new victims of starvation. Last week, Nachman Degenszajn, 69 years old, died, and today, the lawyer Jozef Rosenzwajg.

3.5.1945 Today the elder Szenker, father of the painter, died.

3.13.1945 Borensztejn, with whom I share a bunker, tried to kill himself with a razor blade.

3.19.1945 A general rejoicing — food parcels have arrived from the Swedish Red Cross.

3.20.1945 Messa has arrived from *Auslandstelle*.

3.27.1945 Borensztejn again tried to commit suicide. In the morning he was found dead lying next to me — he died during the night.

4.7.1945 Our camp is being evacuated. We left with the first group at two in the afternoon, going on foot to the railway station. The weather was beautiful. We saw the free world — roads, forests, pretty little German houses. But we could hardly walk. After some time, I had a tragic parting from my mother, who couldn't walk and returned to the barracks. At eight in the

165

evening, the Germans put us on the trains, in which we met our neighbors from the other camp areas — Spanish, Argentine, Hungarians, Slovaks. The train doesn't move.

4.8.1945 There is still no engine. The Germans say that we'll be taken to Theresienstadt.

4.9.1945 At five in the morning, we left Bergen for Zelle. During the night we underwent an air attack.

4.10.1945 We've arrived at Brokhof, and are moving towards Stendhal. We ate our last crumbs of bread, and after some time, got more food. We passed the station Uelzen. On Saturday, we underwent a six hour air raid.

4.11.1945 We arrived at Stendhal. The town had been bombed the day before. There is no water.

4.12.1945 Since yesterday we've moved only a few kilometers. The train began moving into Magdeburg at 10 o'clock. About 20 kilometers out of Magdeburg, we were shelled by Allied artillery. Peasants from nearby villages approached the train. They said that we were very close to the front. That was at three in the afternoon. At four there was an air raid and continuous shooting from the front. We lay in trenches along the track. At five we returned to the train, which began moving. Our transport consisted of about 2,400 people — of that number were 300 Polish Jews, 400 Argentine and Greek, 100 Slovak and 120 Hungarian Jews. We were guarded by about 50 Germans. At midnight, the Germans threw off their uniforms and offered the prisoners canned meat in exchange for civilian clothes.

4.13.1945 Following a night of noise from the heavy artillery, flashes of searchlights and rockets and the sounds of the approaching front, the morning was peaceful. There was neither artillery shelling nor the roar of airplanes. Suddenly, we saw a group of Germans on bicycles. Each of them was leading a riderless bicycle. Our escort ordered a roll call of all the prisoners with their luggage. We left the cars. We were ordered, "Remain in rows in front of the cars until we return. Whoever leaves the line will be severely punished when we return." The SS men guarding us mounted on the bicycles and left with the others. We waited in line, wondering why they had left no one to guard us. After half an hour, some of us became courageous and began to leave the line and went to the nearest village to look for food. After some time, they returned with potatoes, milk, and other products. It was clear that the Germans had simply escaped before the approaching front. We found a box with the prisoners' documents in the car of the escaped Germans.

At one o'clock in the afternoon, the long awaited hour of liberation arrived. The first Allied soldiers arrived. People cried and embraced. The Americans looked at us, at the living skeletons, in terror. One of the American soldiers, a Jew, was very moved.

Suddenly, a group of German soldiers appeared from the woods, their hands up. They surrendered their arms. Our freed prisoners broke their rifles against telegraph poles.

The Americans were in a hurry. They moved in the direction of the Elbe River. Magdeburg was in flames. They told us to await another detachment that would take care of us. At five in the afternoon, a new American detachment arrived. They arranged for us to stay in the nearest village, Farsleben. From there we were taken in trucks to Hillersleben to await repatriation. Freedom came after exactly 21 months of hunger, disease, and the nightmarish life of Bergen-Belsen.

SIMCHA KORNGOLD

. . . I had all of my "possessions" around me in the train — that is to say, the people I had undertaken to care for. We were altogether, eight. The doors of the cars weren't locked.

We looked at each other. We were free! We were afraid to say a bad word, but everyone sat with a pounding heart. In spite of everything that had happened to us, we weren't sure whether it was all real. We didn't trust the criminals. And so the train moved on. On July 14 at midnight the train stopped. We looked out of the windows — we were in the middle of a forest — surrounded by trees on both sides. We heard a sudden command: "*Aussteigen!*" We began to tremble. Our hearts fluttered. What did this mean? We left the cars. SS men stood on both sides of the tracks, armed with rifles.

A new order: "Women and children separately. Luggage separately." Now we were sure that these were our last moments. Midnight, a forest — we all knew what this meant. We would all be shot

One of the women could no longer stand it, and swallowed

167

poison. She fell dead. Her name was Aronovitch, and she was from Warsaw. Our mood was bleak. They took the dead woman away. Trucks arrived and the women and children were taken away. The luggage was taken in another truck.

Now they ordered us to form rows of five and to march under a heavy guard of SS men. But to our surprise, the SS men behaved in a human way. They didn't rush us. They were polite. They didn't order us to walk faster. And so we slowly marched, nobody knew where to. I walked next to a young Warsaw physician, Landberg, a great pessimist. He tortured me with his pessimism. He said that they would soon shoot us all like dogs, that no one would know where we have vanished. I told him that if that were so, their behavior would be different. But my words didn't change his mind — and so we walked on.

Suddenly, we saw huge, bright searchlights in the distance. We came closer. We were marched into a huge yard lined with barracks. Here we met our women and children and also received our luggage. We also met the people who had left the Hotel Polski in the previous transport of July 7th. We had thought that they were in Switzerland. There was great rejoicing, people embraced and kissed. We asked, "Where are we? What is the name of this place?" They told us, "Bergen-Belsen." And they explained, "Before going to Switzerland, we must pass through this camp." I looked around and saw many acquaintances from Warsaw: Godel Kalikstein of 14 Nalewki Street; Dr. Jelen, the well known physician of the Linat Hatzedek; the writer, Joshua Perle, and Natan Buksbaum; Israel Kanal and Israel Geller, two comrades who had left the ghetto together with me through the sewers which began on Karmelicka Street; a number of well known merchants, such as the Friedman brothers of 26 Gensia St.; and the Szenberg family from Twarda. I also met a number of Jewish traitors who worked for the Gestapo, such as Juzek Szpet and Franka Mannowna, and others whose names I don't remember.

We were about 3,000 Jews from Warsaw and were taken into barracks. Everyone got a bunk. We were brought straw mattresses and military blankets. We were also given food: bread, margarine, marmalade and soup. Everyone could help himself to as much as he wanted. Women and children were in separate barracks. There was no fence, and we could visit each other; and so we spent the first night.

Early in the morning, on July 15th, a command was issued: "Everyone leave their barracks!" We stood on line. The camp commandant delivered a speech. We were being counted to see if, heaven forbid, anyone was missing. The Germans appointed barrack commanders, men and women, who would be responsible for cleanliness. Those who broke the rules would be punished. The discipline was harsh, even for the women and children. Early in the morning, everyone must make his bed, cover it smoothly with a blanket, sweep the barrack, take care of cleanliness. Then a German began counting us again. This was repeated every day — the counting and the attendance lists. At first, there was no shortage of food — the wealthy people didn't eat their soup, for they had brought their own food: canned meat, bread, sausages, and other delicacies. The camp was called Polish Sonder Lager. We didn't work. Legally, we were foreign citizens.

Every day, four to six people of each barrack were appointed to bring the cauldron of soup and the other food. This was to be divided according to the number of people in each group. All this continued until October 21st, 1943.

On that day, a political group of the Gestapo arrived, and they established an office from which they started to check the authenticity of our papers. The Gestapo was well aware of the entire affair.

The leader of the Gestapo was a Nazi murderer, Obersturmführer Seidel. He didn't talk much, but succeeded in piercing everyone with his razor-sharp eyes which caused each of us to shudder. We were called to his office one by one in alphabetical order. He had before him all our papers. When a person entered, he looked at him calmly and then asked in a dry voice for his name, place of birth, and who had sent him the papers. He wrote all this down and ordered the person to leave. He was always accompanied by a huge wolf dog. During the questioning, the dog sat in a corner, waiting for his boss's orders.

The procedure continued for several days. When it came to the Palestine group, nobody had any papers, for we were all included on the Palestine list. There wasn't much to investigate. Everyone came back from the identity check completely broken. People became apathetic.

In the meantime, the food situation grew worse and the discipline harsher. People began to starve. The soup, mostly water, was measured with a tape measure. To find a piece of cabbage was considered great luck. The soup stank and contained no fats. People began to lose their human look. Everyone walked around like a shadow. Many became swollen because of the watery soup. Bread was restricted to one loaf for eight people per day. Once a week, the Germans gave us marmalade or a little margarine. Early in the morning, we received a cup of ersatz coffee, hardly sweetened. After drinking it, people would scratch the residue at the bottom of the cup with their fingers. We used to stand near the gate all day looking toward the kitchen, like dogs waiting for a few crumbs from their owner. Everyone wanted to be among those who were sent to fetch the heavy cauldrons, for this gave one a chance of finding potato peelings or a piece of cabbage, which one could sometimes steal from the kitchen. The Germans turned us into starving animals. We became almost feral, real hungry wolves.

There were also some who were more privileged, and who had the gold which they could use in exchange for food. There were also the "strong" ones, the pushers, with whom nobody wanted to quarrel. They always got more from the cauldron than the others. One such "tough guy" once gave me such a slap in the face that I tumbled over three times. This man now lives in Tel Aviv. I don't want to reveal his name, for he is a father of children.

The Jewish camp commander formed a sort of committee which he consulted whenever it was necessary to ask anything from the Germans. We could see that sooner or later we would all die from starvation. There were occasional visits of Red Cross representatives and German generals. They looked at everything and saw what was going on. Previously, the camp leadership had opened a canteen where one could buy a pocket mirror, a toothbrush, or marinated crabs. The canteen would be opened before the arrival of the Red Cross representatives, and closed soon afterwards. The German camp commander visited us once weekly. The daily roll calls were conducted by ordinary SS men. The inmates formed a group of intellectuals who debated such theoretical topics as philosophy. They spoke about spiritual things at a time when our stomachs were empty. *Im ein kemach, ein Torah* — without physical sustenance, there can exist no Torah. The hunger tormented us, and I said to my family that if we ever got anywhere, it would certainly be to our deaths.

We felt that something was going to happen. We didn't know what it would be, but suspected something terrible. We recognized this from the way they treated us — no longer like foreigners, but rather like dogs. People gathered outside the barracks, talking about the criminal Seidel, who was slim, had sharp eyes, and questioned everyone: How did you make your contact abroad in order to get your papers?

First he called the Americans, and finally, the Palestinians. I shall never forget my visit to his office. He asked my name, and how large my family was. I told him that we were two. My "wife" stood next to me. He was holding the list and demanded our papers. I handed him the *Ausweis* and my wife's *Ausweis* with the photos. He barked, "I want your foreign documents!" I said, "I have no foreign documents. I have these *Ausweis*." At the end, he looked at me in a way that I shall never forget. I saw that murderer only the one time, but his depravity is so engraved in my memory that I would recognize him anywhere.

I was sure that this identity check would end in a catastrophe. Everyone else was of the same opinion. We knew that almost all of the American papers were false. Only a few dozen were genuine. We were certain that almost immediate extinction was to be our fate.

We didn't have long to wait. An order suddenly came — all those with American passports and those belonging to the Palestine group were to prepare themselves. They were to be sent to the Exchange in Switzerland. This took place on July 18th. Only the real Americans and Argentines who had come to Poland before the war could remain. It isn't difficult to imagine our mood. We knew that they had carried out the final selection. We all knew this and yet tried to convince ourselves that we were indeed going to be exchanged.

Our entire Palestine group gathered at 11 o'clock in the morning before the barracks. I was desperate. Since we had no luggage, there was nothing to pack. We could see the Jewish Gestapo men grabbing enormous suitcases filled with Jewish goods.

Among the "Americans" I noticed Goldrand, the murderous Betrieb-Leiter of Schultz, his wife and children; the wife of Rakover (he himself had been shot); her son, Mietek Goldrand; Mordechai Perlmutter, carrying bulky suitcases; the young Margolis with his sister and mother; Mrs. Barszowski, the mother of the Jewish scoundrel Menashe Barszowski; and Mieczyslaw

Warcinski — altogether a motley group of criminals and German agents. Among these Americans I also saw the beloved Yiddish writer, Joshua Perle; Natan Buksbaum; Eliezer Geller; and Yudel Kalikstein and Shimon Friedman, two Jewish ghetto fighters who had, together with me, escaped through the sewers; their wives and a son; Dr. Yellen; several converts to Christianity; and also Christians who had Jewish wives from whom they didn't want to be separated — a veritable mélange of people, characters, types, good and bad, waiting for transport. At ten in the morning, there was an unexpected order. The entire Palestine group was to remain, together with the real Americans and Argentinians. And so, only 1,800 were going to South and Central America. Trucks began arriving and the luggage was loaded. The people were being arranged in lines and were marched for six kilometers to the railway station at Bergen-Belsen.

Our Palestine group remained. It is impossible to express our joy. We were saved at the last minute from that unfortunate transport. It was almost as if mysterious powers were watching over my family and me, and saving us from annihilation.

And so the majority left and we remained, a small group of only 1,000. Now they began to bring foreign Jews from other Polish cities — from Tarnow, Lwow, as well as from Holland. Each of these groups was placed separately behind a wire fence. The entire area of Bergen-Belsen covered 40 square kilometers and consisted of camps for various nationalities: German political prisoners, Russian war prisoners, Poles, Dutch, Belgians, French, English, Americans. The camp had many separate kitchens and the inevitable crematorium.

The entire camp was surrounded by towers, each guarded by an SS man armed with a machine gun. After the disaster of November 18, we were moved to smaller barracks which were more crowded and there we remained until January, 1944.

Among the inmates were the rich, and the poor and barefooted. The rich refused to share their possessions, which they had stuffed into their suitcases. Some children suffered from the bitter cold — the winter was extremely harsh. The barracks which were filled with small children, had no doors or windows. Conditions deteriorated, while others gorged themselves with food.

After a few more selections and transports, we remained four hundred, all squeezed into the one barrack number ten. At that time the Germans brought a group of Hungarian Jews, the so-called Kastner group. A number of them were sent to Switzerland. We gave them a Pentateuch in which we inscribed our real names, and asked them to give it to Jewish organizations so that they would shake the world. The Pentateuch arrived in Palestine and reached the hands of my uncle, my father's brother. From this he learned that I, my three children and my sister were alive. We asked for help, but the world apparently had more important priorities.

In 1944 a Jewish family from Poland, the Rabinovitch couple, was sent to Vittel. (They live today in Haifa.) Another family, the Rosenbaums from Radom, was transported to Switzerland.

Our group grew smaller. The barracks were crowded and dirty. We suffered from hunger. We were living corpses, swollen from starvation. It was wild, a veritable madhouse. I walked around in tatters, barefoot, starving, suffering from many illnesses.

One day someone smuggled in a newspaper, and our hearts were full of joy. During the summer there were frequent air raids. There was panic among the Germans, and they ran around like madmen. One of the Palestine women in the camp, the wife of Haim Szarf, got pregnant and was taken to the hospital in Zelle, 25 kilometers from the camp. Many of our people gave her letters to mail. The Germans found out about this, and as punishment organized torturous roll calls and diminished the food rations. She gave birth to a boy. The whole family arrived in Palestine on September eighth.

The year 1944 was approaching its end. A number of Poles who had taken part in the Warsaw uprising were brought to the camp. The Russian army was in the Warsaw suburb of Praga. The people called me "Musulman" — skin and bones. I contacted the camp of Czechoslovaks and we settled on an exchange: I would wash their linen, for which they would pay me half a plate of soup.

April, 1945. An order: "The whole *Sonderlager* is to be moved." All the groups — Poles, Dutch, also Czechs, were to prepare for transport. Only the sick would remain.

I was a Musulman weighing 44 kilos. I could stay but decided not to be separated from the family. What happened to them would happen to me. Maybe I was the lucky one who had protected them until now. I joined the transport. We marched six kilometers to Bergen. Nobody rushed us. We were accompanied by SS guards. We dragged along to the station, falling and lifting ourselves again, but we finally arrived. They put us in a train. The train moved — to where, nobody knew.

On the way they hooked up more cars filled with Jews. Altogether there were 65 cars. All around us were ruins, raging fires. The train was frequently bombed by planes. The last two cars carried artillery which shot back at the planes.

We dragged on slowly for six days, until April 13. We arrived at a place 27 kilometers from Magdeburg. We had passed six days and nights without food or water.

Late afternoon, April 13. The train stopped in the middle of a forest — woods and hills. The engine pulled away the two cars with the artillery guns and disappeared. Our guards, elderly SS men aged 60 to 65, opened the cars and we breathed the fresh air. The SS men, about sixty of them, looked resigned. We left the cars. We saw German refugees running from Magdeburg. They told the SS men that Magdeburg was being attacked from all sides and by low-flying Russian and American planes.

Evening, April 13th. Night approached, but all around us everything was light, for everything was one vast conflagration. We returned to the train, hungry and exhausted. They didn't lock the cars, but we were hungry and unable to sleep.

Suddenly, in the middle of the night, violent machine gun shooting and light artillery fire broke out, and hand grenades exploded. I told my family, "If we survive this night, we are saved. We are close to the front."

April 14, 1945 — 5 A.M. Quiet. No shooting. We waited until daybreak. We left the cars and talked to the SS men. We asked if we could go into the nearby villages to find some food. They shrugged their shoulders as if to say, "It's all the same, do as you like."

We left the cars and walked to the closest village. I took my son along with me. Other people streamed into the villages. We arrived at the first hut. The peasants let us in and offered us as much to eat as we wanted. My dream was fulfilled. I ate a huge bowl of cabbage soup of about three kilos. I told the peasant that

I had children and women under my care who also needed to eat. I took everything I could carry — bread, eggs, potatoes, fatschmaltz, milk, anything I could lay my hands on, and walked back to the train. We cut off branches from the trees and lit a fire to bake the potatoes, and we ate. Everyone brought food to the cars. A delight! We did nothing but eat.

It was 12 o'clock. Suddenly, a group of twelve Germans arrived on horseback: Himmler police. They told the SS men to order the Jews back into the train and be ready to go. An engine had been brought and attached to the train. We sent messengers to the villages to call our people back, but they were in no hurry — they were busy eating. I sat in the train. The door was open. I looked out and admired nature. Suddenly, I saw a man armed with a machine gun crawling on all fours on top of the hill. He got up. I looked closely and saw — an American soldier!

I ran quickly from the car and began shouting, "Hevra, the Americans are here!" Together with a few others, we climbed the hill and came closer. The American soldier asked us in Yiddish, "How many are you? You are all saved. You must immediately disarm the SS men. My name is Moshe Cohen. I'm a Bialystoker Jew and an American army officer."

We ran back and took the arms away from the SS men. Most of this was done by our 11, 12, and 13 year old boys, for we, the adults, had no strength. Our boys began to hit the SS men with tree branches. The SS men were beaten and covered with blood. Yesterday's supermen threw themselves to the ground and beat their heads against the earth, begging us to let them live. Fifteen minutes later, three more Americans arrived and took away the battered Germans. After another fifteen minutes, the first American tank appeared. One of our group, Israel Shapiro, began to recite the *gomel benchen** aloud. We suddenly heard a few soldiers from an American tank answer, Amen!

ROZA GOLDBERG-MATZNER

Roza Goldberg-Matzner was born in Lwow. She was married in 1939 to Dr. Menachem Matzner. Shortly afterwards, the war broke out and the Soviet army occupied Eastern Poland, including Lwow. A few months

*Thanksgiving prayer for being saved from danger.

later Dr. Matzner with his parents and some other members of his family were arrested by the Soviets and deported to a labor camp in Siberia. In the beginning of 1941 Roza gave birth to a daughter, Miriam. During the Soviet occupation a friend of her father, a man named Lauerbach, who had managed to escape to Vilna and from there to reach Japan, obtained two visas from the Chilean consul – one for Roza's father and another for her husband. But both were afraid to apply to the Soviet rulers for permission to leave.

In June, 1941, Germany attacked Russia and the Nazis occupied Lwow. They immediately began to liquidate the Jews. In August, 1942, the Germans gathered the remaining Jews together on Janowski Street.

Standing in the crowd with her child, Roza appealed to one of the SS men, showing him her Chilean documents. He allowed her to leave the group and took her, together with her child, to the Gestapo prison, in which she was interned as a foreigner. But 24 hours later another German ignored the papers and ordered her: "Raus!" Once again she was taken to the Janowski Street where the Jews stood surrounded by SS men and their dogs. The usual selection followed, the separation of men, women and children.

Roza once more showed her papers to the SS men as they began driving the Jews to the train.

. . . Then one of the Germans, whose name was Petrich, looked more closely at my documents and told me to stand aside. I was joined there by a few others who also possessed documents. Soon our group grew to two hundred. We were all taken to a building on Sapieha Street, in which we stayed until July, 1943.

One day a group of SS men told us to pack, and marched us to the railway station. We boarded normal passenger cars and were taken to Bergen Belsen. There we met a number of Jews who had been removed from Warsaw and who held fictitious papers authorizing them as members of a Palestine group.

In April, 1945, we were driven from the camp to a train which took us to a spot not far from Magdeburg. Because of the air raids and incessant bombings, and because the engine was damaged, we stopped in the middle of a forest.

One day we saw in the distance a soldier in an American uniform approaching our train. He was a Jewish officer, Abraham Cohen, a member of an American patrol.

Our joy was indescribable.

HELENA GOLDBERG

Helena Goldberg, whose account of her stay in the Hotel Polski was given in Chapter One, describes here her experiences in Bergen-Belsen.

176

. . . We arrived at the camp, Bergen Belsen. There we met those who had come to the camp earlier. They tried to calm us, saying that nothing bad would happen. I spent my first night (in many months) without fear. I no longer had to make decisions. Life in the camp with its 3,500 people resembled ordinary camp life, with morning roll calls and fines for breaking rules. But here the mood was not tense but generally calm, except for the odor from the crematorium and the wagons full of corpses of Russian prisoners of war which passed close by our camp every day. All this provided a constant reminder of the underlying peril.

Our food consisted of bread, black coffee, margarine (or marmalade) and soup. The children received a special *Millksupper*. Whoever had money had to deposit it with the camp commander. If one had cash one could buy such items as shoe paste, pencils, or washing powder in the canteen.

We began, somehow, to organize our lives. We pulled boards out of the bunks and taught the children to write. In the evening we would wash the boards, replace them, and the next day pull them out again. We bought pencils in the canteen. From time to time, we got hold of the newspaper, *Badenmeister*, which was sold secretly. There were no searches. Every few days we went to the bath where our clothes were disinfected. Some people bought food from the Germans with the diamonds and gold which they had smuggled into the camp. In the winter, the Germans installed iron stoves in the barracks, on which we could bake potatoes stolen from the kitchen.

Cultural life wasn't a very high priority. Some women sang or performed, but most of the time they lay on their bunks and talked about food. There were frequent quarrels centering around accusations that someone had stolen bread from a neighbor's bunk, or about any trifle.

Our Jewish camp commander was the engineer, Soloveychik, who now lives in Haifa. The German commander was Haas, whose attitude towards the inmates wasn't bad, at least by comparison.

In the spring of 1944, a rumor began circulating: the Gestapo had come to check our documents. They set up an office and our Jewish camp commander led groups of people there for a hearing.

I stood before a Gestapo man. I told him that my papers were

177

in Italy. He asked, why didn't I go to Italy? I gave a naive excuse, replying that I had no money to go. He smiled mockingly, "A Jew would sell his quilt to be able to go." and he added sharply, "You're lying." But I saw out of the corner of my eye that he wrote on the margin of his paper, *Zum Austausch geeignet* (fit for exchange).

The document check lasted for several days. The entire camp was in the grips of a terrible nervousness. No one knew what was better — to show the American or the Palestinian documents. Some possessed both.

After the check, there was a roll call. Everyone was there. The Gestapo divided us into two groups. Those who were to leave went to the right; the others to the left. Those who were to remain were the people on the Palestine list, as well as a few elderly people who possessed authentic American citizenship. These Americans had come on a visit to Poland and couldn't leave because of the outbreak of the war and the subsequent occupation of Poland.

We learned later from a young man who had gone with that transport that all those who had left were sent to Auschwitz. He had jumped from the train and then sent a letter to the hospital in Zelle, where it was received by a woman from our camp who gave birth there.

It the meantime, conditions in the camp deteriorated. There was hunger and people were dying of exhaustion. The soup was cooked with ordinary leaves, some poisonous, and people began to suffer from diarrhea. Only once, in the beginning of 1945, did we receive food parcels from the Red Cross. Bergen-Belsen received many inmates of various nationalities, which we recognized from the signs sewn onto their clothing. Our barrack was exclusively for Jews from Poland.

In 1945, the situation became still worse. Our clothes were full of vermin. They would be returned from disinfection even more infested than when they were sent out. There were many cases of typhoid, diarrhea, and bodily swelling from starvation. The chief doctor of the entire camp, a German, supplied us with unclean medications. After an injection, one would get shivers and high fever.

The mood in the camp became desperate. At last, an order was issued one day: all those able to walk must leave. I was too weak to march because of illness, and decided to stay. In all, a few dozen of us, weak and sick, remained.

Two days later, an ambulance took us to the railway statoin and we were locked into sealed cars. We spent thirteen days there without food. Every night, a few people died, and the corpses were removed at short stops, and then the train would move on.

We got off at every station to try and steal some food from other trains. Later, the women baked the stolen potatoes. On the thirteenth day, during a heavy bombardment, our German guards ran away. A few of the more courageous among us dared to leave the cars and they met the first Soviet patrol.

We were free!

ANNA SZPIRO

In Chapter One we gave a lengthy account of Anna Szpiro's experiences in the Hotel Polski. Here she tells briefly of her life in Bergen-Belsen.

. . . Our group consisted of 3,650 people. I belonged to the Palestine group, which had 280 people. The rest were Americans — and Honduras, Uruguay, and so forth. Some time later, we were called to the German commander who began to ask everyone how he got his papers. It appeared that many had false documents. The Germans began to separate us into groups and to send some of them away — allegedly for exchange, but actually to the crematoria. In the end, only our own group, registered on the Palestine list, remained. We stayed in this camp for interned foreigners from July, 1943, until March, 1945. Our living conditions were similar to those in other camps. However, the Germans here didn't beat us, and we weren't obliged to work. On only one occasion, close to the end of the war, did our Palestine group receive food parcels from Switzerland. Of the 280 people in our group, several died of hunger.

About two months before the end of the war, a roll call was taken, and all those who were able to walk were marched to the station of Zelle. There, we were put into sealed railway cars and given a little food. The trip lasted seven days and nights. From time to time, the train stopped because of aerial bombardments.

As we approached Magdeburg, we encountered ground fighting. We were liberated by the Americans about 20 kilometers from Magdeburg.

Chapter Four

PAWIAK,
THE ANTECHAMBER OF DEATH

The Pawiak Prison

The last group of "foreign" Jews was taken from the Hotel Polski neither to Vittel nor to Bergen-Belsen but to the Pawiak prison only a few blocks away, amid the ruins of the Warsaw ghetto.

One of the Pawiak prisoners, the Polish underground fighter and historian, Leon Wanat, wrote a book, Behind the Pawiak Walls, *in which he describes how the Germans and their Ukrainian guards viciously humiliated, tortured and murdered Jews as well as a number of Poles. It was here, in a separate part of the prison which once had been the administrative section, and in the prison cells once designated for women – Serbia – that the foreign Jews were held prior to their transportation to an internment camp.*

Leon Wanat spent several years in the prison and he describes the circumstances under which the last group from the Hotel Polski was brought and how most of them were "liquidated":

LEON WANAT

On July 13, 1942, the Germans surrounded the Hotel and all the people there, 424 men, women and children, were arrested and taken to the Pawiak.

Here, in the courtyard of the prison, and under the surveillance of the SS Untersturmführer Brandt, began the segregation of the arrested people. The Germans checked identity documents and passports, and finally decided that the papers of 262 persons weren't in order. These people were sent to Section VII. There they were more scrupulously searched and the guards took most of the prisoners' valuables for themselves. Among the arrested were entire Jewish families, who had deluded themselves that they could receive the privileges of foreign internees.

The Germans very quickly settled their fates. They were led, in small groups, to the ruins of the house on 27 Dzielna Street and shot.

The remaining group of 162 persons was sent temporarily to the women's section of the prison. On July 17 they were taken to Bergen-Belsen.

BER BASKIND

Ber Baskind, whose account of his experiences in the Hotel Polski we have given in the first chapter, belonged to one of the last groups to be brought to the Pawiak, on July 13, 1943. This is his description of what happened that day:

It should be noted that our group consisted not only of hotel internees, but also of some "Aryan" Poles who had gone to the hotel to bid farewell to their Jewish friends. The Germans had carried out no identity checks but rounded up everyone and forced them into the trucks without distinction.

They left us in the prison's courtyard until 7 P.M., when several officials from the "Passport Bureau" came to check our documents. Their appearance threw our group into a great panic, because no more than about twenty of us had papers in order. It was, unfortunately, easy to guess what would happen to the rest. David Guzik, the director of the American Joint in Warsaw, was in our group. On his initiative we began to look for a way to legalize the status of as many people as we could; we succeeded in doing this only for a few. Guzik, in addition to his own "promesse," possessed a few which had not yet been filled out. Therefore, we could register on these forms a few hastily-created families of about twenty people each. As a result of this ruse, the number of people belonging to registered families rose to 116. They were promptly separated from the others and led into another courtyard which belonged to the "Department of Internees."

We had no luggage, nor any of our possessions. As for food, we were reduced to the meager prison rations. But we didn't

182

complain, for we knew that our brothers and sisters in the other courtyard — numbering about 400 — might be, perhaps within an hour or a day — once more deported or even shot.

After a night in the prison cells, our worst fears were realized for they were all taken the next day to the ruins of the ghetto and shot.

In truth, we knew very little of what might happen, and what the Germans intended to do with us. Although we were for the moment a little reassured, every one of us was full of doubts and fears. We all knew quite well what sort of American he is, by what sort of tricks he had been registered, and we had very little doubt that the Germans weren't altogether blind.

In the Hotel Polski we had lived with the impression that we were surrounded by some sort of invisible and constant protection. But here, behind the walls of the Pawiak Prison and directly before our enemies, we felt deprived of any defense. An entire week had passed, yet no one had come to visit us. No one seemed interested in our fate.

With the help of some Polish prison guards, we tried by all possible means to get in touch with our two patrons and with the engineer. For a long while, our efforts were in vain. But finally, on July 20, the "engineer" arrived. He told us that he had so far been unable to attend to our cases, and that for the present he could do no more than to leave us interned in the Pawiak. The Germans were absolutely against letting us return to the Hotel Polski, simply because they considered it a refuge for many Polish Jews.

The engineer advised us to elect a committee from among ourselves. Every week he would be able to take into town a person or two who could buy for us necessary goods, and who would also make the necessary official petitions to the authorities on behalf of the internees. Finally, at our request, he promised to bring the luggage which we had left in the Hotel Polski, and to come see us the next day.

As soon as he left, we called a meeting and formed the required committee. The directors were the Joint director, David Guzik; the attorney, Kohn; Mieczyslaw Orlean; and myself. The next morning the engineer indeed returned. He took Kohn and me into the town to arrange a few matters. He didn't recover more than a small portion of our luggage — the rest had been completely pillaged.

We worried daily about food, and our hearts were filled with fear for the fate of our relatives. But the main topic of conversation was the fate of those who had left the hotel on July 5th and the 13th. We had received a few letters written during their journey, but since then had no news of how their trip had ended.

As for myself, I continued to live with increasing concern about my wife, and constantly planned ways to save her. I also thought of Rosental. The engineer assured me that he would manage to get my wife out of the camp in Lublin, and that it was possible that he would also manage to get Rosental freed as well. So, despite everything, I still maintained some hopes.

The days passed in passive waiting. Then suddenly, on July 27th and 28th, two convoys of 64 persons each were taken from the prison, leaving us no more than about one hundred. A few days later, the engineer arrived with about twenty people from the Lublin camp, but, alas, my wife was not one of them. The engineer told me that he had searched for her throughout the whole camp, but in vain. Only later did I learn that at that time she was no longer in Lublin — on July 7 she had been taken to Auschwitz together with a few hundred other women. But even now the engineer assured me that he could save her, if I could pay. I once more gave him carte blanche.

The unfortunates who arrived on July 30 were in a terrible state. All of them had swollen legs, and their skin color was green and cadaverous — they looked more dead than alive. They had nothing; they had been robbed of everything. We took care of them as best we could, and gave them as much food as we could spare. After some time they began to gradually return to life. But three of them had contracted typhoid fever and were sent to the hospital. Of the entire group only one didn't survive, a man with a gangrenous leg.

Those who had come from Lublin answered our anxious questions and described their life in the camp. From what they told us, we became convinced that there is no limit to human suffering.

After they arrived at the camp, they had been forced to surrender all their belongings, and were then divided into two groups. The first group was taken to a shower, after which everyone received uniforms made of paper. The other group was also sent to a shower, but from that shower they never returned. That second group consisted mainly of elderly people and children who had been forcibly torn from their mothers.

Those of the first group had been immediately put to work, for — as we knew already — the Germans do not murder outright those still able to work and produce. Their physical strength granted them the privilege of laboring under the most terrible conditions from dawn to sunset. Each person's entire daily food ration consisted of a meager piece of bread and a bowl of soup. While they worked, the Germans stood over them like executioners over their victims. It was forbidden to succumb to fatigue and to interrupt one's work for even a minute. The Germans watched over them, and anyone showing signs of weakness was whipped. And very often people were beaten for no reason at all.

To become sick meant to die, for a sick person was taken directly to the "hospital" from which no one returned. In case a person committed a more serious offense he was hanged in front of his comrades.

A few days after the arrival of these unfortunates, at the beginning of August, we learned that from the group that had been separated from us soon after our arrival at Pawiak Prison, ten were still alive and in another part of the prison (the others, as mentioned earlier, had been shot). These ten survivors were mostly young boys whom we tried, with great difficulty, to supply with food.

A short while later, in the middle of August, my friend Rosental became the citizen of some South American country, as the engineer had promised, and he joined our group. For this favor I paid the engineer 100,000 zlotys, which at that time equalled $1,500. Shortly after that, our group was joined by another few survivors from the Hotel Polski.

We tried to help the other prisoners in Pawiak by giving them food. We also helped some by sending letters to their families or friends. The Germans became suspicious of us and began to threaten us with grave consequences despite our being "Americans." Finally, to put an end to our help for the others, they transferred us to the ground floor to cut us off completely from the other prisoners.

The days passed uneventfully. We became more and more restless because we heard nothing about those who had left the Hotel Polski on July 5th and 13th. We only knew that about 1,000 of them had been sent to a place called Bergen-Belsen. We received no news at all from them although we did receive many letters from other camps such as Vittel, Compiègne, and St. Denis.

Meanwhile it was announced that a group of 64 of us would leave on September 21st. But first we were anxious to know the reason for the silence from Bergen-Belsen. We were also anxious to know if our departure was just another trap. Once again we turned to the engineer for advice. He promised to get letters from our friends through this group that was scheduled to be sent out on the 21st, and indeed, a few days after the group left, the engineer brought us the awaited letters.

We learned that our friends were being held in a camp of a few thousand internees. They lived in barracks, and slept on wretched bunks. They weren't forced to do any work, and had the right to communicate with the outside world. They were told that they were in a temporary camp and that they would shortly be transferred to an open camp with all the rights of American citizens.

The letters only partially reassured us — they didn't remove our uncertainty about our final destination, for we had already learned not to naively believe the Germans' promises. But what could we do but wait? It was impossible to return. We knew quite clearly what the conditions would be were we to hide among the "Aryan" Poles and what it would cost. We were aware of the constant terror we would have to live with under those conditions. And finally, we all knew from our own experiences how difficult it would be to find a safe hideout.

At that time David Guzik was the only man on whose support the hidden Jews could depend. During his visits to the city he distributed subsidies to all of them; he examined their situations and searched, together with them, for possible solutions.

We found ourselves torn between our desire to remain in the prison and the prospect of new departures. A transport was scheduled for October 19. As for myself I couldn't decide whether to leave Warsaw before finding my wife. The engineer assured me that she would arrive before the nineteenth, and renewed his promises daily. But little by little, after so many vain attempts to contact her, I was beginning to lose hope. I realized that I might have to leave without achieving my goal.

For his part, Guzik was unable to decide whether or not to save himself and abandon the hidden Jews, who, without his assistance, would be deprived of moral and material help, as well as his advice.

In any case, it was impossible to remain in Pawiak prison, for all of us must leave that place. The only practical solution would be to accompany the engineer on one of his food missions, and to disappear and begin an illegal life. I wouldn't be able to do anything to find my wife. We found ourselves in a situation with no solution, a veritable dead end.

We once again turned to our engineer. He repeated his promise to return my wife to me, but admitted that I must arm myself with more patience. However, he found a solution which permitted us to wait. Guzik, possessing a "promesse" in his name, was interned as a citizen of Honduras. He also possessed a more precious document, a false passport, also in his name, showing him to be a citizen of Argentina. The engineer used $1,000 given him by Guzik to get the false Argentine passport stamped and legalized. Thus Guzik became an Argentine citizen and was no longer obligated to be interned. He had the right to live and walk throughout the city as a free man. As for myself, in order that I miss the upcoming transport, it was necessary that I feign illness and be sent to a clinic for treatment.

Everything went ahead as arranged, and Guzik and I avoided being sent away, and remained in Warsaw. Thus we would be in touch with each other for some time at least, and we were able to communicate with and help those in hiding. But this was not a long-term solution. It was, first of all, very dangerous, especially for me, for my position was untenable. Also, it tied me to the engineer, without whom I could do nothing for myself.

And, in fact, all our efforts ended in failure. I had to give up any hope of saving my wife. Not only was the engineer unable to find her, but he was also obliged to leave Warsaw. After the departure of the last internees his mission was, in principle, finished. And since his wife and children were in Vittel, the Germans had permitted him to join them. He could now only suggest that Guzik and I accompany him.

This news had a very demoralizing effect on me and plunged me once again into cruel indecision. I was at the end of my resources. I had fought five months in peril of my life, I had sacrificed everything I had in the hope of saving my wife from the Auschwitz camp, and now that last hope was being taken away from me.

All these thoughts of despair threw me into a deep depression. Now nothing seemed of importance. I began to despondently walk the streets without any precautions, although I knew very well that one identity check would lead to imprisonment and probably death.

Guzik and the engineer brought me back to my senses. They made me accept the idea that all I could do was to go to Vittel. Guzik himself preferred not to leave Warsaw. His passport gave him sufficient security, and there seemed little reason the Germans would doubt its authenticity. He preferred to stay and risk his life rather than abandon to the Germans those whose lives depended on him. He insisted that I accompany the engineer.

JULIEN HIRSHAUT

Ber Baskind (and Stanley Osinski, mentioned in the first chapter) belonged to the last group which was rounded up that day in the Hotel Polski and taken to the Pawiak.

There is still another witness to what occurred in the Pawiak that day, a Jewish prisoner there who worked in the prison bath. He watched through his cell window the arrival of the "foreign" Jews from the Hotel Polski, and their selection in the courtyard. He also received an eye witness's account of their slaughter outside the prison walls.

The witness is Julien Hirshaut, a Jewish writer who lives today in New York and edits the Yiddish literary magazine, Tsukunft*. He went through the Warsaw ghetto and was later incarcerated in the Pawiak Prison, from which he managed to escape. After the war he wrote a book,* The Dark Nights in Pawiak.

In one of the chapters of that book he tells how he watched from his cell the group of Jewish "foreigners" who had been brought in from the Hotel Polski:

. . . It was the evening after a hot, sticky day. The air in the basement of our eighth ward was moist and damp. The prison-

188

ers sat as usual on their sacks of straw, one pressed against the other. It was more crowded than ever — three more victims had joined us that day. Our shirts stuck to our bodies. We were too weak to talk. Even the younger ones had no desire to quarrel among themselves as they always did.

Suddenly we heard through the window the rumbling of trucks. This was followed by dogs barking and shouts in German.

Kazik, the *starosta* (cell elder), placed a little stool next to the wall under the window. He climbed upon it and remained there for a while, motionless, holding onto the side of the little window so as not to be visible from outside. He then jumped down and gave a report. "It's a big crowd of people. I can see they're Jews. The women are elegantly dressed. Everyone's carrying lots of luggage, nice suitcases. There are also children."

What could this be? Obviously there had been an "action" somewhere.

One of the new prisoners, a young man from Warsaw named Litwak, jumped up from his place, climbed the stool and, following the *starosta*'s example, stood at the side of the window and looked out at the courtyard. After coming down, he told us, "They've liquidated the Hotel Polski. I know the people, I was there together with them until yesterday morning, when I was caught in the street just a few steps from the gate. I'd left the hotel for a while to help a friend enter a sewer to return to the ghetto, where he had hidden some money. Now they've taken the remaining Jews from the hotel." He added sadly, "Yes, this too has come to an end."

Taking every precaution, we began to use this little window as an observation post to the courtyard. A large number of men, women and children stood lined up in rows in the prison courtyard. Next to them was a mountain of luggage. In the middle of the courtyard stood a long table, behind which sat two Gestapo officers: Brandt, the well-known mass murderer of the Warsaw Jews, and his assistant, Mende. Next to them stood several Gestapo men of the prison staff, headed by Obersharführer Alberts.

Brandt, with his broad, porcine face, ordered the Jews to approach his table one by one. He looked at their documents and commanded some to go to the right, and others to the left.

189

The number of people on the right side kept growing while the line on the left remained small, with no more than a few dozen people.

We immediately knew what this scene meant: it was one of their "selections." To those who didn't go through the hell in Poland, this word means little. But it designated the method by which the Germans had murdered millions of Jews.

The Gestapo had evidently come to the conclusion that it was no longer profitable to continue the Hotel Polski affair. They had won the game. They had managed to get a few thousand more Jews into their hands. The transports which had already been sent to Vittel and Hanover wouldn't get lost either. The Gestapo could lay their hands on them at any time they wanted and finish them off.

I risked my life and remained standing a while on the stool looking out of the little basement window, and watched the parade of death. My own life was in danger, for if any German saw me staring out the window he would kill me instantly. But I ignored that risk. I couldn't tear myself away from this sight of cynical bestiality and helplessness. I was above all shattered by the sight of the children — their blond little heads and round rosy faces, their eyes wandering all around as they pressed against their mothers, shivering.

Yes, this I could see distinctly: they all shivered. They all knew why they had been brought here. I thought at that moment of my own little child who had suffered this same fate.

The Germans continued their work calmly. Treating the Jews almost politely, they asked for their documents and then let them return to their places. The line on the right was now enormous, and the left line wasn't growing. I knew what that meant: the right side was death, the left was life — or, rather, a temporary reprieve.

The selection lasted until well into the evening. Later we learned how a huge crowd had been driven into the prison building and how the heavy gate had been shut behind them with a resounding loud clang. The smaller group from the left side had been taken to the women's section. And the others were driven into our section, which was the ward of death.

We later learned that the few dozen Jews who had been led into the women's section because of their allegedly "better" documents were later sent to the camp in Hanover. Only a few survived.

The next morning, those people from the Hotel Polski who had been locked into our part of the prison were again brought to the courtyard. Then they were led in groups of five outside the prison building, from where we could hear bursts of machine-gun fire.

A few days later prisoners in the cells overlooking Dzielna Street told me about the execution, which had been carried out opposite the prison gate in the ruins of 25 and 27 Dzielna Street.

The prisoners saw from their windows how Ukrainians armed with clubs drove naked Jews, in groups of five, from the prison gate and across the empty street to the ruins. Among the ruins a deep pit had been dug out, over which was suspended a little wooden bridge. The Ukrainians drove the Jews towards that bridge. When they reached it, there was a burst of fire from an automatic weapon and the five naked people fell into the pit.

One of the prisoners who had witnessed this scene from his window noticed, among the ruins from where the shooting came, the outline of a man whom he recognized as Alberts, the *Scharführer* of Pawiak. Alberts stood there, elegantly dressed as usual, holding an automatic gun in his gloved hands. When the group of five reached the little bridge he raised the gun, pressed the trigger and then gracefully lowered the machine gun muzzle. That day Alberts by himself murdered over 300 people, among them many women and children.

Chapter Five:

THE PALESTINE LIST,
THE CINDERELLA OF THE DRAMA

The only group to go through the Hotel Polski and survive consisted of the few who had Palestine passports and the 170 plus who were registered on a so-called "Palestine list." From diaries and testimonies it appears that only that group of pariahs, those destitute few who could not afford the exorbitant prices of the tempting documents for such legendary countries as Honduras, Nicaragua and Costa Rica, had no choice but to resign themselves to joining the Palestine list.

In connection with this we must mention a Mr. Engel, who sat in the hotel in possession of a copy of that list, in charge of adding more names. But no one until now had explained the origin of that list, not even Mr. Engel.

Jonas Turkow, in his book The End of an Illusion, *contributes some information about the case of Mr. Engel – but more revealing and sensational is the story told to the author by a man who was one of the creators of the Palestine List.*

We shall first quote Mr. Turkow:

JONAS TURKOW

"Many Jewish families which had been living in Eretz Israel since before the war made great efforts to bring their relatives over from Poland and other occupied countries. Some of these families succeeded in getting permits from the Palestine Mandatory Authorities and in bringing over their relatives via Turkey or Switzerland. They were supposed to be exchanged for Germans in Palestine.

"An example of such an exchange is the following case:

192

Among the candidates for exchange on the Palestine List was the Engel family from Lodz. During the war, they lived in the Warsaw Ghetto. Mrs. Engel received a letter from her relatives in Eretz Israel informing her that they had acquired a permit for her family from the Mandatory Authorities to be exchanged, and that the appropriate papers had already been dispatched. Mr. Engel had an acquaintance on the Aryan side of Warsaw, a Swiss citizen who worked as a governess with the Christian family of Rotwand. The governess, whose name was Ivonne, was friendly with a Gestapo officer, the SS Obersturmführer Grishe. She went with Mr. Engel to the Gestapo, where the officer looked through the Palestine list of names and found Mr. Engel's, his wife's and their little daughter's names. The Obersturmführer gave him a signed document authorizing Engel and his family to move freely on the Aryan side until their departure for Turkey, where the exchange was to take place.

"The Palestine list also contained the name of Mr. Engel's brother, who by that time was no longer alive — he had been sent to Treblinka during the great deportations. Engel asked the Obersturmführer if his brother's place might be filled by somebody else. The SS man agreed. And so it began. . .

"The Obersturmführer himself suggested that Mr. Engel find illegal' Jews who would take the place of those whose names were on the Palestine list but who were no longer alive. In this way, a group of one hundred Jews were formed. For his idea, the Obersturmführer received golden watches, diamonds and other valuables. The Swiss woman received one hundred American dollars and many gifts from Mr. Engel. After Engel gained possession of the document authorizing him to move freely on the Aryan side, he felt so secure that he visited his friends in the ghetto. But during one of these visits, an "action" (deportation) began. In vain did he show his foreign papers. He was taken to the *Umschlagplatz* and put on a train. The transport was travelling to the death camp of Maidanek. With the help of a little saw, which he always carried with him, Engel managed to open a little window and, together with his friend, Mr. Tomkiewicz* jumped from the train. The German guard shot at them and Mr. Tom-

*The husband of Mrs. M. Tomkiewicz, the author of the account in this book, Chapters One and Three.

kiewicz was killed, but Engel managed to escape and returned to his wife and child on the "Aryan" side.

"On another occasion, when a new deportation from the ghetto took place, Engel was caught again, but this time he had better luck. At Engel's request, one of the SS men called the Gestapo and they found that he was indeed on the list of foreign citizens to be exchanged. On the advice of the Obersturmführer Grishe, Engel went first to the Hotel Royal and, later, to the Hotel Polski."

* * *

This account, however, still doesn't explain how and under what circumstances the Palestine list originated.

I learned more about that from a conversation with Mrs. Niuta Gutkowska, the wife of a well-known Israeli lawyer, Moses Gutkowski.

During my interview with Mrs. Gutkowska in her Tel Aviv apartment, she told me the following story.

One day, upon leaving her apartment on Warsaw's "Aryan" side on her way to the ghetto, she was told that there were two letters for her in the ghetto post office. She found a Palestine laissez passer and a letter from Istanbul advising her to take the document and go with her child to the Gestapo and register for an exchange.

Her husband Moses Gutkowski had in the first weeks of the war escaped from Warsaw to Vilna. This was all the information she had concerning him. From that letter she learned for the first time that he was alive, and in Palestine. But even then she knew nothing of how the certificate had been sent to her or the meaning of the Palestine list which Mr. Engel in the Hotel Polski possessed.

Her husband, who was present at our interview, afterwards explained. He told how the list had come into being, and how approximately 270 Jewish lives were saved thanks to the desperate attempts of some, and in spite of the shortsightedness and stubbornness of others.

Mr. Gutkowski had arrived in Palestine as a refugee from Vilna in 1940. Immediately following his arrival, he began to search for a way to bring his wife and child — who he believed to be in the Warsaw ghetto — to Palestine. He looked around and

194

found other Jews whose families were similarly trapped in Nazi-occupied Poland.

They finally hit upon the following idea: At that time, several thousand German women lived in Palestine whose husbands, members of the sect of the "Templars," had obeyed the call of the Führer and left for their homeland, to join the Nazi army. The British, who at that time ruled Palestine, planned to send all these German women to an internment camp in Australia.

Mr. Gutkowski and his friends decided to ask the Jewish Agency (the Sokhnut) in Tel Aviv to convince the British that rather than deport these women to Australia, they should be exchanged for the Polish Jewish wives and children of their Palestine relatives. A delegation consisting of Mr. Gutkowski; the lawyer, Moszkowicz; A. Klarman; Meir Griffel of Agudath Israel; Rappaport; and Eksztejn went to the Sokhnut leaders — Itzhok Greenbaum and Maximilian Apolinary Hartglas, ex-deputy of the prewar Polish Parliament. Both Sokhnut leaders rejected the idea outright. Mr. Greenbaum said that all this news about German atrocities, about Treblinka and Auschwitz, was just panic-propaganda. Mr. Hartglas raised another objection: he said that the British Empire was fighting for its existence and therefore couldn't risk the possibility that the Germans might include spies among the exchanged Jewish women!

The shocked members of the delegation tried once more, this time appealing to other Jewish leaders, Dov Yosef and Moshe Sharett. Again, they achieved no satisfactory result.

They therefore decided to appeal directly to the British High Commissioner in the King David Hotel in Jerusalem. They went there with little belief that after their refusal from the Sokhnut they would meet with more success from the British. But to their astonishment and joy, they were immediately received by the Chief Secretary of the High Commissioner, Mr. Newton, who listened with great attention and compassion to their story, told in a broken English. At the end of the meeting, he asked them to leave a telephone number so that he could get in touch with them.

A few days later, Mr. Gutkowski received the impatiently-awaited call. Mr. Newton told him that he had discussed the possibility of such an exchange with the "Protecting Power" (Switzerland), and he now asked them to submit a full list of names, dates and photographs of the family members in Poland. When the news of that successful intervention reached the leaders of the Sokhnut, they made similar applications for two hundred additional people.

The problem now was how to get in direct contact with the Germans about this proposed exchange. While the Sokhnut tried to arrange the matter through Spain, Mr. Gutkowski and his friends found a quicker and more direct solution: Istanbul.

In Palestine at that time there existed — and still exists today — a cigarette factory, Dubek. Its representative, Mr. Simcha Glikson, used to make occasional trips to Turkey to purchase tobacco. Mr. Gutkowski and his friends gave him a sum of money to send food parcels from Istanbul to their relatives — and also, more important, they gave him the list of names of their families and asked him to get in direct touch with the Gestapo center in Istanbul.

The result of Glikson's intervention was the arrival of the Palestine laissez passer for Mrs. Gutkowska and a number of others in the ghetto post office and in the Gestapo office of Warsaw and several other Polish cities. This was the origin of the Palestine list, which saved the lives of about 270 men, women and children.

ANNA BERGER

The repeatedly asked question of whether or not the entire affair of the exchange of foreign Jews was a trap invented by the Nazis to exterminate the few surviving Jews is too complex for a simple answer.

The exchange took some of the Jews to so-called transfer camps like Vittel and Bergen-Belsen with Auschwitz as their final destination; some managed to survive; and in other cases, as here described by Anna Berger, from the Polish city of Radom, the scheme was used by the Nazis as an opportunity to carry out indescribable atrocities. (Source: Nasza Trybuna, New York, 1946).

On the first of January, 1943, all that was left of the 45,000 Jews of the ghetto of Radom was a remnant of 5,000. But just then, despite all logic, a ray of hope descended upon the small ghetto. We began talking about an exchange of foreign citizens.

The Judenälteste of our group received an order to register all foreign citizens, as well as those who had relatives in foreign

196

countries, even in Palestine. Our sick brains began fabricating various ideas. There was one thing in which we all believed, or, rather, wanted to believe: the world was beginning to care about us, they wanted to save us. Of the 5,000 Jews, 2,500 registered as having relatives — fictitious — in Palestine. It was sufficient for someone to find an address with a name similar to his in Palestine, to claim that person as a close relative.

On January 13, 1943, at five in the morning, a group of armed SS men surrounded our camp. Ten minutes later, we were all gathered outside. Ten Gestapo men asked the Judenälteste for the Palestine list. Our group began buzzing like a beehive. The Germans began to read aloud from the list and those called out were sent to the left. We were all gripped with terror. We knew that this was a selection between life and death. We just didn't know which side meant death and which meant life.

As a nurse of the camp clinic I was dressed in a freshly laundered white uniform, and I ran around the whole place. The Germans liked uniforms and symbols of power. My white uniform made me stand out from the rest of the crowd, and none of the SS men stopped me — they obviously believed that I had the official right to move about freely. I was looking among the gathered people for my husband. He too was on the Palestine list.

I still didn't know whether it was good to stand on the left side with those called out from the list, or whether I should help him get over to the right.

The reading of names lasted until three P.M. The frost was sharp and the SS men kept drinking vodka. Towards evening all those who weren't on the list — mothers with children, old and young people — were marched away. The silence was terrifying. Not a single child cried, nobody coughed. The Jews went in silence, resigned, to their death.

After that, life again resumed with the customary rhythm it follows in a camp. Every morning we marched in lines of five to work, and every evening at dusk we returned exhausted to the barracks. Every few days several Jews were shot for the most insignificant infractions. The hope of getting out of this hell alive slowly died. So passed January, February and the first half of March. The holiday of Purim was approaching.

One day in the second half of March, at ten in the morning, the Gestapo called the Judenälteste on the phone and told him to compile a list of the "intelligentsia." Only those who were in possession of university diplomas had the right to be registered. To this day I cannot understand how a logical and wise man like Dr. Szenderowicz, our Judenälteste, could have confused the registration of intelligentsia with the Palestine list. Immediately, with lightning speed, the news spread that those with university degrees would be allowed to go to Palestine. A new ray of hope entered our sick minds. People began to comment, to create new ideas. "The registration is a good thing, the proof is that all those who were on the Palestine list are still alive." Dr. Korman, our only Roentgenologist, formed a completely new and tragic hypothesis: "Evidently the world is in no position to save all the Jews, so they're trying, for a high price, at least to get the professionals out." People were once more going berserk.

As the order was to register not only those with diplomas but their parents as well, people began to use all their shrewdness and ruses in a desperate search for ways to get their names on the new list. As a result, the Judenälteste registered sixteen physicians together with their families — a total of about 150 people — as well as several engineers, lawyers, professors, and many more professionals and pseudo-professionals. Many among them had, during the first selection, lost their families, and now, in order to save others, had come forward with new artificial families. The others begrudged these happy ones chosen by fate. Still others silently ridiculed human naivete and stupidity.

The departure from the ghetto was to take place in three days. The people could no longer sleep. They had the most wonderful dreams about freedom and Palestine, and began to pack their suitcases. There were others who had more common sense, who cried, "People what are you doing? What Palestine? It's a new bluff. The Germans are preparing a new trap. Never trust the Germans."

But these were words shouted into the wind. Nobody wanted to hear them. The hope was sweet, and nobody wanted to listen to the "black crows."

The departure was set for Sunday afternoon. There was a new order: "Remove from the list two physicians, the nurses and some of the camp functionaries." People were again overcome with fear and new doubts.

To this day I cannot forget a tragic farewell scene between a mother and daughter in my room. A friend of mine who was also a clinic nurse was at the last moment taken off the list at the order of the camp commandant. Her mother, who was on the list under an assumed name as the fictitious wife of one of the engineers, didn't want to go without her daughter. She said that life had no meaning for her without her child. But her daughter cried and begged her to go. "Go, Mama, darling. I want you to. If I know that you're living in safety, I'll run away and will also try to live." The scene continued until the last moment before the departure.

At two o'clock a number of trucks arrived. Mrs. Naghaus was still saying to her daughter as she boarded one of them, "Marysia, I feel that I'm going to my death." The girl kept back her tears and believed deeply that her mother was being sent to freedom. Half an hour earlier Fryd had said to me, "I don't know why, but I have a strange premonition of death. I've never felt like this before." Five minutes after the trucks left, they were followed by two cars carrying Ukrainians armed with machine guns. We knew them well from many previous "actions." This was the ill-famed execution squad of our region. We understood everything in a flash, but nobody dared put it into words. It was a new Satanic plan of the Germans. Our uncertainty lasted until midnight.

Then two of the trucks arrived at the camp gate. Ten people, pale, with savage looks in their eyes, descended from them. Among the group was Bela, our youngest nurse. And this is what she told us:

"When I saw, earlier, how the trucks arrived before the camp and how the happy people entered them with their luggage, my longing for freedom was so great that I turned without thinking to the Untersturmführer and begged him to let me go along. I was afraid that he might recognize me, for he had seen me at work and often asked for something. He shouted, 'Weg von hier!' But my determination was strong. I crawled cautiously toward the gate and jumped into one of the trucks. A second later we departed. I breathed the free air of our native town. But my joy was short lived. When we left the town the trucks accelerated and we suddenly saw the cars with the armed Ukrainians behind us. We suddenly understood everything. They had cheated us shamelessly. We became aware that they're taking us to our death. Under the excuse of 'Palestine' and 'intelligentsia' they had prepared a nightmarish Purim play, a present for Hitler on the occasion of the holiday of Jewish victory. The younger people began to jump from the trucks, and were killed by the well-aimed bullets of the Ukrainians. The older Jews said Psalms. Others recited kaddish. We came to the cemetery in Szydlowiec, near Radom. The view before us was indescribable. Among the graves and under the trees lay the blood-soaked, deformed bodies of those who had come in the first trucks. I saw the well-known brutal faces of the Ukrainians. All of them were drunk. I felt the dull smell of blood mixed with the odor of vodka. The Ukrainians had just finished shooting the people from the trucks before ours. Now it was our turn. People descended from the truck paralyzed with terror. Several men threw themselves with empty hands on the armed Ukrainians. One succeeded in grabbing a rifle from a Ukrainian and shot him to death. A second later he fell with a bullet in his head. He fell like a hero with a rifle in his hand. That was Dr. Fryd.

"Suddenly, in the face of imminent death, I terribly desired to live. I looked around. It was impossible to escape. I didn't want to die. I was so afraid of a bullet. I closed my eyes not to see but the noise of constant shooting prompted me to quick action. I looked behind me. Fifty steps to the rear stood the Obersturmführer smoking a cigar as he watched the execution, like a general observing a successful war operation. I bolted toward him, fell on my knees and mumbled that I wasn't on the list, that I was here illegally, that I was young and finally that I craved to live.

"I heard his command: '*Hier, stehen bleiben!*' I realized that I was going to live. My escape became a signal for others. Dr. Witonski's wife, holding her two children, came to us. Behind us came a few others. Together we were ten. The Germans sometimes coupled their degenerate bestiality with caprices of generosity. Satiated with blood, the arch-murderer had had enough of his amusement. He shouted, '*Aufhören!*' and the Ukrainians stopped their shooting."

And thus ten people returned from their trip to the cemetery, instead of to Palestine.

Chapter Six:

AUSCHWITZ, THE END OF THE TRAIL

There are several versions of what happened to the first transport of Jewish "Ausländer" – foreign nationals – who were sent from Bergen-Belsen to a fictitious camp called Bergau and said to be near Dresden, in 1943. Actually, these people were transported to Auschwitz, and murdered. Josef Gitler Barski, at that time an inmate in Bergen-Belsen, writes in the introduction to his "Diary of a Prisoner in Bergen-Belsen":

JOSEF GITLER BARSKI

. . . The majority of Polish Jews were deported. In October of 1943, a high official of the Office of German Security Affairs had arrived at the camp and ordered the immediate "departure" of 1,800 Polish Jews. During one roll call, they were informed that they had been chosen to be part of an exchange, and that for the time being, they would wait in a transfer camp called Bergau near Dresden. The transport included Antoni Buksbaum, a well known political activist; Czerski; Joshua Perle, the Yiddish writer; Grzybowski, the ghetto fighter; Galka Leszczynska, daughter of a well known labor activist; the physicians Dr. Chorazycki, Dr. Gedborski, Dr. Weintal, and many others.

As it appeared later, these people were transported not to Bergau, but to the death camp of Auschwitz. After the war, it became known that upon arriving, these people began an uprising. They threw themselves at the SS men, tore away their guns, and broke the barbed wire fence. These facts were later verified by Rudolf Hoess, commander of Auschwitz, at his trial.

Another, more detailed version of what happened when the Jews of the Bergen-Belsen transport arrived at Auschwitz was given by Mrs. Tom-kiewicz:

M. TOMKIEWICZ

... This is what happened to the transport from Bergen-Belsen. One of the men who worked in the gas chambers told the newly arrived group that they were going to be gassed. He therefore asked them to give him their valuables along with their currency, for they had no further need of these things, while he could try to save himself. He also told them that after their death, everything would be taken by the Germans.

That worker, a survivor, testified after the war in Paris, and when the shocked audience asked how he could be so heartless and talk in this manner to the unhappy victims, he replied that a man forced to take part in the annihilation of his own family had no sentiments left in his heart. And besides, he maintained, by telling them what to expect, he gave them a minute chance of defending themselves — either to escape or to die in a less painful way than by gas.

We also learned that after they arrived, the people who were so elegantly dressed and in possession of such 100% perfect documents, didn't believe what they saw. Scenes of despair, hysterical screaming, crying, and madness ensued. In a mad reflex of despair, they began to throw everything they had at the Germans — bottles, thermoses. Some tried to resist. Miss Mann, the dancer, known in Warsaw as a Gestapo agent, ended her infamous career as a blond traitor with a heroic gesture. She threw herself at one of the SS men who had accompanied the transport, wrested the revolver from his hand, and shot him and then herself. A most terrible death for the entire group followed.

I learned all this much later, at the end of the war. In the meantime, we preferred to live in benign ignorance of our friends' fate. Subconsciously, I knew that the end of the war would not prove to be a moment of joy for me, and that, on the contrary, all the gaping wounds would open and that my losses would stand out more conspicuously against the background of a normal life. I frankly admit that in my mind, I tried to push away the moment so desired by everyone. I didn't feel psychologically ready. I had no faith in my strength.

Mrs. Miriam Novitch, who was interned in Vittel, and who later became one of the founders of the Kibbutz of Ghetto Fighters in Israel, writes in her diary about the group of 173 Polish Jews who were deported from Vittel to the French camp of Drancy, and from there to Auschwitz:

Their train arrived in Auschwitz at 11 p.m. on the night of April 30, 1944. The group was separated from the other deportees and conducted to the crematoria . . . In 1964, I was in Frankfurt at the trial of the former SS men from Auschwitz. I learned from one of the survivors, a woman prisoner who worked in the so-called "Schreibstube," that this first group of Polish foreigners, as well as those from the two trains that came from Bergen-Belsen filled with Jews bearing South and Central American passports, fought the SS. The deportees threw bottles and other heavy objects at them.

This is the version given by Mrs. Miriam Novitch during a recent visit to the Irgun Asirei Naziim Misheavar in Tel Aviv, I met a witness of this event, Mr. Chaim Frosz, who is today in charge of this organization of former Nazi prisoners, and who lives in Ramat Gan.

Mr. Frosz is a native of the Polish town of Opoczno, from which he was taken with a group of Jews to Auschwitz on April 26, 1942. He remained there for over 30 months, until October of 1944. The date of his deportation was not accidental. This was the birthday of the "Führer" which the Nazis celebrated in occupied Poland by deporting a tenth of the Jewish population to Auschwitz.

In Auschwitz, Chaim Frosz was assigned to the Bekleidung Kammer, a unit whose task was to repair and sew numbers on clothing taken from murdered Jews and distribute to prisoners in various blocks. For that reason he was in daily contact with the prisoners on the Sonderkommando, who worked at the gas chambers where the victims, before they died, were ordered to strip.

On October 22, 1943, the prisoners of the Sonderkommando told Chaim Frosz and the other members of the Bekleidungskammer who had happened the day before upon the arrival of the "foreign" transport from Bergen-Belsen.

It was an unusual sight. The victims arrived, not in the usual cattle trains, but in comfortable passenger cars. Most of the men and women were elegantly dressed. Some women wore expensive fur coats and hats, and the men wore fashionable suits and coats. Many of the children were similarly dressed. They descended from the cars like real foreigners who had arrived at their peaceful destination. But their faces upon closer inspection could be seen to be marked with fear, for they had seen through the train windows that they were being taken back to Poland. The fear changed to unspeakable terror when, upon descending from the train, they were immediately surrounded by SS men with bestial faces, armed with guns and whips. They also saw the skeletal figures of the Jewish Sonderkommando and heard the SS men savagely shouting at them to undress.

The majority was too paralyzed to move. Others, driven by wrath and despair, began hurling insults at their executioners. At that moment, one of the most vicious and sadistic of the SS men, infamous for his bestiality, Obersturmführer Schillinger, arrived, and began roaring at the victims. At that instant, one of the Jewish women, Gestapo agent and dancer Franciszka Mann, tore her blouse and shouted at the criminal, "Come on, you animal, shoot!" Before he could reach for his gun, she tore it from his holster and shot him dead. She then shot and wounded another SS man, Emmerich, and wounded a third. A few of the young Jews in the transport, survivors of the Warsaw ghetto uprising, threw themselves on the SS men with knives, but they were all executed — all 1800 Jewish men, women and children.

In 1947, during a Congress of Jewish Culture, which was held in Paris with the participation of delegates from many countries, Mr. Chaim Frosz, who was at that time director of the regional committee of the DP camp in Bamburg, described this incident to the assembled delegates. According to him, the news about the heroic act and death of Franciszka Mann spread all over the camp and was the direct cause of the rebellion of the Sonderkommando later on.

FILIP MÜLLER*

But the full story was recounted by a first hand witness, Filip Müller, who later wrote the book *Eyewitness in Auschwitz*. Müller was born in 1922 in Sered, Czechoslovakia. He was deported to Auschwitz in April, 1942, where he was assigned prisoner number 29236. He worked in the Sonderkommando until the evacuation of the camp in 1945. He witnessed the atrocious scene of "foreign" Jews arriving unsuspecting that October night — a scene that exceeded anything that was conceived even in the diabolical minds of Hitler or Goebbels.

... This evening as I went on night duty the crematorium yard was deserted, dimly and scantily lit by a few arc lamps. Every oven had been fired since morning. We were ordered to keep the fires going which meant feeding them with two wheelbarrowfuls of coke every half hour.

Contrary to their wont, several SS leaders including *Oberscharführer* Voss and his aides, Gorges, Kurshuss and Ackermann were in the crematorium before us, busily dashing about and poking their noses into all sorts of things. They checked to see that the fire in the ovens was burning well; they checked the door to the mortuary to make sure it was properly locked; they checked that there were no traces of blood anywhere; they checked the fans; and they switched the light in the gas chamber on and off a few times. Normally the concrete floors in the gas chamber as well as in the changing room were damp; today they were carefully dried. To this end a few coke-burning stoves had been set up and kept going all day. Kurshuss was running about holding a large atomizer from which he sprayed clouds of a sweetish fragrance. Quite obviously the people expected today must not be met by the customary musty odor, but rather the impression must be created that they were in fact inside a perfectly hygienic bathhouse. The notices at the entrance to the changing room were replaced by new and larger ones. The red letters announcing that this was the "entrance to the baths and disinfecting room" stood out well against a pale blue background.

Another party of *SS-Unterführers* arrived, among them Quackernack, Hustek, Emmerich, Schillinger and *Obersturmführer* Schwarzhuber, together with Dr. Thilo, medical officer on duty. All was now ready to receive this clearly out-of-the-ordinary transport.

After a while a convoy of trucks covered with tarpaulins entered the crematorium yard. The SS men who had come with the transport leapt down from the running-boards, ran to the back and let down the tail-boards. Then they raised the tarpaulins and asked the people to step down. This was done so

205

courteously that I could hardly believe my eyes and ears. I was puzzled: what sort of people were these who had just arrived? I noticed that not one of them wore a Star of David. As the people were climbing down from the trucks there was none of the usual shouting, beating and general harassment. On the contrary, the SS men were at their most polite and helpful wherever required. After a short while some 1,000 people were standing in the yard. There were more men than women; all were well dressed, none had any baggage; that, too, was unusual.

A wooden box was set up in the center of the yard arousing the interest of the people who craned their necks to see what was going on. Climbing onto this improvised speaker's platform was *Lagerführer* Schwarzhuber, followed by a man in a leather coat and grey hat with the brim pulled well down. I thought he might be a member of the Gestapo who had been assigned to a special mission. In the yard all was hushed. The crowd stood expectantly, waiting to be addressed.

Schwarzhuber spoke first: "Ladies and gentlemen!" he began. "On behalf of the camp administration I welcome you. We have been instructed to do everything possible to expedite your departure abroad. For this purpose a representative of the Foreign Ministry is here to tell you how the rest of your journey has been organized, and he will now speak to you."

The so-called representative of the Foreign Ministry now mounted the platform. "Ladies and gentlemen!" he said. "I have been instructed by the Foreign Ministry to organize your journey to Switzerland. This is your last stop in the territory of the Third Reich. We have brought you here because the Swiss authorities insist that each one of you must be disinfected before you cross the frontier." He went on officiously: "Here we have the facilities for carrying out large-scale disinfection proceedings. In this building," he pointed at the crematorium, "a large bath-house has been installed where you are to go later. Another thing! After your bath, please have your travel documents ready so that we can certify that you have been disinfected. Once more, may I point out that the Swiss authorities have declared that nobody will be allowed to cross the frontier without this certificate in his passport. Your special train is waiting at the station. It is scheduled to depart at 7 tomorrow morning and will take you to the frontier. I would therefore ask you in your own interest to follow the instructions of the camp personnel. May I end by wishing you a pleasant journey for tomorrow."

It seemed to me that these words had the desired effect. Instinctively many people reached into their breast pockets as though to make sure that their passports were still there. For at that moment they meant more to them than anything else in the world.

The way in which the so-called representative of the Foreign Ministry behaved, his gestures and, above all, his voice, seemed familiar. He was indeed none other than *Obersturmführer* Hössler.

Not long after Hössler's address all the people had left for the underground changing room. Hössler's promises and the courteous and correct conduct of the SS men helped to make everything go off smoothly. We prisoners of the *Sonderkommando* were kept away. Perhaps they thought that our presence might make the people hesitant or give us a chance of speaking to them.

The order for the *Kapo* of the stoker team to fill up the ovens with coke came about a quarter of an hour later than usual. No doubt the delay had been carefully planned: first, it was necessary to wait until the yard had been cleared of people; and second, the noise of coke being fed into the ovens might have made the crowd suspicious.

The lift linking the underground rooms with the cremation room was constantly going up and down. The nervousness displayed by the SS men indicated that, after initially all going so perfectly according to plan, their well-organized murder operation had struck a snag. Kaminski, our *Kapo*, was ordered to stand by with eighteen prisoners, of whom I was one. Some time later an SS man took us down in the lift. There we waited in the corridor from which doors led to the gas chamber, the mortuary, and the changing room. From the latter came a humming of voices, and, at intervals, firm commands ordering the people to undress.

Eventually *Oberscharführer* Voss took us into the mortuary. There behind a pile of emaciated corpses six hand-painted signboards were propped against the wall. They had the letters A-D, E-H, and so on, down to Z, painted on them in black letters and had arrived at the crematorium some days earlier; nobody could imagine what they were meant for. And now the mystery was to be resolved. *Oberscharführer* Voss lined us up in rows of three. Then we marched into the changing room where we took our places along one of the walls, facing the people who had come with the transport. Each board was turned so that they could read the letters.

Naturally we attracted their attention and suddenly there was silence while the crowd was looking at us and at the boards. Hössler, that cunning fox, who was still playing his part as representative of the Foreign Ministry, swiftly exploited the silence. He stepped before the crowd and started to speak again: "Ladies and gentlemen!" he began. "You can all see the boards with the letters of the alphabet which have just been brought in. Now please look at them carefully." Here he pointed at the boards, one after the other, from A to Z. Then he went on: "When you have dressed after your bath, kindly queue up at the board with the first letter of your surname where you will be given a certificate confirming that you have been disinfected. Please also remember the number of your hook in the changing room so that the necessary formalities can be dealt with as quickly and as smoothly as possible. And do not regard this disinfection business as something we have thought up to annoy you. It is, let me reemphasize, the Swiss authorities who insist on it. It is therefore in your own interest to submit to this unavoidable procedure as quickly as possible. You must also remember that railway tracks are often blocked through enemy terror raids. So please hurry up if you want to get away from here without delay!" While he was finishing his speech Hössler gazed at the people facing him like a priest eager to gain the confidence and credibility of his congregation.

When he was finished, the people went into huddles to consult each other. They were talking in Yiddish, and some of them had clearly become suspicious. They were Jews from eastern Europe who doubtless had heard rumors of mass extermination. And yet Hössler's words had impressed many so that they now began to undress. But there were others who were still standing around undecided, ignoring the constant urgings by the SS men that they should hurry and undress. Hössler's speech had not convinced them. They knew somehow that they were in a trap and that their lives were at stake. Therefore they thought it best not to take off their clothes which contained their travel documents.

After a few minutes' hesitation the SS men began to usher the ones who had undressed into the gas chamber, possibly in the belief that once they had them out of the way they might be able to deal with the recalcitrant ones more efficiently. Presently more than half the people were behind the great door of the gas chamber. It seemed that the others still in the changing room were trying to gain time. Time for what, though? The crematorium was surrounded by armed SS men. None of us prisoners was willing to join them in what would be a senseless attempt to get away. Nor was there any chance of telling the people that they were about to be gassed. This might have persuaded them that it was more honorable to die fighting than meekly inside the gas chamber. However, every phase, from their arrival on the ramp to the moment when they were coerced into the gas chamber was deliberately carried out in a tearing hurry leaving the victims no time to think or take decisions.

Surreptitiously *SS-Unterführers* Quackernack, Hustek, Voss, Boger, Schillinger, Gorges, Emmerich, Kurshuss, Ackermann and others left the changing room one by one, returning after a short time armed with sticks. No doubt *Lagerführer* Schwarz-huber had given them the green light to deal with these people in the usual way. Instead of their earlier marked courtesy and lying talk there were now terse requests of "Get undressed! Hurry up! Get ready for your baths! Come on, come on!" The people did not respond, but simply kept standing about, doing nothing. It was not surprising therefore that the SS men grew nervous. In order to demonstrate that they meant business they shifted their holsters round to the front and opened the flaps. Then they came closer to the crowd and, assuming a menacing attitude, began to shout. When this had no effect either, they started to strike blindly at the crowd with their sticks. Now the ones standing in front, in an attempt to dodge the blows, tried to back away while those exposed in turn tried to get out of the way, so that there was utter chaos. The SS increased their furious, merciless beatings. By now many people were bleeding profusely from blows they had received. And finally the rest realized that resistance was useless. There was no way out. They began to undress, whereupon the SS men stopped beating them. Why we were still standing by the wall holding our boards no one knew.

It was obvious that the SS felt themselves once more to be

masters of the situation. Quackernack and Schillinger were strutting back and forth in front of the humiliated crowd with a self-important swagger. Suddenly they stopped in their tracks, attracted by a strikingly handsome woman with blue-black hair who was taking off her right shoe. The woman, as soon as she noticed that the two men were ogling her, launched into what appeared to be a titillating and seductive strip-tease act. She lifted her skirt to allow a glimpse of thigh and suspender. Slowly she undid her stocking and peeled it off her foot. From out of the corner of her eye she carefully observed what was going on round her. The two SS men were fascinated by her performance and paid no attention to anything else. They were standing there with arms akimbo, their whips dangling from their wrists, and their eyes firmly glued on the woman.

She had taken off her blouse and was standing in front of her lecherous audience in her brassiere. Then she steadied herself against a concrete pillar with her left arm and bent down, slightly lifting her foot, in order to take off her shoe. What happened next took place with lightning speed: quick as a flash she grabbed her shoe and slammed its high heel violently against Quackernack's forehead. He winced with pain and covered his face with both hands. At this moment the young woman flung herself at him and made a quick grab for his pistol. Then there was a shot. Schillinger cried out and fell to the ground. Seconds later there was a second shot aimed at Quackernack which narrowly missed him.

Panic broke out in the changing room. The young woman had disappeared in the crowd. Any moment she might appear somewhere else and aim her pistol at another of her prospective executioners. The SS men realized this danger. One by one they crept outside. The wounded Schillinger was still lying unattended on the floor.

After a while a few SS men came in and dragged him hastily to the door. Then a third shot was fired: one of the SS men pulling Schillinger let go of him and started to limp to the door as fast as he could. Then the light went out. Simultaneously the door was bolted from the outside. We, too, were now caught inside the pitch-dark room.

The people who had lost their bearings in the dark were running about in confusion. I, too, was afraid that this might be

210

the end for all of us. Just now, I thought ruefully, when our plans for a rebellion were progressing, and when we had a not inconsiderable hoard of arms and ammunition, why did it have to be just now? I began to grope my way along the wall towards the exit. When I finally reached it I found nearly all of my companions, but also many of the others who instinctively had made for the door. They were weeping and bemoaning their fate, some were praying, others bidding each other farewell. There was considerable speculation as to the identity of the woman who had fired the shots.

A man who was standing near us had noticed that we did not belong to their group. He spoke to us in the dark and wanted to know from where we came.

"From the death factory," one of my companions replied tersely.

The man was very agitated and demanded loudly: 'I don't understand what this is all about. After all, we have valid entry visas for Paraguay; and what's more, we paid the Gestapo a great deal of money to get our exit permits. I handed over three diamonds worth at least 100,000 zlotys; it was all I had left of my inheritance. And that young dancer, the one who fired the shots a little while ago, she had to pay a lot more."

Suddenly the door was flung open. I was blinded by the glare of several searchlights. Then I heard Voss shouting: "All members of the *Sonderkommando*, come out!" Greatly relieved we dashed outside and ran up the stairs and into the yard. Outside the door to the changing room two machine guns had been set up, and behind them several searchlights. Steel-helmeted SS men were lying ready to operate the machine guns. A horde of armed SS men were milling about in the yard.

I was on my way to the cremation room when a car drew up and *Lagerkommandant* Höss climbed out. Then there was the rattle of machine guns. A terrible bloodbath was wrought about the people caught in the changing room. A very few who had managed to hide behind pillars or in corners were later seized and shot. In the meantime, the "disinfecting officers" had thrown their deadly Zyklon B gas down into the gas chamber where the credulous, placing their trust in Hössler's deceitful words, had gone less than an hour earlier.

Next morning we learnt that Schillinger had died on the way

to hospital, while *Unterscharführer* Emmerich had been wounded. The news was received with satisfaction by many camp inmates; for in section B2d of the men's camp Schillinger had been regarded as an extremely brutal and capricious sadist.

The body of the young dancer was laid out in the dissecting room of crematorium 2. SS men went there to look at her corpse before its incineration. Perhaps the sight of her was to be a warning as well as an illustration of the dire consequences one moment's lack of vigilance might result in for an SS man.

As for us, these events had taught us once again that there simply was no chance of escape once a person entered the crematorium: by then it was too late. The promises of the SS, ranging from work inside the camp to emigration to Switzerland, were nothing but barefaced deception, as they had proved to be for these wretched people who had wanted to emigrate to Paraguay.

THE RESCUE THAT FAILED

And so the story which had begun with fear ended — for alas, so many — in death. The Jews who had lived hidden and in terror on the "Aryan side" had gone to the Hotel Polski, following the thinnest thread of hope. From there, they set out on one of three journeys — to Vittel, to Bergen-Belsen, or to the Pawiak Prison.

Ironically, it was those few that belonged to the disdained "Palestine list" who survived in the end. They suffered more fear than those "privileged characters" who possessed Latin American papers, but they lived.

In this book we read the stories of those survivors as they told them in their own words. And the more we read, the more puzzling the total picture becomes, the more tormenting the questions: Did the Jewish collaborators serve the Germans with the deliberate intention of delivering their fellow Jews into the hands of the executioners? What were the hopes, the dreams and the delusions, or how great was the despair, that led Jews to the Hotel Polski? Who, besides the German killers, bears guilt, direct or indirect, for this tragedy?

Who was responsible for this cruel hoax? Was it conceived at the headquarters of the Gestapo on Szuch Avenue in Warsaw, or did it originate at the Central Gestapo headquarters in Berlin? Or was it a brainstorm of Jewish collaborators, born of their own delusions, of their desperate efforts to save themselves along with their fellow Jews?

What was the mysterious role of Dr. Stabenow, the bigwig in the dreaded *Sicherheitsdienst* (Security Service) of Warsaw? How are we to explain the strange behavior of David Guzik, the director of the JDC in Warsaw? Guzik threw the full weight of his prestige behind the Hotel Polski project. He not only lent

213

credibility to this affair but actually gave many victims the money to buy the precious documents. He himself and his closest families had acquired foreign papers. Yet, at the last moment, he chose not to leave Warsaw. Why did he decide to remain, and how could he manage to do so?

The Hotel Polski affair received wide coverage during the trial of Dr. Ludwig Hahn, who had served as chief of the Warsaw Gestapo. The trial took place in Hamburg. On July 4, 1975, Hahn was sentenced to life imprisonment.

Among the witnesses at the trial were survivors of the Hotel Polski, such as Max Gerstmann, Stanley Osinski, Jozef Miodowski, Meyer Bielicki, and David Gilbert. These five men traveled from the United States to Hamburg in order to testify.

Gerstmann was one of those who had bought his Argentine passport from David Guzik. He was taken from the Hotel Polski to Pawiak Prison. He survived the "selection" as an artisan.

Osinski, too, survived the "selection" by working as an artisan. He escaped later from the prison, but his father perished. Meyer Bielicki survived Pawiak as an artisan. David Gilbert bought his papers at the Hotel Polski from Engel, and managed to survive the "selections" first at the Pawiak Prison and then at Bergen-Belsen.

The court which tried Ludwig Hahn spent days hearing testimony on the Hotel Polski case, but could elicit no additional information, neither from the witnesses nor from Hahn himself. The Warsaw butcher Hahn was certainly familiar with the intricacies of the affair but he chose not to share his knowledge with the court.

The more questions we ask, the more illusory the answers become. As in the Japanese motion picture, *Rashomon*, we see different individuals live through the same experience but unable to agree on the facts. For instance, was it sufficient to come to the hotel and state, "I'm Jewish," for the gate to swing open immediately, or was the entrance closely guarded by men in police uniforms? Was the show the work of a few individuals, or was it a systematic operation by an organized gang?

There are glaring discrepancies in facts and figures. How many Jews were victimized at the Hotel? How many were sent to Pawiak Prison — four hundred, five hundred or six hundred? How many transports went to Vittel? To Bergen-Belsen? How many people were in each transport, and on what dates did they set out on their journey? No official lists are extant, so our only sources of information are accounts written much later by the survivors themselves, who are naturally in no position to deal objectively with statistics.

From the diaries, court testimonies and other documentary material stemming from survivors we may assume that between four and five thousand Warsaw Jews went through the Hotel Polski and that of these almost all who held Latin American papers perished in Auschwitz. The sole survivors were the approximately 170 person who had been registered on the so-called "Palestine list."

But there are psychological questions which are still unanswered. What made the Jews believe the false promise of a last-minute rescue held out by the Hotel Polski? And what of the Jewish collaborators who helped the Gestapo perpetrate this monstrous hoax? Was the swindle their own idea, or were they duped into believing that, by participating in the operation, they were helping to save other Jewish lives?

* * *

In December, 1943, the Germans ordered the "internees" in Vittel and Bergen-Belsen to surrender their foreign documents for scrutiny. Chapters "Vittel" and "Bergen-Belsen" in this book describe the terror that seized the "foreigners" at Vittel and Bergen-Belsen when they learned that representatives of the Gestapo's *Auslandsstelle* (Foreign Department) had arrived at the two camps to verify their Latin American documents. Panic-stricken, they used every means available to broadcast their plight to the free world.

Later, it became known that their calls of distress had reached some ears, and also some hearts, in Allied and neutral countries, but the few rescue attempts which were made ended in failure and shame.

The U.S. War Refugee Board appointed by President Franklin D. Roosevelt sent out secret messages, through the State Department, to all U.S. embassies in Latin American countries, imploring the Latin American governments to intercede "in a situation in which so many human lives are at stake." The War Refugee Board tried to persuade the governments of Peru, Costa Rica, Ecuador, Honduras, Venezuela, Paraguay and

Nicaragua to declare their documents held by the Jews in the Hotel Polski as valid, at least until the end of the war. Even if these countries did not actually open their doors to these Jews, an official statement that the papers held by the Jewish "internees" were authentic might have protected the Jews from deportation.

But what was the response from Latin America to the appeals from the United States?

In Peru, the newspaper *Verdades* declared that

> hospitality should not be extended to elements that might endanger the solid basis of our Ibero-American personality, our Catholic tradition. . . . Under no circumstances should we accept the imposition of offering asylum to foreigners who hold religious beliefs contrary to our own, and who follow excessively liberal customs and moral norms different from our own.

When the Germans, through the good offices of the Swiss government, submitted to the Peruvians a list of 48 Jews who held Peruvian papers and were interned in German camps, the Peruvian government flatly denied the authenticity of the documents, thus condemning all the 48 Jews to the gas chambers.

From Caracas, Venezuela, the U.S. embassy reported that

> upon applying for a Venezuelan visa the applicant is asked as to his race, religion and nationality; and if the person is Jewish or of Jewish origin, even though [now] professing another religion, a visa is refused.

From Cuba, the U.S. embassy reported that the attitude of the Cuban government was "indifferent if not slightly hostile." As for Getulio Vargas, President of Brazil, he "showed no inclination to commit Brazil to the reception of refugees of any kind."

Jacob Rosenheim, president of the World Agudas Israel Organization, "implored" the U.S. Department of State to intercede, particularly with the government of Paraguay, to confirm the authenticity of many hundreds of their papers held by Jews under the Nazi yoke. The State Department thereupon advised the Latin American governments that although "it did not condone the sale of unauthorized documents," such documents at that point might mean the difference between life and death for those who held them.

But the State Department did little more than that. The sorry tale was recorded by Arthur Morse in *While Six Million Died*:

216

On February 21, 1944, the War Refugee Board sent the draft of a cable to the State Department, addressed to the American minister in Bern, who would instruct the Swiss to insist upon German protection of the Vittel internees. The State Department refused to send the message because it imposed excessive pressure upon the Swiss and represented a defense of fraudulent documents.

On March 16 the board submitted a more restrained version of the cable. This, too, was rejected by State.

On March 20, three months after their passports had been seized, 240 of the Jews at Vittel were rounded up and isolated from the others. It was clear that they would be sent to Poland [Auschwitz].

The American minister to Switzerland informed the State Department on April 4 of the pending deportation and the following day John Pehle received a desperate plea from [Dr. Isaac Halevi Herzog] the Chief Rabbi of Palestine: "Have received news of imminent danger deportation to Poland of . . . most respected Jewish families now in Vittel. . . . They left Poland over year ago furnished with citizenship Paraguay and other South American countries. . . . Deportation means death. . . . In Heaven's name pray take every step save them particularly through intervention neutral countries. . . . Rest not may Almighty bless your efforts with success. . . ."

Pehle and his staff tried frantically to budge the State Department. They deluged [Secretary of State Edward R.] Stettinius and other officials with phone calls, memoranda and personal visits. On April 7 the department's Policy Committee finally agreed to communicate with the Swiss. After a three-week delay they sent the restrained draft of March 16. It was too late. Before the Swiss could approach the Germans, the first group of 173 Jews was sent from Vittel to the transit camp at Drancy. On April 29 about sixty of them — men, women and children — left Drancy for Auschwitz, never to return. At the instigation of the War Refugee Board, the Swiss made an earnest effort to intervene in behalf of the deportees, but German authorities claimed they did not know the whereabouts of the Vittel group.

In all, 238 Jews of Vittel died in Auschwitz. Among them were the distinguished Yiddish and Hebrew poet-playwright Itzhak Katznelson and his eighteen-year-old son. Earlier, Katznelson's wife and two younger son had been arrested in the Warsaw ghetto and put to death at Treblinka; the poet and his son, Zvi, had escaped to a bunker dug deep beneath a hothouse outside the ghetto. In May, 1943 they were given Honduran passports by a resistance fighter. Soon after, they were arrested in Poland by the Germans and sent to Vittel. During the next ten months Katznelson, wracked by the memory of his murdered wife and children, poured his agonizing lament into a diary, several plays and his epic poem, *The Song of the Murdered Jewish People*. Before he was taken from Vittel the poet placed his finely written, rolled-up manuscripts into bottles, which he buried beneath the sixth tree in a row of pines. He divulged this hiding place to several companions and one of the survivors later dug up the bottles. Other Katznelson writings were smuggled out of Vittel by a courageous French laundress who had sewn them into rags.

Twelve days after Itzhak and Zvi Katznelson were taken to Auschwitz, the Germans responded to the Swiss plea that they honor Latin American passports. On May 11, 1944, the Nazis agreed to stop deporting Jews with identity papers from Latin American countries. If the State Department had not held up its cable to Switzerland for three weeks, Katznelson and the Jews of Vittel might have survived.

Of course, the State Department's sluggishness was not the sole responsible factor in the tragedy of Vittel. As already pointed out, much of the blame must be placed on the Latin American foreign ministries, which refused to validate the papers issued to Jews by their consuls in Europe.

Most of the Latin American countries had imposed restrictions on the immigration of Jewish refugees even before the war. Such restrictive legislation was passed in Argentina as early as October, 1938, by Bolivia in August, 1939, by Cuba in January and May, 1939, by Colombia in May, 1939, by Paraguay in January 1930, and by Uruguay in May, 1939.

The Latin American reluctance to accept Jewish refugees was undoubtedly inspired by anti-Semitism. Brazil, Argentina and Chile had compact German minorities whom the governments did not wish to antagonize by admitting Hitler's victims. When Stephen S. Wise and Dr. Nahum Goldmann planned a trip to South America in December, 1940, they were cautioned by Assistant Secretary of State Adolf Berle that their visit "might energize the anti-Semitic feelings" in these countries. Anti-Jewish riots had occurred in Mexico, and the Federation of Mexican Farmers had requested restrictions on Jewish immigration because "almost all of them came in under false pretenses and did not engage in work as they (had] promised. They have all become merchants and gangsters." Bolivia at the time was considering the adoption of a resolution prohibiting Jews, Mongols and Negroes from entering the country.

"Supplementing the traditional anti-Semitism," Professor

218

Henry L. Feingold comments in his book, *The Politics of Rescue*, "was the fear of the indigenous merchant class that Jews, whose reputation for sharp business dealings preceded them, would create keen competition for the local market. Few Jews became gangsters, but many of them did become merchants. Much of the hostility was stimulated by a 'drift back' phenomenon which saw refugees who had entered the country as farmers move into the cities to take up their old way of life."

However, there was yet another reason why the governments of Latin America were averse to admitting Jewish refugees or even to "platonically" endorsing their documents for the duration of the war. The Latin American passports, visas and *promesas* had been procured by Dr. Abraham Silberschein and other Jewish individuals and organizations in Switzerland from Latin American diplomatic officials in Bern. Some of the consuls and other officials who issued these documents were motivated not solely by humanitarian feelings. Widespread rumors were circulated in their homelands about the wealth which these officials allegedly amassed as their reward for the documents. These transactions were carried out on a strictly local level, without sanction from the governments concerned. When these governments were then requested to authenticate the documents, they were shocked at the shady dealings of their consuls. So it was small wonder that they gave less than a wholehearted reception to demands that they verify the documents issued by their consular officials in Switzerland.

* * *

Let us return to the Jewish collaborators who worked at the Hotel Polski. Did any of them act in good faith? We know that many of them sent their own families with the transports and finally set out on the journey themselves. There is, of course, the possibility that the Nazis had promised them immunity for themselves and their families if they "delivered" the Jews who had escaped from the ghetto and were hiding out in the "Aryan sector" of Warsaw. We know now that if these collaborators ever believed promises of personal safety made by the Germans, they found themselves cruelly deceived in the end. Four members of the family of Leon Skosowski perished *via* Vittel in Auschwitz. Pawel Wlodawski did not survive Bergen-Belsen, where he served as a *kapo*. Franciszka Mann, too, perished in Auschwitz.

In my interview with him shortly before his death in the summer of 1981, "Antek" Zuckerman, the leader of the Jewish Fighting Organization (ZOB), spoke in the harshest terms about the Jewish collaborators. However, he quoted the words of David Guzik, who, though working with the collaborators by lending his name to the Hotel Polski project, was a loyal member of the underground. "We should be grateful to [the collaborators]," Guzik had said, "even if they had helped save only one single Jewish life."

Elie Wiesel returns to this theme over and over again. In *One Generation After* he writes:

> In dealing with the victims, in an effort to break their morale before annihilating them, the executioners assumed the role of God. They alone could, by decree, proclaim the limits of good and evil. Their idiosyncrasies were law and so were their whims. They were above morality, above truth.
>
> Prisoners of such a system, many deportees chose the easy path of abdication. How is one to judge them? I do not. I cannot condemn anyone who failed to withstand trials and temptations. Guilty or not, the ghetto police, the *kapos*, may plead extenuating circumstances. They arouse pity more than contempt. The weak, the cowardly, all those who sold their soul to live another day, another anxious night, I prefer to include them in the category of victims. More than the others, they need forgiveness. More and in other ways than their companions, they deserve compassion and charity. Their guilt reflects on their tormentors.
>
> Still, I sometimes read books presented as evidence for the prosecution. Their authors are harsh, their judgments devoid of compassion. Whether their words hurt or shock matters little: they will be heard. Of necessity fragmentary, they do not reflect the whole, but are part of it. In fact, this can serve as a general rule: every witness expresses only his own truth, in his own name. To convey the truth of the Holocaust in its totality, it is not enough to have listened to the survivors; one must find a way to add the silence left behind by millions of unknowns. That silence can have no interpreter. One cannot conceive of the Holocaust except as a mystery, begotten by the dead.

Hannah Arendt went so far as to accuse the entire Jewish leadership in Nazi-occupied Europe of actively helping in the annihilation of their people. Her judgment is heartless. In her cold, impersonal condemnation, in which she set herself up as an outsider, referring to the Jewish people as "they" — as if she herself had not been a Jew — she avoided the obvious fact that all the evil which existed in the camps and the ghettos had been triggered by the Nazis.

Even if some Jewish individuals, as Elie Wiesel puts it, "chose the easy path of abdication," the guilt still lies with those who had created the universe of horror.

* * *

The Hotel Polski affair was but a tiny episode in that German-created "absolute reign of evil." The hotel had been built a number of years before the war. It was razed by the Germans, along with thousands of other buildings in Warsaw, methodically and cold-bloodedly. Only a short time before a detonation bomb turned the building into rubble did the Hotel Polski rise for a brief moment from its anonymity, to become the scene of the hoax described in this book.

The Hotel Polski no longer exists but its memory refuses to vanish. We will not forget the Jewish men, women and children who declared their Jewishness and thus risked death for the privilege of entering that "island of hope." We will not forget the terror that filled their hearts when they were herded into German trucks in the courtyard of the hotel for their journey not to Treblinka but to the "paradise" of Vittel or to the relatively "peaceful" camp of Bergen-Belsen. Nor shall we be able to erase from our memory the "courtesy" with which the German murderers in Auschwitz lured the "privileged foreigners" into the showers that dispensed not water but Zyklon B gas.

And we are still left with the mystery of the Hotel Polski affair. Was it a Nazi trap, diabolically conceived and efficiently managed? Was it the product of an impossible dream by terrified human beings grasping at a last straw? Or was it a genuine rescue effort which, for reasons beyond the control of its engineers, ended in failure?

NOTES

1. Dr. Nathan Eck, a Zionist activist and historian in prewar Poland, who survived by jumping from the train which took the internees from Vittel to the Drancy camp in France, and who now lives in Israel, is the author of many books on the Holocaust. In his essay, "The Rescue of Jews with the Aid of Passports and Citizenship Papers of Latin American States," in the *Yad Vashem Studies,* I (1957), he gives an account of what occurred in Warsaw on the eve of the great deportations.

> In Warsaw, citizens of the United States of America and the British Commonwealth were required to register with the authorities on the 14th of April, 1942, — about three months prior to the first transport of Jews from the Polish capital to Treblinka. Five days before the extermination operations were launched, namely on the 17th of July, 1942, hundreds of persons holding such passports were arrested and detained in the Pawiak prison. It was an open secret, however, that these arrests indicated that the lives of the Jews of the Ghetto rather than those of the detainees were in jeopardy. The general opinion was that the Jews of the Ghetto would be engulfed in a wave of destruction. Many believed that something similar to the calamity which had overtaken the Jews of Lublin, who had been slaughtered on the concluding day of the Passover festival, was imminent. The detention of aliens was regarded as a precautionary measure to remove them from impending danger. Such indeed proved to be the case. During the *aktzia* no harm befell those incarcerated in the Pawiak prison.
>
> During the summer months, when the most fearful atrocities were a frequent occurrence in the streets of the Ghetto, these Jews were given the asylum of the Prison. Subsequently, they were transferred in groups to concentration camps, some to Vittel and others to Tittmoning. Also incarcerated at this time in the Pawiak prison was a group of Jews from Lwow who were subjects of countries then at war with Germany. Members of this group were transported together with the Warsaw group. In the Mon-

telupi prison in Cracow, a similar group was detained at the same time; the members of this group were transferred directly to a detention camp for enemy aliens.

After the conclusion of the first deportation of Jews from Warsaw (the operation came to an end on the 10th of September, 1942), there remained only about forty to fifty thousand Jews in the diminished Ghetto and in the German workshops. This deportation was followed by a short period of comparative quiet. Obviously, very few believed that this respite would continue for long. Whoever was able to do so sought asylum beyond the walls of the Ghetto, in the "Aryan" section of the city. Many of these fugitives dispatched pleas to relatives and friends in the free countries, asking them to send them "papers" which could help them to survive. They recalled the case of the Jews who had been detained in the Pawiak prison from whom favorable letters from Vittel and other camps began to arrive. Some individuals were even successful in transmitting funds clandestinely to Switzerland for the purchase of passports. In the Ghetto itself, a public committee was formed (comprising Dr. I. Schipper, Dr. E. Ringelblum, L. L. Bloch, Menachem Kirszenbaum, Zisha Friedman and other leading personalities) which drew up a list of notables, who because of public considerations should be allowed to acquire passports gratis. These lists were secretly transmitted abroad. They included not only passports but also "promesas," namely, letters from consuls of various countries to the effect that the citizenship of the country the consul represented had been granted to the addressee and his family. The recipient was informed that upon the receipt of the requisite photographs and relevant data, a proper passport would be issued in due course.

The "papers" began to arrive, but many of those for whom they had originally been intended were no longer alive and for that reason they were sold to other interested persons.

Some Jews, however, were successful in acquiring passports for comparatively little money. These passports were of local Warsaw manufacture. One witness gave evidence of passports of this category purchased from a gentile who prior to the war had been employed in the consulate of one of the Latin American countries. This gentile had in his possession the necessary forms and stamps. These documents were no less efficacious than those emanating from Switzerland. All holders of foreign passports were arrested and dispatched in May 1943 to Vittel.

2. Thousands of Latin American papers were sent to Poland from Switzerland by the Agudat Israel and mainly by the organization of Abraham Silberschein. The name of this organization was: RELICO — Hilfskomitee zur Hilfeleistung für die durch den Krieg betroffene jüdische Bevölkerung. This Com-

223

mittee was established by Dr. Silberschein immediately following the outbreak of the war. Its activities were financed by the contributions of individuals and Jewish organizations throughout the world, including the World Jewish Congress, the Palestine Rescue Committee (Constantinople), the Histadrut — Jewish Federation of Labor, the Galician Jews Organization, etc.

According to Dr. Nathan Eck, (in his essay in *Yad Vashem Studies*),

> . . . Virtually none of those for whom papers had been sent were living at the time. The Gestapo resolved to issue these papers to other Jews. The only place where such Jews were to be found was in concealment in the "Aryan" quarter. The task of seeking out these Jews and of inducing them to purchase (at a very high price) these "papers" was entrusted by the Gestapo to its Jewish agents. The place where such customers for these "papers" were to assemble was first the Royal Hotel. Later the venue was changed to the Hotel Polski.
>
> No great effort was necessary to persuade the Jews to purchase the "papers" offered for sale. The fact that transports had been dispatched to Vittel and other camps was already common knowledge. It was also known that the inmates of these camps lived in safety and that they suffered from no discrimination in respect of the non-Jewish inmates of the camps. Moreover, many of the Jews were the true owners of the papers now offered for sale. They presumed that somehow Jews abroad had discovered some means of salvation of their brethren from the hands of the murderers. Furthermore, it must be remembered that very few Jews felt secure in their hiding places. They were liable to be denounced and apprehended at any time. In case of discovery those who had sheltered them were equally in danger of summary execution. We can assume that, generally speaking, any person whose refuge was reasonably safe, did not go either to the Hotel Royal or the Hotel Polski.
>
> The agents of the Gestapo, engaged in this traffic in "documents," appointed a "public committee" stationed inside the Hotel to fix the prices of the documents. Wealthier customers were sometimes required to pay fantastic prices. Lower prices were established for those of humbler means, while there were even cases of documents being given away gratis. Every document was issued to a family of at least five persons, in order to ensure the maximum benefit. Generally prolific "families" comprising eight, nine, or even ten persons were created. All members of such families were equipped with the necessary Polish documents establishing their identity. It is imperative to point out that the documents were made out in the names of Jews who were well-known in Warsaw, for it was mainly to such members of the

Warsaw community that Silberschein sent "papers." In this manner thousands of Jews congregated in the "Hotel." Among them were a number who had been brought — at a price — from the provincial towns and even from the Poniatowa and Trawniki labor camps, to which the notorious workshops of Toebbens and Schultz had been transferred, together with their labor forces from the Warsaw ghetto. prior to its destruction.

Among the Jews in Hotel Polski there were a number of immense wealth, some of whom had become rich during the war, others who had in their possession precious stones acquired before the outbreak of war, and also owners of real estate, who possessed very little ready money. The last class sold landed property — buildings, shops, factories, even orange orchards in Palestine — to those who possessed cash. These transactions were ratified by witnesses and by a handshake, the date of execution being set after the cessation of hostilities.

3. **German Documents.** According to nearly all materials, reports, diaries and interviews it is apparent that the Hotel Polski Affair started some time after the uprising and destruction of the ghetto and after the first group of "foreign Jews" had passed through the Hotel Royal. But, strangely, there exist two documents from German sources which indicate that Jews in possession of foreign papers had entered the Hotel Polski while the ghetto still existed and even during the very time of the Uprising.

The subject of the Hotel Polski was mentioned during the trial of the major Nazi war criminals in Nuremberg before the International Military Tribunal.

On February 24, 1946, the Nazi SS and Police Leader of Warsaw, who carried out the final destruction of the Warsaw ghetto, Jürgen Stroop, testified before the investigating officer, Luke P. Rogers. Jürgen Stroop was asked to testify concerning the actions against the Warsaw Ghetto, and in particular Himmler's and Kaltenbrunner's responsibility.

This is the affidavit of Jürgen Stroop, in which he mentioned the Hotel Polski.

> My name is Jürgen Stroop. I was the SS and Police Leader of the Warsaw district from April 17 or 18, 1943, until the end of August, 1943. The action against the Warsaw Ghetto was planned by my predecessor, SS. Oberführer Dr. Ferdinand von Sammern-Frankenegg. On the day when the action began I took over the command and Dr. von Sammern-Frankenegg explained

225

to me what had to be done. He had before him the direct order from Himmler. In addition to this I had a telegram from Himmler who gave me the order describing how to clear the ghetto and to obliterate the entire area.

In order to comply I had two Waffen-SS battalions, one hundred Wehrmacht soldiers, units of Ordnungspolizei and between seventy-five and one hundred Sicherheitspolizei.

Jürgen Stroop proceeds to explain the part played by the Obersturmbannführer, Dr. Ludwig Hahn, (head of the Warsaw Gestapo), and the involvement of Kaltenbrunner; both received their orders from Berlin.

After the people were removed from the ghetto, between fifty and sixty thousand of them were taken to the railway station. The Sicherheitspolizei had full control over these people who were transported to Lublin.

And now he mentions the Hotel Polski:

Directly after the action against the ghetto was completed there were about three hundred foreign Jews assembled in the Hotel Polski. Some of them were there from before the action. Others had been taken there during the action. Kaltenbrunner had ordered that these people be transported. Hahn himself told me that he received this order from Kaltenbrunner. All executions were ordered from the Reichssicherheitshauptamt [Reich Security Main Office], Kaltenbrunner.

Three months earlier, on November 9, 1945, another witness gave his testimony before the same Major Luke P. Rogers — Karl Kaleske, the adjutant to Jürgen Stroop's predecessor, Dr. von Sammern-Frankenegg. Here is the full text of the document:

Before me, Major Luke P. Rogers, being authorized to administer oaths, personally appeared Karl Kaleske, who, being duly sworn through the interpreter, made and subscribed the following statement:

My name is Karl Kaleske. I was Adjutant to Doctor von Sammern-Frankenegg from November 1942 until April 1943, while he was SS and Polizeiführer of Warsaw. I then was Adjutant to SS and Polizeiführer Stroop until August 1943. The action against the Warsaw ghetto was planned while von Sammern-Frankenegg was SS and Polizeiführer. General Stroop took over the command on the day of the commencement of the action. The function of the Security Police during the action against the Warsaw ghetto was to accompany the SS troops. A certain number of SS troops were assigned the task to clear a certain street. With every SS group there were from four to six Security policemen, because they knew the ghetto thoroughly. These Security policemen were under Doctor Hahn, Commander of the Security Police for Warsaw. Hahn received his orders not from the SS and Polizeiführer of Warsaw, but directly from Kaltenbrunner in Berlin. This pertains not only to the ghetto action but to all matters. Frequently Doctor Hahn came to our office and told the SS and Polizeiführer that he had received such and such an order from Kaltenbrunner about the contents of which he wanted to inform the SS and Polizeiführer. He would not do this with every order, but only with certain ones.

I remember the case of the three hundred foreign Jews who had been collected in the Hotel Polski by the Security Police. At the end of the ghetto action, Kaltenbrunner ordered the Security Police to transport these people away.

During my time in Warsaw the Security Police had been in charge of matters concerning the underground. The Security Police handled these matters independently of the SS and Polizeiführer, and received its orders from Kaltenbrunner in Berlin. When the leader of the (Polish) underground in Warsaw was captured in June or July 1943, he was flown directly to Kaltenbrunner in Berlin.

I have read the statement over and I have understood it completely. I have made the statement freely and without compulsion. I swear before God that this statement is in accordance with the full truth.

[Signed] Karle Kaleske

Subscribed and sworn to before me at Wiesbaden, Germany, on this 24th day of February, 1946.

[Signed] Luke P. Rogers
Major CMP
Investigating officer

These are the only two known instances in which the Hotel Polski Affair was mentioned at the Nuremberg Trials. The testimony of the two Nazi criminals, that "foreign Jews" were assembled in the Hotel Polski while the ghetto had still existed and during the uprising, has not been confirmed by any of the Jewish survivors who were directly or indirectly involved in this sinister affair.

4. In the above mentioned essay, Dr. Nathan Eck continues:

Passports, citizenship papers and similar documents issued by Latin American countries, and member-states of the British

227

Commonwealth, provided protection, against the nefarious designs of the Nazis, not only when the issuing states were neutral, but even when they were belligerents. The diplomatic representatives of the neutral states — as long as they maintained their neutrality — made provision for the safety of their citizens both in Germany itself and in the German-occupied territories. When these countries became belligerents other neutral countries (the "protector states") assumed this responsibility. The members of the Gestapo and the SS, into whose hands the extermination plans had been committed, endeavored to seize these Jews who were citizens of countries overseas, too, but they were overruled by the central German authorities.

And here Dr. Nathan Eck quotes the instructions issued by the Nazi Chief of Security Police and SD in France on June 26, 1942, in regard to the deportation of Jews.

These instructions state that all able-bodied Jews, both male and female, from sixteen to forty-five years of age are to be arrested. An exception is to be made in the case of Jews who have intermarried with Gentiles, and those who are subjects of the United States, the British Commonwealth, Mexico, belligerent enemy countries of Central and South America, neutral countries of Central and South America, neutral countries and the Allied Powers.

He also mentions the memorandum of Luther (a top-ranking official in the German Foreign Ministry) to Ribbentrop, of 4th December, 1941, in which *inter alia* it is stated: "Special consideration was generally only granted Jews of American [USA] citizenship because these States have the possibility of taking reprisals against Reich Germans." NG 4667, Trials of War Criminals before the [American] Nuremberg Military Tribunals, vol. XIII, p. 196. The documents were issued by the diverse Latin American countries. . . . Most of the passports were obtained through agents in New York. Paraguayan papers, however, were issued by the consul of that country in Berne, Switzerland.

These passports were genuine and were issued by duly accredited representatives of their various countries. It may, of course, be questioned whether the consuls were authorized to issue such documents to persons who had never been within the borders of the issuing states, and whether, accordingly the passports were valid. The Soviet authorities, however, did not go into this aspect and were willing to issue exit visas to holders of such documents, although, it is reasonable to assume, they were not ignorant of their dubious validity.

And further:

The cost of such documents was not exorbitant and in New

228

York fluctuated between two and three hundred dollars. The major part of this fee ended up in the pockets of the middlemen. We may assume, accordingly, that the consuls were actuated not by mercenary but by humanitarian motives. At the time, of course, these documents represented not salvation from death, but from a nomad existence, from disintegration of the family, from political dangers and other important, but not fatal consequences.

5. In Israel, in the Kibbutz of Ghetto Fighters, I had a conversation with one of the founders of the kibbutz, Antek Zuckerman. His is a name which is rarely mentioned without the accompanying adjective, "legendary," in respect of his heroic role in the underground struggle against the Nazis. What he told me throws additional light on the Hotel Polski Affair.

Antek said that the Joint director, David Guzik, was well aware of the role played by the few Jews who collaborated with the Germans, but, like many others, he nourished the hope that some of those who sought refuge in the Hotel would indeed be saved. Guzik expressed on many occasions the view that those who collaborated with the Germans should be praised even if but one Jew would be saved as a result of the Affair.

According to Antek, not only wealthy Jews who were able to buy foreign documents for fantastic amounts of money came to the Hotel, but also groups of ghetto fighters, some of them directly from the sewers and burnt-out houses. Guzik, according to Antek, was an honest and naive man and the Jews who collaborated with the Germans used him to give the Affair an air of respectability.

6. The many letters sent by the internees in Vittel were received in Switzerland. "At about this time," says Dr. Nathan Eck in his account:

> The consulate maintained in Switzerland by the Polish Government-in-Exile intervened on the grounds that the required documents were intended to succor Polish subjects. Thus a situation emerged in which the Paraguayan consulate, previously the main source of such documents, refused to continue this branch of its activities except through the channels of the Polish consulate. The monopoly thereby created caused the price of documents to rise and a number even diverted this traffic for their private profit. Dr. Silberschein stood in need of a large number of these "documents" and for that reason was unable to pay the high prices demanded. After considerable effort, how-

ever, he was successful in forming contacts with the consulates of other Latin American countries, including Honduras, Peru, Haiti, Chile and Bolivia. Dr. Silberschein first conceived the issue of "promesas" — described above — which did not call for large sums of money. He was instrumental in securing such "promesas" from the Honduras consulate, for members of the Agudat Israel. The Honduras consul sincerely sought to assist the work of rescue and issued "promesas" for a very low fee, almost gratis in fact. We must place on record the efforts of Mr. Mandel-Mantello, then an official employed in the consulate of San Salvador, who issued documents free of charge, even covering part of the expenditure involved out of his own pocket.

It was Dr. Silberschein's practice to send documents to applicants with whom he was personally acquainted. The circle of his friends, particularly among the public personalities of many countries, was very extensive. He also dispatched papers in response to requests from public committees, such as had been set up in Warsaw and Bedzin. Various Jewish organizations also submitted to him lists of names of persons who should be provided with passports. Among these were the Rescue Committee of the Jewish Agency and the Ichud Poalei-Zion Hitachdut, the Jewish World Congress and the Jewish Workers' Councils in U.S.A.

Dr. Nathan Eck writes about the political efforts on behalf of the holders of foreign passports:

> Efforts to secure recognition of the passports commenced towards the end of 1943. Frequent and extensive reference to these efforts is made in the reports and documents of the World Jewish Congress, the Rescue Committee of the American Agudat Harabbanim (Agudat Israel) and of the War Refugee Board established by President Roosevelt.
>
> One writer, a leader of the Agudat Israel, then close to the Rescue Committee of the Agudat Harabbanim, relates as follows:
>
> "There were dramatic moments in the efforts made to rescue the members of that group (i.e. the holders of passports). As a result of the stormy and persistent demands made by delegations of Rabbis on behalf of the Rescue Committee, Cordell Hull and Henry Morgenthau acted with dispatch to obtain recognition of the validity of the passports."
>
> Dr. Tartakower, a leader of the World Jewish Congress tells us: "In December 1943 I was dispatched by the Congress to London on a dual mission: i. to persuade the Governments-in-Exile in London to establish Rescue Departments; ii. to establish contact with the Inter-Governmental Committee for Refugees in regard to rescue activity, and *inter alia* to urge them to take steps for the recognition of the passports issued by various Governments. I

had several talks with Mr. Herbert Emerson, the British Representative on this Committee, who gave me his assurance that he would take the matter up. I know that he endeavoured to honor his promise, although I have no knowledge of the details or to what degree his efforts were successful."

The official report *Unity in Dispersion* published by the Congress in 1948 also discusses this matter.

"Following representations made by the Congress, the Inter-American Advisory Committee for Political Defence resolved: i. to warn the German government to grant recognition to the documents and permits held by persons in whose names they were issued; ii. to draft exchange arrangements on a collective basis with a view to securing the release of these persons."

The Roosevelt War Refugee Board in its report also recounts its efforts on behalf of the holders of these passports, going so far as to declare that this was one of the most successful instruments for relieving the victims of persecution. These three organizations urged leaders of the United States to act. Meanwhile the panic-stricken detainees of Vittel anxiously waited, hoping against hope that the efforts being made on their behalf would ultimately prove successful.

On the 18th of April, 1944 a transport comprising 163 persons, all of whom held "papers" of this kind left the Vittel camp. They were followed a month later by another comprising sixty persons. They (and the entire international community of detainees, the majority of whom were non-Jewish aliens holding British Commonwealth and American citizenship), were informed that the Germans had waited patiently for six months after the documents held by these persons had been found to be invalid. The detainees had been granted an opportunity to explain the situation to their friends abroad; the latter had possessed adequate time to secure the recognition of the passports — but in vain. The passports had not been recognized. It was impossible to detain these people any longer, even for a single day, in a camp established for aliens. For this reason it had been resolved to transfer them to another camp.

The "other camp" was the Drancy Camp near Paris, via which the detainees were despatched to Auschwitz. Only fourteen or fifteen persons who had remained behind in the Vittel Camp survived.

However, the political efforts made by the various bodies referred to above nevertheless bore some fruit, apparently after the Jews of Vittel were transported to Drancy. Finally the passports were recognized as valid.

Dr. Nathan Eck writes at the end of his report that an official decision recognizing the passports was taken only on May 31st, 1944. On that day those included in the first transport despatched from the Vittel Camp were no longer alive, while the members of the second transport, left — if we are not mistaken — the Drancy Transit Camp on that very day in the wake of their unfortunate brethren.

We are in possession of an official letter, written by Else Robinson, President of the American Section, Camp Vittel. Here is its content:

> Vittel, Sept. 26th 1944
> CIVIL AFFAIRS DETACHMENT
> **VITTEL**
> Dear Sirs,
> The following statement concerning the Citizens of Central and South America was made in my presence by Dr. Feissler, delegate of the Swiss Legation in Paris on his visit to this camp on the 6th of July, 1944:
> "THE DOCUMENTS, CERTIFICATES OF ALL CENTRAL AND SOUTH AMERICANS IN THIS CAMP, ARE CONSIDERED LEGAL BY THEIR RESPECTIVE GOVERNMENTS."
> Else ROBINSON
> President of the American Section

The letter was written on September 26, 1944. It is evident from the tone of the letter that its writer was elated by the good news. The "respective governments" of Central and South America came forth too late with their recognition of legality. All the recipients had by then perished in Auschwitz.

7. Dr. Nathan Eck, in his Yad Vashem report on "Passports and Citizenship Papers," underlines the efforts of Dr. Abraham Silberschein in Geneva, Switzerland, with regard to Jewish holders of foreign documents.

> During the war years Dr. Silberschein was stationed in Geneva where he conducted an intensive and ramified work of rescue, which included, among other things, the provision of "rescue papers" for Jews in Poland, Holland, Germany and other countries. In effect Dr. Silberschein headed the efforts in this sphere. . . .
> The writer himself [Nathan Eck] was the recipient, while in German-occupied Poland in 1943, of a Paraguayan passport, coming from Dr. Silberschein. As a holder of such a document he was detained in a camp for foreigners, first in Tittmoning-Laufing, Germany, and subsequently in Vittel.

8. Henry L. Feingold, in his book, *The Politics of Rescue*, reports how the Roosevelt administration dealt with the problem

of protecting Jews who possessed foreign documents:

> Under continuing pressure, the State Department also moved to safeguard those Jews who clung to life by means of passports and visas from neutral nations. Until the final months of 1943, the possession of papers could make the difference between life and death. Such papers would be passed from hand to hand after the death of the original owner. Through the efforts of Dr. Abraham Silberschein, head of the Relief Committee for Jewish War Victims who worked out of Geneva, hundreds of these life-saving documents were smuggled into Axis Europe. Sometimes the Gestapo itself trafficked in such papers. In November 1943 the operation was endangered when the governments in exile began to acquire such papers for their own purposes resulting in a price rise to exorbitant levels and placing their continued usefulness in jeopardy. In December Berlin officials, who had honored such documents and interned their possessors in a special camp in Vittel, France, began to rescreen the documents. Apprehension for the safety of the Vittel inmates rose to a fever pitch. Jacob Rosenheim, of the World Jewish Congress, "implored" the State Department to make inquiries and to use its influence especially with the government of Paraguay, where many of the papers originated, to affirm their legitimacy. The Department complied. It informed the Latin-American governments involved that although it did not approve the sale of unauthorized documents, the situation was so critical that the governments ought at least to delay cancelling false passports so that the holders might remain alive. But the Department became restive when rescue advocates and the WRB suggested that the Swiss government be used as intermediary to transmit to Berlin the government's concern for the continued welfare of the internees at Vittel. Enough pressure had already been placed on the Swiss government and it was not expedient for the United States to be involved with the protection of people who held fraudulent documents. After considerable pressure by the War Refugee Board, the Department finally forwarded a toned-down request to the Swiss government in April, 1944. By that time 240 Vittel Jews had already been earmarked for Auschwitz. Only two were ever heard from again. In May, as suddenly as it had begun, the Nazi authorities reversed themselves and began again to honor Latin-American documents. Alas, the owners of the documents were no longer alive.

9. In his book, *The End of Illusions*, Jonas Turkow writes that Dudelzak and Ajzenstadt succeeded in crossing the border to Switzerland. Their accounts of the German atrocities and gas chambers in occupied Poland resulted in the Swiss government changing its policy toward Jewish refugees. The government also began to show interest in the Jews who were being sent to

Vittel, Bergen-Belsen and other camps for the purpose of a supposed exchange. Unfortunately, their "interest" came too late.

10. In his book, *The Final Solution*, Gerald Reitlinger writes about the origins of the Bergen-Belsen camp:

> There were many Germans interned in the U.S.A. and Latin America, but very few natives of the New World interned by the Germans, Himmler therefore ordered Eichmann to find a special camp for these useful if bogus foreign subjects. A new concentration camp had been under construction at Bergen-Belsen since April, and to this camp 367 Jews with Spanish passports were brought from Salonika on August 2nd, 1943, while on September 15th, an additional 305 owners of foreign passports arrived in wagons that had been detached from the Westerbork-Auschwitz death train. There were already 3,000 Jews in Bergen-Belsen, and in the next twelve months, an increment of 3,750 arrived from Holland alone. Eventually the Dutch Jews in the exchange camp at Bergen-Belsen were to number 4,594.
>
> From the very beginning, the purposes of Bergen-Belsen were confused and uncertain. *Obersturmführer* Nowak wrote to Zöpf from Eichmann's office on September 9th, 1943, that only Jews from the "exchange list," Jews with relatives in Palestine, and "Honduras and Paraguay" Jews should be sent there. But further categories were introduced among the 1,037 Jews who arrived from Westerbork on January 11th, 1944; diamond workers, men decorated with the German Iron Cross and their families, half-Jews belonging to the Dutch Confessional Church — and Trotsky's nephew. This confusion of purpose appears in the variety of terms by which Bergen-Belsen was officially designated "convalescence camp," "transit camp," and "exchange camp."

11. According to Dr. Nathan Eck's report

> the camp at Bergen-Belsen comprised little more than a number of wooden huts, remaining from a prisoner-of-war camp dating back to the First World War. The Germans proceeded to establish a camp for Jews whom they did not intend to send — for the time being at any rate — to the extermination centers. The inmates included Jews from whom the Germans hoped in due course to derive some benefit and who could, for example, be exchanged for Germans living outside German-controlled territory. Former residents of Poland constituted a separate unit in this Camp, maintaining no contact with the other units which developed in the course of time. They were not required to work, nor to wear any mark on their clothing indicating that they were Jews. They were merely to wait "for their journey abroad." Cruel disappointment was not long in coming, however. In August or September 1943 Dr. Seidel, a Gestapo officer, conducted a

meticulous examination of the documents and of the inmates themselves. The latter assembled in families on the grounds. The sight of these prolific families, the members of which, as any child could immediately discern, were bound by no blood relationship whatever, made a ridiculous spectacle. The final installment came a few weeks later.

On a day in October 1943 1,800 of the detainees were ordered to pack as they were to be transported to another camp, at Bergau near Dresden. Their luggage and possessions they were instructed to leave behind at Bergen-Belsen. These would follow without delay. (Sometime later the inmates who had remained in the Bergen-Belsen Camp, discovered that the luggage had not been sent but had been stored in one of the huts.) All members of this group held "promesas."

Only a few days earlier a transport comprising seventy persons, who had been included in the lists drafted in Hotel Polski but whose departure to the Camp had been delayed for some reason, arrived. They were immediately attached to the transport "leaving for Bergau." The destination of the transport was Auschwitz.

This was followed shortly afterwards by a second and a third transport, the latter comprising the remaining holders of "promesas" and passports. Only a few hundred detainees remained in the camp, the majority of them belonging to the Palestine List, the other holders of documents which the Germans for some reason chose to regard as authentic. . . .

The tragic fate of the holders of documents who had been incarcerated in Bergen-Belsen was not yet known in the free countries. Unlike those detained in the Vittel. Tittmoning and Liebenau camps, the inmates of Bergen-Belsen did not correspond with their relatives abroad. Once or twice they were given postcards upon which prisoners conducted their correspondence, but the cards never left the Bergen-Belsen camp. For this reason, indeed, rescue organizations and private agents (who also engaged in these transactions) continued to obtain "papers" from the consulates, which they despatched to the Nazi-occupied countries, even after 2500-3000 holders of such documents had been despatched from Bergen-Belsen to Auschwitz.

12. This description of Nazi atrocities with regard to some of the so-called "foreign Jews" wasn't an isolated case. Dr. Nathan Eck in his Yad Vashem report on "Passports and Citizenship Papers" writes that

In some areas, particularly in more isolated districts of Eastern Europe, the Germans would murder their victims with the utmost dispatch without making any attempt to ascertain their nationality; elsewhere, however, these Jews enjoyed a totally different status in respect to the overall campaign of repression and murder.

Bibliography

Most of the materials in this book are based on documents, diaries and witnesses' reports in the archives of the Yad Vashem in Jerusalem and in the Kibbutz of Ghetto Fighters in Israel, as well as from direct interviews with survivors of the Hotel. In addition, many printed sources have been consulted, among them the following:

Auerbach, Rachel. *Baym Letstn Veg* ("The Final Road"), Tel Aviv, 1977.
Baskind, Ber. *La Grande Epouvante* ("The Great Terror"), Paris, 1945.
Berg, Mary. *Warsaw Ghetto – A Diary*, New York, 1945.
Borzykowski, Tuvya. *Between Tumbling Walls*, Ghetto Fighters' House, 1972.
Celemenski, Jacob. *Mitn Farshnitenem Folk* ("With My Slain People"), New York, 1963.
Czerniakow, Adam. *Ghetto Diary*, New York, 1978.
Dawidowicz, Lucy S. *The War Against the Jews 1933–1945*, New York, 1975.
Eck, Nathan. "The Rescue of Jews with the Aid of Passports and Citizenship Papers of Latin American States," *Yad Vashem Studies*, I, Jerusalem, 1957.
Feingold, L. Henry. *The Politics of Rescue*, New York, 1980.
Goldstein, Bernard. *The Stars Bear Witness*, New York, 1949.
Hilberg, Raul. *The Destruction of the European Jews*, Chicago, 1967.
Hirshaut, Julien. *Fintstere Nekht in Pawiak* ("The Dark Nights in Pawiak") Buenos Aires, 1948.
Katznelson, Yitzhak. *Vittel Diary*, Ghetto Fighters' House, 1972.
Klin, David. *Georemt Mit Toyt* ("Arm in Arm with Death"), Tel Aviv, 1968.
Meed, Vladka. *On Both Sides of the Wall*, New York, 1979.
Morse, Arthur D. *While Six Million Died*, New York, 1967.
Mueller, Filip. *Eyewitness Auschwitz*, New York, 1979.
Novitch, Miriam. *Notes from Vittel*, Ghetto Fighters' House, 1964.
Reitlinger, Gerald. *The Final Solution*, South Brunswick, 1968.
Ringelblum, Emanuel. *Polish-Jewish Relations During the Second World War*, New York, 1974.
Rudnicki, Adolf. *Ginacy Daniel* ("The Perishing Daniel"), Warsaw, 1946.
Seidman, Hillel. *Togbukh fun Varshever Ghetto* ("Warsaw Ghetto Diary"), Buenos Aires, 1947.
Tomkiewicz. Mieczyslawa. "Tam się też żyło (Life in Bergen-Belsen"), *Nasza Trybuna*, No. 53, New York, 1945.
Trunk, Isaiah. *Judenrat*, New York, 1972.
Turkow, Jonas. *Azoy Iz Es Geven* ("That's How It Was"), Buenos Aires, 1948.
Turkow, Jonas. *Der Sof Fun An Iluzye* ("The End of an Illusion"), Tel Aviv, 1972.
Wanat, Leon. *Za Murami Pawiaka* ("Behind the Pawiak Walls"), Warsaw, 1958.
Wiesel, Elie. *One Generation After*, New York, 1965.

INDEX

238

Lange Michal, 60, 62
Lauerbach, 176
Lawrence Mrs., 29
Lender Joshua, 102
Leszczynska Gala, 50, 157, 201
Lewin Pinchas, 26
    Mindel, 26
    Sara, 26
Lipszyc Yoszke, 46, 47
    Ester, 46
Lopata, 81
Lubraniecki, 51
Lusternik, 82

Machno Madame, 43
Mann Franciszka, 94, 100, 101,
    152, 202, 204, 219
Mandel Mantelo, 230
Margolis Alexander, 27, 171
Matzner, Dr., 165
Meed Vladka, 51, 94
Mende Gerhart, 24, 62, 189.
Mendzyrzecki (Meed) Benjamin,
    56, 94
    Wladka, 51, 94
Miller Artur, Mrs., 27
Mincberg Pinches, 158, 160
Minzberg Yechiel, 81
Miodowski Josef, 214
Morgenthau Henry, 24, 230
Morse Arthur, 216
Mosciuk, 62
Moszkowski (lawyer), 195
Müller Filip, 204

Najhaus Mrs., 199
Natanson Wladyslaw, 126, 128
Neustat, 27
Newton Mrs., 195
Nicolaus (Nikolaus), 24, 29, 31, 33,
    34, 35
Novitch Miriam, 114, 126, 127,
    129, 130, 134, 139, 203

Orf (SS), 31
Orlean Mieczyslaw, 183
Orzech Maurycy, 49
Osinski Stanley, 91, 92, 93, 94, 95,

188, 214
Menachem, 93

Pehle John, 217
Perle Joshua, 49, 81, 101, 102, 103,
    158, 168, 172
    son, 81, 102, 103, 157, 158
Pilpul Robert, 135
Pinczanek, 76
Pinczow, 128
Przedborski, 151, 157

Quackernack (SS), 205, 209, 210

Rabinowicz, 2, 158, 160, 173
Rakower, 171
Rapaport Szabse, rabbi, 27, 124
Reitlinger G., 234
Remarque, E. M., 146
Ribbentrop J., 228
Ringelblum Emmanuel, 13, 14, 21,
    103, 131, 223
Robinson Else, 232
Rogers Luke P., 225, 226, 227
Rolnik Jacob, 85, 87, 88, 89, 90
Rosenman Samuel, 24
Roosevelt F. D., 23, 24, 215
Rosenheim Jacob, 216
Rosental Abraham, 73, 74, 76, 184,
    185
Rotblat Lutek, 160
Rozanykwiat Tadeusz, 128
Rottenberg, rabbi, 124, 128
Rosenbloom Noah, 130
Rozencwajg Jozef, 160, 165
Rubin Mrs., 146, 149
Rubinstein Danuta, 59, 61, 62
Rucinska Barbara, 95
Rudnicki Adolf, 41, 104
Rutowski, 152

Salomon, Dr., 126
Schillinger (SS), 204, 205, 209,
    210, 211
Schipper I., Dr., 23, 223
Schorr Tamara, 27, 33, 121, 124
    Moses, Dr., 27
Schwarz Herbert, Lagerführer,

239